SPIN
DOCTORS

Other books by the author

Raw Meaty Bones: Promote Health 2001
Work Wonders: Feed Your Dog Raw Meaty Bones 2005
Multi-Billion-Dollar Pet Food Fraud: Hiding in Plain Sight 2023

SPIN DOCTORS

JUNK PET FOOD
PARTNERS IN CRIME

DR TOM LONSDALE

RIVETCO PTY LTD

First published in 2026 by:
Rivetco Pty Ltd
PO Box 6096
Windsor Delivery Centre
NSW 2756
Australia

Email: info@rivetco.com.au
Phone: +61 2 4577 6236
Website: www.thepetfoodcon.com
www.rawmeatybones.com

National Library of Australia Cataloguing-in-publication entry:

Lonsdale, Tom, 1949–
Spin doctors: junk pet food partners in crime

Includes index

ISBN 978-1-7642455-0-0
ISBN 978-1-7642455-1-7 (ebook)
ISBN 978-1-7642455-2-4 (audiobook)

A catalogue record for this book is available from the National Library of Australia

This book has been written and published in good faith. However, when dealing with biological systems, for example the health of animals, problems can occur. The publisher is therefore unable to guarantee that, in every circumstance, the information presented here will be of benefit, and neither does the information constitute professional advice upon which you should rely.

The author and publisher have made efforts to trace the copyright holders for borrowed material. If they have overlooked any, they will be pleased to rectify matters at the first opportunity.

If you find errors of fact or interpretation contained within these pages, please contact the publisher.

Editor's note: The main text of this book consists of *Raw Meaty Bones Newsletters* published from 2001 to 2011. The minor differences are corrections of any typing errors, and consistent use of accepted Australian spelling (-ise rather than -ize, for example), punctuation, dates and measurements.

PREFACE

Welcome to *Spin Doctors: Junk Pet Food Partners in Crime*, a compilation of all 45 issues of the online *Raw Meaty Bones Newsletter* from 2001 to 2011.

It's a rolling commentary on the veterinary-junk pet food industrial complex—a system based on fraud, protected by bogus science and endless spin.

We see the failings of an unregulated capitalist system where deception is the norm; a system where regulators are subject to regulatory capture by powerful corporate interests, veterinary interests and animal welfare lobbyists.

The pet food industry began in the 1860s when Jack Spratt first made his Wheat Fibrine Dog Cakes. Now, after 150 years, there's a large population of pet owners who know no alternatives. So thorough is the cultural conditioning that many pet owners appear to like and defend their dependency on the vet-endorsed industrial junk. Pets become helpless addicts and get no say.

Making matters worse, censorship and suppression create an isolated and uninformed populace. However, by reading this book and by sharing it with others you can help to create an informed community empowered to make a difference. Together let's try.

Wishing you and your pets the best of good health,

Tom Lonsdale

January 2026

CONTENTS

ABBREVIATIONS

AAFCO   Association of American Feed Control Officials
AAP   Australian Associated Press
ABC   Australian Broadcasting Corporation
ACA   *A Current Affair* (ABC)
ACVS   Australian College of Veterinary Scientists
AHAW   Animal Health and Welfare
AIDS   acquired immune deficiency syndrome
AVA   Australian Veterinary Association
BARF   Born Again Raw Feeders
BMJ   *British Medical Journal*
BSAVA   British Small Animal Veterinary Association
BVA   British Veterinary Association
CEO   chief executive officer
CPD   continuing professional development
DEFRA   Department for Environment, Food and Rural Affairs
EDM   early day motion
EFRACom   Environment, Food and Rural Affairs Committee
EU   European Union
FDA   (US) Food and Drug Administration
FLUTD   feline lower urinary tract disease
FOI   freedom of information
IMO   in my opinion
JAVMA   *Journal of the American Veterinary Medical Association*
NHMRC   National Health and Medical Research Council
NSW   New South Wales
NZ   New Zealand
OVC   Ontario Veterinary College
PETA   People for the Ethical Treatment of Animals

PFMA	Pet Food Manufacturers Association (UK)
PGF	Post Graduate Foundation
PHC	primary healthcare centre
PR	public relations
RCVS	Royal College of Veterinary Surgeons
RMB	raw meaty bones
RSPCA	Royal Society for the Prevention of Cruelty to Animals
RN	Radio National (ABC)
RVC	Royal Veterinary College (University of London)
TV	television
UK	United Kingdom
UofG	University of Guelph
US	United States
USA	United States of America
VIN	Veterinary Information Network
WCPN	Waltham Centre for Pet Nutrition
WDJ	*Whole Dog Journal*
WSAVA	World Small Animal Veterinary Association
WWF	World Wildlife Fund

INTRODUCTION

———

spin doctor
a political spokesperson employed to promote a favourable interpretation of events to journalists

partner in crime
a (habitual) criminal accomplice
New Shorter Oxford English Dictionary

Past, present and future

Back in the early 1990s, the pet food industry and its veterinary and animal welfare partners in crime were revealed in their true colours. 'Raw meaty bones' principles were established and written into the historical record.

After the publication of *Raw Meaty Bones: Promote Health*, from 2001 to 2011, I published periodic updates and commentaries in the *Raw Meaty Bones Newsletter*.

All 45 editions of the newsletter are now reproduced in the pages of this book. For the future, and to keep faith with pets, people and the planet, George Santayana's wise words carry across the ages: 'Those who cannot remember the past are condemned to repeat it.'

Three themes predominate

1. Corrupt science and bogus research underpin the junk pet food fraud.
2. The pet food industry, veterinary medicine and animal welfare partners in crime impose massive costs on pets, people and the planet.

3. Cunning opportunists push fad raw recipes and concoctions that further cheat animals and defraud consumers.

What have pets, the voiceless victims, done to warrant relentless cruelty and abuse? Why is the community held to ransom by spin doctors, white collar and organised corporate criminals? Are there no effective checks and balances?

Questions such as these can be framed and reframed in numerous ways, resulting in ever more complicated answers. However, at core, I believe much can be explained by reference to us as humans, and who we truly are. We are hard-wired with a double dose of cunning arising from our early evolution as both predators and prey.

Imagine a band of early humans lacking sharp teeth and claws but possessed of large brains, out on a hunt. Trickery and deception were their potent weapons enabling them to capture prey without falling prey themselves. Subterfuge—cheating and lying—enabled our ancestors first to survive and then to thrive. Nowadays it's ever more the method of predatory groups, partners in crime and their spin doctors who push deception to the limit.

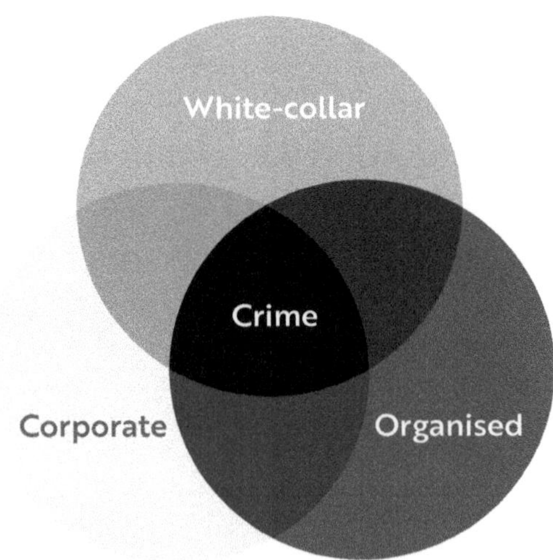

Let's consider the groups that most concern us here: the groups that prosper by helping themselves at the expense of pets, people and the planet.

Scientists and administrators

The word 'science' has acquired almost magical connotations. It's a powerful word holding large swathes of the population in awe. In the farm animal sphere, useful research does get performed and published. But, alas, in the pet feeding realm, what passes for 'science' is more often fashionable posturing by researchers beholden to commercial interests. Forget any thoughts about high-minded individuals searching for the laws of nature. No, the so-called science that underpins pet diets and veterinary care is all part of the pet food crafted subterfuge.

In fact there's a simple test, the laugh test, that can inform us as to the validity of their science. If their so-called science deems that ultra-processed, grain-based junk is suitable for everyday feeding of carnivores for the entirety of their miserable lives, then we can be forgiven for our peals of laughter. Either their scientific method is risible, or their scientific conduct is risible or both. I favour both in equal measure.

Note that long-term feeding trials have never been published showing that industrial products are suitable or safe for pets as compared with the natural standard—whole carcasses or raw meaty bones. I emphasise 'published' because it is almost certain that the companies (primarily Mars, Nestlé and Colgate) have secret internal research comparing outcomes for pets fed artificial junk and those fed raw meaty bones.

The refusal to provide scientific validation is perhaps the clearest indictment of the junk pet food merchants and their vet school and vet journal allies. It's a clear indication that they have something to hide—that they're covering up a multi-billion-dollar crime.

Meanwhile we can and must rely on:

1. The dictionary definition of the word 'carnivore'.
2. The realisation that dogs and cats know what's best. Dogs crave to gnaw on raw meaty bones and cats spend hours waiting patiently at the mousehole.
3. Switching dogs and cats from a junk food diet to a raw meaty bones diet. If vets were to conduct this simple retrospective comparison,

they would soon see with their own eyes that old dogs and cats regain the vitality of puppies and kittens.

Unfortunately, government regulators ignore established truths and instead swallow the marketing spin, the bogus 'science'. They are complicit. In more than 50 years as a vet, I've never encountered an official who acknowledged the enormity of the pet food fraud.

Alliance of pet food industry, vets and welfare groups

Having corrupted the research and administrative arms of the vet profession, the pet food companies employ the utmost cunning as they push their harmful products—with general practitioner vets and fake animal welfare propagandists in the front line.

We may assume our distant ancestors, efficient killers, were indifferent to the suffering of their quarry. Pet food makers, the organised vet profession and fake welfare groups show similar indifference. If they felt even a smidgen of concern, then surely they should realise that forcing animals to survive on ultra-processed junk inflicts lifelong cruelty, suffering and untimely death.

Notice how the multinational companies seldom take to the media, the podcasts and blogs to defend their products. No, it's the vet and fake welfare groups that provide protective cordons around the industry. (A minority of nonconformist vets and groups oppose the junk pet food alliance.) They repeat over and over the company weasel words: 'Complete, balanced and scientifically formulated—complete, balanced and scientifically formulated—complete, blah ...'.

And making the most of their opportunities, there's a vast array of interlinked commercial enterprises dependent on the vet-pet food complex—supermarkets, pet groomers, boarding establishments, transport companies, toy makers and many others. At first glance, they are legitimate activities with little or no connection with the corrupt pet food giants powering the system. They do, however, provide a buffer, a protective cordon for the pet food fraud hiding in plain sight.

Fad raw diet proponents

These days there is a sizable population of pet owners who distrust the veterinary-industrial pet food complex. Seeking refuge, fleeing decades of exploitation, pet owners are vulnerable and fall easy prey to the 'bait and switch' tricksters who promise raw-meaty-bones benefits, but then switch to their fad recipes and junk raw concoctions. If the vet profession had provided leadership, there would be no space, no opportunity for the hucksters and their scams.

The hucksters don't speak against the unholy pet food/vet/fake welfare alliance. They want the alliance to continue with its cavernous failings providing niche opportunities. By drawing attention to the ultra-processed product failings, they promote themselves as experts, thereby setting the stage for their niche FADs (Financially Advantageous Diets).

They bait the trap by touting the importance of raw meaty bones and by encouraging owners to stop feeding industrial junk. Then comes the switch. Instead of promoting optimum pet health with the feeding of raw meaty bones, the tricksters divert consumers to their fad products advertised as 'low carbohydrate', 'natural', 'grass-fed', 'evolutionary', 'biologically appropriate', 'additive-free', 'lightly cooked' or 'freeze-dried'. Duped into believing the diet gurus, pet owners become unwitting cult followers. Cult followers recruit more followers *ad infinitum.*

There is another failing of the raw (Righteous And Wrong) diet gurus. They have scant dentistry knowledge, no diagnostic and treatment acumen, no understanding of the essential interplay between raw meaty bones, gum health and systemic health. Undeterred, many raw product manufacturers simply lie, claiming that their products improve dental health. Pet owners remain oblivious to their entrapment, to the essential need for their carnivore companions to do their own processing, do their own ripping, tearing and gnawing of raw meaty bones.

Escaping one cult only to fall into the clutches of the next[1]

Finding solutions

OK. So we're beset with problems and need to find solutions. If we look to the history of the medical profession, we find that it (eventually) reinvented itself in response to compelling scientific evidence provided by Ignaz Semmelweis, Joseph Lister and Louis Pasteur. Dentists emphasise prevention—and thus less need for treatment—through healthy diets, tooth brushing and fluoridation. But of course, doctors and dentists are primarily patients themselves, and only secondarily gain their livelihood from sickness and disease. As patients, they can press for better treatment for themselves and their families.

Our companion animals don't speak for themselves. They have no bargaining power over vets whose livelihood and primary focus depend on a procession of sick pets. Hidden and intermingled with the vet majority there is a minority who, to some degree, support the feeding of raw meaty bones to carnivores. Finding those vets, building bridges, and encouraging them to stand up and speak out will be an important ongoing task.

Otherwise, hoping for miracles is pointless; there are no magic wands. Appealing to the better nature of pet food companies, vet institutions and niche marketers is a forlorn prospect. Also, they have no shame. If we are to succeed, we need to lobby politicians and regulators, and we need to use the law.

Existing laws should be strong enough to prosecute widespread animal cruelty and consumer fraud. Animal cruelty is a crime in most jurisdictions and a matter for government prosecutors. Fraudulent sale of goods or services can be prosecuted as a criminal offence by governments. Consumers can bring civil actions. Prime targets should be the pet food companies, vet schools and corrupt regulators. There is scope for class actions where numerous litigants band together. In the United States, better still, the Racketeer Influenced and Corrupt Organizations (RICO) Acts, both state and federal, provide excellent mechanisms with which to sue companies, vets and welfare group conspirators.

Successful prosecutions can yield massive payouts. Lawyers can advise the best course of action.

When legal actions get underway, the media may follow court proceedings. Traditionally, the media does report when small-time researchers are found guilty of doctoring data in private. In the future, whether through court hearings or on their own initiative, will journalists gain courage and investigate the pet food companies and vet spin doctors who commit their mega-fraud in plain sight?

Please review the following chapters, weigh the evidence and help generate informed discussion leading to effective, lasting solutions.

1

———

2001: LAYING THE FOUNDATIONS

Ten years after its commencement, a new phase of the Raw Meaty Bones (RMB) Campaign gets underway. Beginning with the fight for free speech, the omens are not good and destined to get worse. Signs of industry corruption and media suppression foretell of developments ahead.

October 2001: The First Amendment

Dear Reader,

Thank you for subscribing to the *Raw Meaty Bones Newsletter*.

With a majority of the world's pets suffering the effects of an artificial diet and a majority of the veterinary profession—the pet health-care professionals—endorsing these diets, there's a huge job to be done. But we must start somewhere, and where better to start than by staking a claim to freedom of speech—the subject of this first *RMB Newsletter*.

Over the coming months the *Newsletter* will evolve. Your feedback is especially welcome.

Let's make this interactive.

Until next time,
Best wishes,
Tom Lonsdale and the Raw Meaty Bones Crew

———

The First Amendment

If we can't speak about it, we can't fix it—and that's what they want.

Who are the ubiquitous 'they'?

They are the artificial pet food makers and their allies.

What is it that they don't want us to fix?

They don't want us to fix the multi-billion-dollar industry where pet owners are deprived of cash and pets are forced to consume harmful foodstuffs and vets promote treatments which, at best, serve as a stopgap but don't deal with fundamental issues.

And as we know, it's fundamental issues that are important and that's why we are going to talk about them.

The US Congress identified the need for people to be able to speak about the things that concern them. That's why, in September 1789, they proposed the First Amendment to the US Constitution: 'Congress shall make no law ... abridging the freedom of speech, or of the press ...'

Now, 212 years later, the First Amendment has as much validity, but sadly is often forgotten—by governments, corporations and professional groups. Recent Australian experience provides illustration and a salutary lesson.

Raw Meaty Bones: Promote Health has been a long time in the writing. When the time came to launch the book, I approached three journalists and invited them to read the book, make inquiries and publish an article. (Names are suppressed to protect the individuals, but they were from the *Australian*, the *Sun Herald* and AAP.) All three were cautious, as befits people in positions of public trust, but happily I can recount that each committed to the task of publishing important information. A photographer working for the *Australian* took photos for illustration of their story and on the weekend of 18–19 August, nationwide coverage was scheduled.

But events unfolded in a different way. It's true that the AAP article was circulated to the media:

Canberra, 19 August 2001

Pet cats and dogs are suffering and dying from health conditions caused by convenience food foisted on the community by the multinational pet food industry with the connivance of many vets, a new book claims.

The book *Raw Meaty Bones: Promote Health*, by maverick vet Tom Lonsdale, argues that carnivores are ill-suited to a diet of processed meat and cereal which produces dental disease and a wide variety of other health ailments.

That includes what he terms as diet-induced AIDS in which the animal's immune system is depressed, leading to a variety of health problems.

What pets really need, he says, is a diet of fresh water, table scraps and raw meaty bones including fish, chicken necks and wings, animals' carcasses and offal.

Dr Lonsdale's views have won him no popularity from the pet food industry and even from his own profession.

He points to linkages between pet food manufacturers and vets. In what appears to be a marketing triumph, pet food companies have won the endorsement of vets who recommend the use of premium pet foods to new pet owners.

'What we are saying is so dramatic in its implications for the health of animals that they (the vets) can't in all honesty or justification simply wipe their hands of it and say we are not interested,' Dr Lonsdale told AAP.

'The pet food industry got under way in the 1860s and has been gathering momentum ever since. If something so woefully inadequate or harmful can gain momentum over that period, then there is something seriously wrong with the gatekeepers who are supposed to be protecting the community from harm from these sort of things.'

Dr Lonsdale said a diet of raw meaty bones produced another benefit besides the better health of pets—an end to messy dog poo all over backyards, paths and parks. The output from pets fed with meaty bones turns white and crumbles away.

Dr Lonsdale said he expects the pet food industry will respond with the usual public relations spin. 'It is all about conditioning the consumer into believing that in order to be a thoroughly sophisticated consumer you feed your pet out of a can, at the same time obscuring the downside of these products,' he said.

'They will get their spin doctors working overtime. The Veterinary Association will lament that they have rebels in the ranks. They have tried to bring actions against me. Fortunately that has finally come to nought.'
AAP mb/cd

But the AAP media release went largely unnoticed except by the *Border Mail*:

The Border Mail

Monday, 20 August 2001
Albury–Wodonga, Australia

Book links pet food, poor animal health
The actions of pet food manufacturers, including the Wodonga-based Uncle Ben's company, have been blamed for the poor health of pet cats and dogs in a new book written by a Sydney veterinarian.

Dr Tom Lonsdale released his book, *Raw Meaty Bones*, on Saturday.

It traces his 10-year campaign against processed pet food, which he argues produces health problems, such as dental disease and a weakened immune system, in dogs and cats.

Dr Lonsdale said he had named Uncle Ben's in his book, which was fully scrutinised by three different lawyers before publication.

'This is about empowering the community against the predilections of a multinational,' Dr Lonsdale said.

'I know you've got a responsibility to readers and your town derives its livelihood and well-being from this factory, for which I'm sorry, and I am not poking the finger at the workers from Albury–Wodonga.

'It's unfortunate for them but they might like to get the book and see what's happening because I'm not in the business of distorting evidence; woe betide me if I do.'

Dr Lonsdale supports pets eating food as close as possible to whole raw carcasses and favoured consumption of raw meaty bones and table scraps.

The external affairs manager for Uncle Ben's, Dr Duncan Hall, who is a veterinarian, strongly rejected Dr Lonsdale's views.

He said many of Dr Lonsdale's theories were not supported by nutritional science and he understood there was not widespread backing of his stand from other veterinarians.

'We would clearly state that we regard prepared pet foods as a convenient and nutritious way for pet owners to feed their animals,' Dr Hall said.

Dr Hall said Dr Lonsdale's campaign over 10 years had failed to create a dent in Uncle Ben's production levels.

'It's not something which has made a huge impact on us,' he said.

Dr Lonsdale said he believed governments should become involved in the argument by taking action against advertisements for pet food.

The *Australian*, despite its three-week-long investigation and photos, canned the story, as did the *Sun Herald*. The editor of the *Australian* has not returned phone calls or answered correspondence on the matter. Things at the *Sun Herald* are arguably worse.

On 19 August 2001, the day the *Sun Herald* was due to alert its readers to the dangers of artificial pet foods, they published an advertorial:

> **New food helps pets live longer**
> An experimental pet food makes cats and dogs live longer by reducing the damage to genetic material linked with the diseases of aging.
>
> Preliminary evidence was presented recently to a gathering of academics and vets in Vancouver, Canada.
>
> Patents are pending on the food, which mixes antioxidants, notably vitamin C and E, which mop up damaging chemical intermediates, called radicals.

Readers were not told that premature aging is a major problem associated with commercial pet foods, nor were they told which giant multinational conducted the experiments and hosted the 'gathering of academics and vets'. But readers were primed for things to come—Mars Inc.'s Advance and Waltham pet diets, which, the company claim, 'add life to the life of your pet'.

On 10 September 2001, Uncle Ben's of Australia (a Mars subsidiary) promoted the new products to veterinarians with the assurance: 'Remember every product in the Advance and Waltham ranges is 100% guaranteed for palatability, performance and dating.' Dr Mark Lorschy, professional services manager at Uncle Ben's of Australia, told veterinarians that if they had any questions they should call him on 0417 259 187. The address for correspondence is Unit A3, 3–9 Birnie Avenue, Lidcombe NSW 2141. Phone: +61 2 9737 5300. Fax: +61 2 9737 5399.

In fact this episode raises many questions, not least whether a 'free' press should stop publication of information vital to the wellbeing of pets and their owners, and at the same time publish commercially inspired propaganda.

———

We welcome copies of correspondence/emails/faxes for possible inclusion in future *RMB Newsletters*. Please circulate, distribute or reproduce this newsletter as you wish.

November 2001: By crikey

Dear Reader,

It's summer in Australia and it's hotting up. In the pet food struggles, things warm up a bit on the commercial TV stations too—despite their dependence on the pet food dollar. (The taxpayer-funded ABC TV stays mute on the $1.5 billion scandal.)

In this second edition of the *RMB Newsletter* the stories by *Crikey* come from the newsletter.[1]

Although strong on Australian flavour, the stories are relevant to the situation everywhere. For that's where the multinational pet food monster intrudes—everywhere.

Until next time,
Best wishes,
Tom Lonsdale and the Raw Meaty Bones Crew

———

By crikey

Crikey Newsletter, 1 November 2011

Dodgy doggy tucker
Speaking of dead and dying animals, *Crikey* was delighted to see that *A Current Affair* picked up on our piece (the *ACA* producer rang to thank us) by vet Tom Lonsdale and gave his story about dodgy dog food a really good airing last night (31 October 2001) on prime-time national television.

The story alone will wipe millions off the annual $1.5 billion in sales that pet food companies like Uncle Ben's reap each year. The argument really is compelling. Dogs are carnivores being made to eat crappy grains-based product by hugely profitable multinationals who fund the vets and any other interest group who'll talk up pet ownership and pet food sales. And these crappy diets lead to a lot of sick puppies which keeps Australian vets nice and busy.

All the dog owners and breeders featured on *A Current Affair* feed their animals raw meaty bones and never have to visit a vet as a result.

Uncle Ben's have 65% of the market and are owned by the Mars Corporation, which is the world's biggest family company, controlled by the eccentric American Mars brothers. Yes, they own Mars bars.

They are also incredibly secretive, so it was no wonder that Uncle Ben's and the Australian Petfood Association refused to co-operate with *ACA*.

It remains a shame that the newspapers are so worried about all that pet food advertising and refuse to give Tom Lonsdale's book the decent airing it deserves.

These multinationals have used devious tactics to grow their sales way beyond what is good for Australian pets and pet-owners and it is about time we saw a bit of a downward trend. Boycott Uncle Ben's everyone and feed your pets Raw Meaty Bones.

Check out Tom's original article below:

Poison your pets with multinational offerings

by Tom Lonsdale
Vet and author

Veterinarian Tom Lonsdale is selling plenty of his book Raw Meaty Bones *in the US but the Australian media seems to have blacked him out because the multinational pet food companies don't want their dodgy doggy tucker exposed.*

Poisons injure health or destroy life. Some are quick-acting —strychnine and cyanide—others act slowly—alcohol and tobacco—although addiction speeds up the process. Sometimes packet labels warn about the contents. 'Smoking kills' say the labels, but only now after years of anti-tobacco lobbying.

Alcohol containers sometimes carry labels recommending limited intake of the poison, but generally carry no warnings. Some poisons are banned and some are sanctioned and some aren't even recognised as poisons. Take artificial pet foods for instance—widely available in supermarkets, petrol stations and corner stores (do they still exist?)—they injure the health of a majority of the world's pets, but few folks know or are allowed to know.

As a veterinary practitioner confronted by the procession of bedraggled, diet-affected pets attending my clinic I was, at first, too busy dealing with the problems to notice their origin. Besides, I was handicapped by a university education and constant bombardment by pet food ads. But eventually I woke up to my naivety, my complicity, in promoting artificial modern diets to the pets under my care. Pet owners accepted my apologies for past misleading advice and together we set about helping their artificial-diet-addicted pets.

By the early 90s a group of Australian vets, the Raw Meaty Bone Lobby, started to chip away at the artificial pet food dogma encasing the veterinary profession. The Australian Veterinary Association (AVA), itself in receipt of pet food company funds, led the counterattack. Within the professional journals the AVA banned discussion of diet and diet-induced dental disease and issued media statements against the dissident members.

Hostilities escalated and spilt over into the UK veterinary profession with the US pet food regulator, the FDA (Food and Drug Administration), involved in exchanges too. Along the way the Western Plains Zoo, WWF (World Wildlife Fund), ABC *Science Show*, a professor at the NHMRC (National

Health and Medical Research Council) and numerous university lecturers and university departments were shown to be involved with, or actively promoting the interests of, the artificial pet food industry. High court judge, Justice Michael Kirby, patron of the RSPCA (Royal Society for the Prevention of Cruelty to Animals), justified that organisation's involvement with Colgate-Palmolive, makers of 'Science Diet', on the basis that the RSPCA needed the money.

Beside the toothpaste maker the other major players are American transnationals Mars Inc. and Procter & Gamble and the Swiss giant Nestlé. Money talks and the watchdogs stay silent, whether they be protecting against cruelty to animals, truth in labelling or the welfare of children in our schools. A book was needed to tell it the way it is and attempt to get some sort of debate going.

Starting in October 1996 I sat in my garret scribbling away at Happy Zone, for that was the working title. I hoped that by working in the 'Zone' I could make people happy by revealing sombre truths and showing how things could be better. Natural pet food is cheaper, pets live healthier longer lives, vet bills reduce and the environment gets a better deal. Except for the artificial pet food companies and their veterinary allies, it's a win, win, win situation.

Richard Potter the defamation lawyer, two barristers and four other lawyers commented on the text and Happy Zone metamorphosed into *Raw Meaty Bones: Promote Health*. By August 2001 the book was ready to be launched, but instead more layers were added to the multi-layered scandal. The *Australian* newspaper had exclusive rights to a story about the book scheduled for Saturday 18 August—but the story and the colour photographs finished in the can. Michael Stutchbury, the editor of the *Australian*, failed to return calls or answer correspondence regarding the newspaper's back flip.

On Sunday 19 August the Sydney newspaper the *Sun Herald* scheduled to publish an 800-word exposé based on revelations contained in *Raw Meaty Bones*, but that finished in the can too. Worse still, an advertorial headline in the paper's science pages told readers: 'New food helps pets live longer'. (The Mars company Uncle Ben's of Australia have since released a new line of pet foods which they claim: 'Add life to the life of your pet.')

Messrs Laws, Jones and Carlton were sent copies of *Raw Meaty Bones*, as were 50 other journalists. Almost all appear to have ignored the information and their employers still broadcast pet food ads. Bert Newton, on his *Good Morning Australia* program, went to air with a sanitised version of the story—the book *Raw Meaty Bones* didn't get a mention; neither was it acknowledged that the diet-affected Labrador dog in Bert's story was filmed at the author's veterinary clinic in 1994! Regarding the multi-layered pet food scandal, viewers were spared the details, but Bert did encourage us to feed our pets raw meaty bones.

Is truth too hard to bear; is the full story too difficult for Australia's journalists? Will a slow poison affect us all? Time may tell, but at least we have a benchmark.

Tom Lonsdale

Crikey Newsletter, 1 November 2001

Dodgy dog food

A subscriber writes:

I was interested in your reference to Tom Lonsdale's book and remember some years ago a NSW vet published an article indicating that a form of immunodeficiency was emerging in pets and that cause was a diet filled with commercial dog food. His advice was the same as Lonsdale's but he wasn't having much success selling his message.

As an ABC radio producer at the time we followed up the story but also found it difficult to get a response from pet food manufacturers and some veterinary organisations. It is also interesting that one of the first people to successfully sell a program idea to the ABC, after it decided to outsource most of its light entertainment programs, was a vet working for one of the major associations who were sponsored by a pet food company. From memory there were concerns about the independence of the vet and the implications for the programs content. I believe she resigned from the association shortly after getting the nod from the ABC.

Regards, John

Crikey Newsletter, 2 November 2001

Crooked cat food

A well-connected subscriber writes:

There was an article on Tom Lonsdale a few years back in the *Fin Review* on the ABC pet series and the conflict-of-interest trip with industry. It might be in Tom's book but interesting when you look at Pal/Pedigree brand from Mars (Effem was/still is I think the holding company in Australasia) you'll find a classic front group on pet food packaging from Mars claiming, 'developed with Waltham, the world's leading authority on pet care and nutrition'. Was bankrolled and controlled by Mars a few years ago unless they have got clever with the money trail. You'll also find a little tactic of Uncle Ben's sales reps is to eat Mars pet food to prove its quality. While they'll do that on the premium cat and dog brands, they steadfastly refuse for

Pal/Pedigree. Top breeders still recommend it though.

We've also picked up that the 'ABC journalist, former vet' is Jonica Newby, none other than Robyn Williams's girlfriend. Questions were asked at the time about how Robyn was able to use his impeccable *Science Show* credentials to convince RN management to get a four-part series of people and their pets for a lightweight fluffy PR piece for a multinational. At that time Jonica was working for the doggie food people—*Media Watch* picked it up.

But this did not stop her career and some cynics would suggest it is Robyn's ABC clout that sees Jonica appearing each week on *Catalyst* these days, which is a far cry from the old *Quantum*.

December 2001: A pet food vet speaks on the radio

Dear Reader,

Christmas is coming and it's a time for relaxing with the family—in front of the TV maybe. Will the pet food admen give us a break? Or will we, and our children, be treated to the usual stream of carefully crafted messages delivered with high-tech precision?

But what do the pet food people say when they are not scripted, when someone asks them a few straight questions? Recently Uncle Ben's, the Australian pet food division of Mars Inc., were asked for public comment. In this edition of the *RMB Newsletter* we bring you two (lightly edited) transcripts from ABC radio. Long-time Mars vet Duncan Hall was the company spokesperson in both interviews—in the first via a 'hands-free-speakerphone'.

We welcome your comments on Dr Hall's contribution to the raw vs processed debate.

Until next time,
Wishing you a Merry Christmas and Happy New Year,
Tom Lonsdale and the Raw Meaty Bones crew

———

A pet food vet speaks on the radio

Derek Guille ABC Radio 3LO 774 Melbourne, Australia, interviews Dr Duncan Hall, external affairs manager, Uncle Ben's of Australia, 20 August 2001

Interviewer: Duncan Hall, good afternoon, welcome.

DH: Good afternoon Derek and thank you very much.

Interviewer: You've had a chance to listen to some of the things that Tom Lonsdale is saying. First of all, I guess we would all agree that, yes, in the best of possible worlds a raw meat, raw meaty bones diet with a few supplementary table scraps or whatever you'd like to call them, would be a great diet for a dog.

DH: Thanks Derek, there's a few things there. Firstly, we would certainly endorse feeding of the occasional large uncooked bone to dogs as part of an overall dietary plan—providing that the bones are not cooked—providing that they are not chop bones and providing that the dog doesn't have an underlying veterinary problem—say an enlarged prostate or some sort of colonic problem that could lead to constipation.

So, if people want to feed the occasional bone on top of a good quality diet, we have no problem with that. I think it's important though to recognise that raw meaty bones are a long way from nutritionally complete, they don't provide the whole range of nutrients required and that what we do, with good quality manufacturers, is make sure that in consuming a meal made of high-quality prepared pet food the whole gambit of nutrients, being protein, you know carbohydrate—rather the whole series are consumed in the right level. So for good bone development of puppies, you need very close mix of calcium and phosphorus—minerals in the diet so they get strong bones and healthy teeth to start them off right.

Interviewer: Duncan, sorry the technical problem from our operator, are you on a hands-free speaker phone?

DH: Ah yes.

Interviewer: Yeah 'cause it's difficult for us to hear you unfortunately, it's not coming through very clearly, would you be able to pick the phone up?

DH: Ah I can't do it ... I can dial in again.

Interviewer: Oh we'll keep going and see what we can get from the position you're in then.

DH: OK

Interviewer: So you're suggesting that a variety, or a diet of raw meat and meaty bones is not going to provide the nutritional requirements even though it might be much closer to what a natural diet in the wild would be.

DH: Oh I think that in the wild—if you do look at animals in the wild—they do consume the whole carcass and what we're effectively doing is we're providing the whole range of nutrients in a convenient and nutritious format.

Interviewer: So there's the equivalent of eating offal of eating the stomach contents of prey, those sorts of things.

DH: Absolutely because that's the balance of vitamins and minerals that are provided in a quality prepared food. The, the issue really is ... also is what we've done is, we've done all the hard work of balancing up the nutrients, we've made sure that the digestibility of the food is good so that the animal can easily digest it and extract those nutrients and we've provided it in a convenient format in different versatile formats like dry or canned format so people can mix and match whatever suits both them and what their pet prefers.

Interviewer: Well I mean that's a really interesting question. Is it really about convenience for pet owners rather in the best interest of the dog or do you believe you've found a balance for both.

DH: Oh it's all so paramount, to us is the nutritional integrity and one thing that prepared pet foods offer is validated nutrition in as much as the testing has been done and we know what the levels of those nutrients are on a daily basis. Now, people can certainly feed dogs on a variety of different formats and if you put the work in, yes people can feed good quality prepared, sorry, home-prepared meals for their dogs. The way our lifestyle has developed though is that, you know, many people are not prepared to put the work in to finding out what the nutrient profiles of all of those raw materials are, therefore, what we offer are high quality prepared pet foods that are ready to go that we know will provide a good balance of nutrition for that pet.

Interviewer: Good, Duncan, well thank you very much for being with us this afternoon.

Ian Rogerson interviews Dr Duncan Hall on ABC 2BL 702 Sydney, Australia, 26 October 2001

Ian Rogerson: We heard from Dr Tom Lonsdale, who's a veterinary surgeon, with a book out entitled *Raw Meaty Bones: Promote Health*. Well for the other side of his argument we've now got on the line, Duncan Hall, he's the external affairs manager of Uncle Ben's, he's joining us right now, are you there Duncan?

DH: I certainly am, good evening.

Ian Rogerson: Good evening, well Duncan you've certainly heard Dr Lonsdale's criticisms of pet food, I hope you were listening beforehand. What do you say to claims that pet food is, you know, unnatural and potentially dangerous, as he says.

DH: Oh well Dr Lonsdale's certainly entitled to his view and I'd make that point.

Ian Rogerson: Mmm.

DH: His views aren't supported by science or the scientific community, or indeed the vast majority of the veterinary community either. They're primarily anecdotal views that he's formed, they're personal views.

Ian Rogerson: Mmm.

DH: And I'd make the point we, we undertake a lot of studies and a lot of science goes into, nutritional science goes into formulating our foods based on proven and internationally accepted standards. But perhaps more importantly, somewhere around two thirds of Australian pet owners choose to feed prepared pet foods and really, I think it's ah, the pet owners can judge for themselves. If they have a look at their pet right now, or out in the back yard that they can judge for themselves whether their pets are healthy, contented and full of vitality. And I think that that's the key point that we're not enforcing anyone to adopt feeding of pets by prepared pet food, that's entirely, how they feed their pet is entirely up to themselves.

Ian Rogerson: Mmm.

DH: And we actually accept that pet owners should have their choice in how they feed their pets. It's just a fact that the majority of pet owners choose, of their own volition to feed prepared pet food due to convenience, ah for the nutritional quality, the safety, the cost effectiveness and in the end, the measure is, as I said, the health of their pets that they see on a day-to-day basis.

Ian Rogerson: Mmm, I actually am a pet owner as well, Mr Hall, and I must admit I've never really ever looked at the tin food on the side. Do you have all the ingredients and the various additives and everything that goes into the tin? And pardon my naivety if you do.

DH: Yes, we do, we have a comprehensive listing of ingredients on the sides of any packs and it's there for all to see.

Ian Rogerson: Yes.

DH: I'd also, I think there's some important points that, you know, we have no problem if pet owners want to feed large raw meaty bones for their pets, we would endorse that, that's exactly what the Australian Veterinary Association endorses.

Ian Rogerson: Mmm.

DH: Recommends, and their recommendation is the basis of the diet should be on a high quality, nutritionally balanced diet, and they recommend that large bones are fed on a, on a, you know maybe a weekly or so basis to not only improve the dental health but also to provide relief from boredom in many cases or to entertain the animal in their environment, so we have no problem, so, if you know, if people choose to do that.

Ian Rogerson: Yes.

DH: As well feed a balanced prepared pet food, they're not only getting complete nutrition, they're getting all the vitamins, all the minerals et cetera they need, they also get the benefits that bones can bring in, in regards to, you know, both entertainment and improved oral health.

Ian Rogerson: Yes, Dr Lonsdale actually says that in his book that big companies don't really care about pet health, that they're only interested in making money, I mean, what would be your response there to that Mr Hall?

DH: My response would be, I think the large companies would be out of business if we weren't producing like any other organisation in this market economy, we would be out of business, if the products weren't of a high quality and, you know, maintain the, and enhance the pets' health.

Ian Rogerson: Yeah.

DH: You know, we're not, we're, of course we're interested in pets' health, both from a moral view, but also from a, from a, that's what we do.

Ian Rogerson: Yes.

DH: We have a very large investment goes on behind, in maintaining and even driving forward nutritional science relating to pets.

Ian Rogerson: Yeah, and what sort of things have you come up with in some of that science? Obviously some of it you don't want to give away for trade reasons, but, you know, are you moving forwards towards, you know, a healthier diets like that or a more sort of bone-orientated meals?

DH: Well, it's one of the things that have come about it, that in some cases, bones, people, you know, may not choose to feed bones, either on veterinary advice, sometimes you find for instance dogs that may have predisposing medical conditions, whereby they get constipated if they consume bones. What we've gone and evolved is an alternative whereby we have a product called Pedigree Dent-a-Bone, which people can choose to feed as a very hard, but a biological-based product that people can choose to, to feed to their pet, which also enhances the oral health of the dog.

Ian Rogerson: Mmm, have you ever been in a situation where, and by the way I'm talking with Duncan Hall, who's the external affairs officer of Uncle Ben's. Have you ever been in a situation where people have actually asked questions of health food makers and yourselves in that area?

DH: Oh, we regularly have customer inquiries on all sorts of matters relating to pet health. We actually employ somewhere around about ten veterinarians at our organisation and many of those are engaged on a daily basis in responding to any consumer inquiry or customer inquiry that we may have on a whole diverse range of topics.

Ian Rogerson: Mmm, OK, well listen, thank you very much for joining us here this evening, it's good to get both sides of the argument in this circumstance, thank you for talking with us Duncan Hall, external affairs officer from Uncle Ben's.

DH: My pleasure, thank you very much.

2

2002: INDUSTRY STRIKES BACK

Industry pushback intensifies as media outlets refuse to acknowledge diet-related health concerns. The pet food industry and veterinary profession become more aggressive in silencing dissent.

January 2002: An Australian Veterinary Association vet speaks on the TV

Dear Reader,

How was your Christmas? Good, I trust.

Down here in Australia we had a scorcher with some devastating bushfires. Conditions were right with plenty of dry undergrowth, eucalyptus oil and hot winds. Once ignited nothing mankind could do could stop the blazes.

Happily, the flames have died down and the smoke has cleared as I prepare this first *RMB Newsletter* of 2002. Following on from the previous newsletter we shall take a look at veterinary utterances in the public domain—how some veterinarians, healthcare professionals, defend the artificial pet food industry. And of course, this fits within the general theme of this newsletter:

1. Stop the harm done by processed food and the proponents of processed food.
2. Promote the healthy feeding of pets.
3. Promote a healthy human economy.

4. Promote a healthy natural environment.

It's a bit like fighting bushfires. Whilst it makes sense to fight the fires and to take all precautions in case bushfires occur, the main strategy must surely be to prevent folk lighting bushfires in the first place. If pet food companies and their vets stopped promoting harmful products, then improving pet health, the human economy and natural environment would be a much easier task.

This edition carries a couple of readers' responses to the last newsletter. Your responses are encouraged; we would be delighted to hear from you.

Until next time,
Wishing you a terrific 2002,
Tom Lonsdale and the Raw Meaty Bones Crew

An Australian Veterinary Association vet speaks on the TV

On 31 October 2001 the Australian national broadcaster Channel 9 went to air on the popular *A Current Affair* program, with a segment on the pet food industry[1] and based around the recent publication of *Raw Meaty Bones: Promote Health*.

A researcher from the program had seen a news item about *Raw Meaty Bones* and contacted me to inquire further. They recognised the merits of the story and scheduled reporter Jane Hansen and a camera crew to spend two days filming. Leah Ryan's pack of rough collies were shown gambolling and playing. Pups eagerly searched for the chicken backs on offer for lunch. Leah told how, when she used to feed commercial foods, she had huge veterinary bills for her kennel of between 10 and 20 pedigree dogs. She was spending around $1000 per month on vet bills for a variety of ailments. From the day she started more natural feeding, the ill health seemed to miraculously disappear. When asked what she now spends on vet bills, Leah responded: 'Oh, zilch!'

Diana Trickett has been feeding her Burmese cats and two small dogs raw meaty bones from the beginning. Simba, the 14-year-old Burmese, chewed on a rabbit carcass for the benefit of the cameras.

'He's been eating this way since he was 12 weeks old, when I got him as a kitten,' said Mrs Trickett. 'I wouldn't do it any other way … They are happy, they are contented. It doesn't cost me a fortune.'

At this point the picture cut to Dr Paul Hanson, president of the New South Wales division of the Australian Veterinary Association (AVA). Dr Hanson was filmed in a Sydney veterinary hospital and the soundtrack goes thus:

> **Dr Paul Hanson (AVA representative):** Most GP [general practitioner], day-to-day vets, would advise caution in feeding a raw meaty bones diet as a sole diet.
>
> **Jane Hansen (reporter):** Dr Paul Hanson, from the Veterinary Association … Why should cats and dogs eat rice and corn and cereals and vegetables that you find in these canned foods?
>
> **Dr Paul Hanson:** A lot of commercial diets, particularly of the supermarket variety, are often formulated in a form to appeal to us rather than to our pets—like any marketing program.
>
> **Jane Hansen:** Yes, meat and three veg.
>
> **Dr Paul Hanson:** Exactly.
>
> **Jane Hansen:** So you would agree that there's some marketing trickery.
>
> **Dr Paul Hanson:** Like any commercial product that's designed to appeal to a consumer, there is an element of that.

'some marketing trickery'

An element of 'marketing trickery' appears to be acceptable to Dr Hanson, who endorsed the commercial offerings with the words: 'If it's an appropriate product, there's no reason not to use it.'

Acceptance of 'trickery' and blandishments about 'appropriate products' seems an inappropriate stance for the Australian Veterinary Association. But when seen in the context of the pet food industry declining to speak in its own defence, the performance of the AVA seems even more problematic.

Rather than appear on the program, pet food company Uncle Ben's of Australia (a division of Mars Inc.) sent a statement. Here's a transcript of the soundtrack as Jane Hansen, the reporter, reads to the camera:

The multinational Mars Corporation and its Australian subsidiary, Uncle Ben's, has 65% of the local pet food market, but they didn't wish to discuss Tom Lonsdale's theories. They sent us this statement and it says, 'there's absolutely no scientific or other basis for the claims'.

We also received a fax from the Pet Food Industry Association of Australia and they say: 'The raw food versus processed pet food debate has caused unnecessary alarm amongst pet owners, and on that basis alone, it is the debate that we no longer wish to take part in'.

Jane Hansen made no comment about the pet food industry's reluctance to answer straightforward questions—their failure to appear spoke volumes. The Mars' statement that 'there's absolutely no scientific or other basis for the [health risk] claims' beggars belief.

———

In the December 2001 *RMB Newsletter* we reviewed two radio interviews featuring Dr Duncan Hall, external affairs manager of the Mars Company, Uncle Ben's of Australia.

A reader comments:

My main comment is on why pet owners feed commercial food and I doubt that most even give it any thought—they are shown on television and on posters in the shops that dogs and cats live healthy active lives being fed out of bags and tins, so that is what they do. When their pets get skin problems, joint problems, teeth problems, etc. it doesn't occur to them that the diet is the cause, any more than they link their own processed food diet with their own health problems.

Their vet is not going to tell them that the reason they are living in his surgery is because of what they are feeding their pet. He can make lots of money selling them special diets instead. I find it interesting that Pedigree Pet Foods have this year actually come out and said that dogs are carnivores. And this is after years of feeding dogs soya, peanut hulls, grains, etc. If pet food companies were interested in what was best for dogs and cats to eat, they would not need to carry out laboratory research but just look at what wild carnivores eat. What they are really doing is finding ways they can use up the garbage from other processes they would otherwise have to find ways of chucking away. As it is, instead of having to pay for disposal, they charge pet owners for it. Since they said at the start that their foods were complete and all that a dog or cat would need, how come they keep changing them?

(Name and address supplied.)

Stop press 23 January 2002
The Post Graduate Foundation in Veterinary Science at the University of Sydney is a leading source of postgraduate education for veterinarians. Dr Michele Cotton, associate director of the Foundation, has reviewed the book *Raw Meaty Bones*.[2]

November 2002: The good, the bad and the misguided

Dear Reader,

In 2002 the good toiled valiantly, the bad conformed to type and the misguided failed to convince—the subject of this *RMB Newsletter*.

But first an apology is due for the long interval since the last newsletter. I plead pressure of work because 2002, for me, has been a whirlwind of meetings, lectures, planes and trains a long way from Sydney.

How has your year progressed? Are your animals thriving? Are you making headway spreading the good-health message whilst combating the efforts of the merchants and the 'competent authorities'? I hope so and hope you continue to receive lots of positive feedback.

I'll try to write again soon, but it's my guess it will be after Christmas.

So here's wishing you compliments of the season and happy New Year, Tom Lonsdale and the Raw Meaty Bones Crew

———

The good, the bad and the misguided

The good

The good, selfless and highly motivated folks are among us and we owe them a huge debt of gratitude. I met some exceptional people during 2002, in particular the organisers of the four components of the Raw Meaty Bones lecture tour.

Kim Roberts, assisted by Liz Tilley and staff, organised the inaugural Raw Meaty Bones lectures at the University of Western Australia, Extension. From conception, several years ago, through to completion in March 2002 I enjoyed wonderful hospitality, encouragement and support.

Kim Roberts, director of the UWA Extension, signs his emails with the following:

> Unless we change direction, we are likely to end up where
> we are headed.
>
> Old Chinese proverb

Ever on the lookout for essential truths, I incorporated the saying into subsequent lectures because it seems to me that we are stepping out in a new direction and need the support and encouragement of clear-sighted folks like Kim and the ancient Chinese.

In June, Swanie Simon organised the second anniversary get together of the Gesunde Hunde (healthy dogs) internet discussion group. And what a delightful week it was. I'm smiling as I write this, thinking of the happy folks and contented canines who gathered in a marquee in a sports ground somewhere in the middle of Germany an hour from Frankfurt.

At first, I was apprehensive about speaking, given my lack of German, but I was mistaken. Swanie, Christiane and Sylvia were superb. They translated the questions for me and made my answers intelligible to the audience—and the enforced wait between questions gave me time to think about the subject under discussion. I almost wish all audiences could be German.

The dogs of all shapes and sizes were catered to—a raw meaty bones truck pulled up with supplies. Lots of good food, good weather and good cheer marked this major initiative by Swanie and her helpers. I'm filled with admiration.

Tony and Carol O'Herlihy of Bark Busters UK organised the most ambitious series of lectures through August at various venues in the UK. It's true they enlisted the help and resources of an enthusiastic force of Bark Busters licensees, but even so I cannot help but be in awe at the thought, commitment and effort that went into ensuring the success of the tour.

Everyone in Bark Busters UK, on a daily basis, sees and understands the need for carnivores to be fed as closely as possible to the way Nature planned it. They feed their own animals a predominantly raw meaty bones diet, help their dog training clients find information and supplies and generally advance the cause of dog health and behaviour across the UK. I am grateful to have been hosted by such a health-conscious enterprise.

Next stop after the UK was Atlanta, Georgia, USA. Alison Tyler is a renowned 'raw feeder', internet discussion list owner and moderator, organiser of the Southeastern Natural Rearing group and raw meaty bones cooperative. Besides holding down a busy professional career and feeding 22 carnivores she still managed to organise a four-city tour of the USA.

The 4 August, 'Welcome to the USA and Raw Meaty Bones book launch' was held in the grand Atlanta residence of Glo Ghegan—Southern style and hospitality at its finest. More a social event than a work gathering, the occasion marked the announcement of the proposed class action proceedings against the artificial pet food industry.

Alison and her helpers put on four wonderful all-day discussions. My thanks go to Sue Cosby in New Jersey, Chris Ostrowski in California and all those who helped make my stay so enjoyable.

The bad

Whilst the few toiled valiantly, communicating the raw meaty bones message, Nature's message, the majority were otherwise engaged. In Australia three veterinarians came to the Raw Meaty Bones talks, in Germany one, in the USA three and in the UK eight veterinarians attended.

We cannot know for sure why veterinarians prefer the tried, tested and failed methods they were taught in veterinary school. We cannot know why, for them, ignorance is bliss and why they prefer not to see, hear or speak evil against the poisonous artificial pet foods. But we do know that the majority of the world's pets are fed artificial foods and we also know that veterinarians are kept busy attempting to treat the diseases directly or indirectly arising from the consumption by pets of the manufacturers' offerings.

The dark satanic pet food mills churn out thousands of tons of disgusting pap which is then packaged in glossy packaging promising good health, longevity and vitality—a message reinforced by glossy advertising ratified by indolent regulators. But behind the façade not all is well with the artificial pet food industry. After much goading and provoking they seem to be prepared to acknowledge they have a problem with periodontal disease. Their public utterances don't say as much, but we know that they know processed pap does nothing to clean the teeth of carnivores. And failure to clean the teeth sometimes slowly, sometimes rapidly, but always surely, brings about nasty periodontal disease. (Waltham statistics show 100% of dogs over 12 years suffer from the disease.)

You and I, if we knew we had sold products which were 'linked to vital organ disease—most notably kidney and liver'—and if we knew our products were the 'most common reason for anaesthesia' then we would most likely withdraw those products immediately and hope to avoid massive damages claims. If we knew, as we do, that chewing on raw meaty bones is essential to ward off periodontal disease that gives rise to the kidney and liver disease and need for anaesthesia, then we would recommend raw bones.

But in the case of the Mars Corporation, aided by elements of the veterinary publishing industry and the veterinary profession generally, they recommend and sell not raw meaty bones, but biscuits shaped like a bone.

The timing was uncanny. Midway through the UK Raw Meaty Bones tour on 15 July 2002 the *Veterinary Times*—which boasts a net circulation of 13,172 copies and introduces itself as 'The weekly news journal for the profession'—published a bright yellow four-page wraparound advertising piece.

'Pedigree Denta' they said 'is a range of oral care products developed in close conjunction with the vets at Waltham and designed to improve the overall health of dogs' teeth and gums. 80% of dogs over the age of three have some form of gum disease, so there is plenty of scope for advances in dental health.' They went on to say:

> The major health implications of gum disease has been one of
> the major motivating factors for the vets at the Waltham Centre

for Pet Nutrition in their development of new Pedigree Daily DentaStix. 'If we can improve the overall oral hygiene of dogs, we hope to improve their long-term health prospects,' a WCPN spokesperson said.

Tens, perhaps hundreds of thousands, of pounds have been poured into this effort to dumb down the UK veterinary profession, who in turn dumb down their clients into believing that an artificial bone-shaped biscuit is the answer to cut down or eliminate life-threatening diseases of dogs. (Cats and ferrets don't get a mention.)

The misguided

While the cooked processed pet food industry is, rightly, concerned about the periodontal implications for dogs fed on pap, the raw processed pet food industry seems rather unconcerned. What's going on, how did it come about and what's to be done?

The road to Hell, or so they say, is paved with good intentions. And that seems to summarise what's happened in the raw processed pet food scramble.

Just stopping feeding manufactured pet foods out of the can or the packet will likely bring about an improvement in the health of carnivores. (It's a bit like stopping banging your head against the wall— you feel better when you stop.) The trouble is those who stop feeding cooked artificial foods often then start feeding cooked or raw recipes processed in the kitchen instead of the factory. The situation becomes confused and further compounded when the cooked grains, vegetable pulp, minced meat and additives are given the credit for the perceived good health.

Juliette de Bairacli Levy, back in 1955, was one of the first to recommend feeding meat raw. Unfortunately, in her 'Specimen diet for an average size adult dog' Levy starts by recommending: '100% flaked whole-grain wheat, rye, or barley, softened with either raw milk or vegetable juice'. Pitcairn subsequently published a series of minced meat, grain and vegetable-based recipes in his *Natural Health for Dogs and Cats*. Billinghurst, in a 1986 article, quoted Levy and Pitcairn as sources of information.

In 1991 Dr Breck Muir, Dr Alan Bennet and I, subsequently known as the Raw Meaty Bones Lobby Group, discussed the lamentable state of pet nutrition. As the name suggests, the RMB Lobby emphasised that carnivore diets should be based on raw meaty bones. By concentrating on the physical features of carnivore diets, the RMB Lobby were able to show that concerns regarding quantity and quality of chemicals—the fats, vitamins, minerals etc.—assume less significance.

Soon a major campaign within the Australian veterinary press, on the TV and radio brought the fundamental RMB philosophy to a wide audience of Australian vets and pet owners. The simplicity and convenience and health-promoting aspects made the message suitable for a much wider audience. But unfortunately, the RMB message stayed mostly in Australia.

Part of the message did find its way into various books which then found their way to various parts of the world. But almost without exception the RMB message was adulterated with notions of human vegetarian cooking—the addition of yoghurt, kelp, garlic, vegetables, apple cider vinegar, flaxseed oil and a medicine cabinet full of additives.

Word began to circulate that dogs are allegedly not carnivores but omnivores or even vegetarians—and persuading reluctant dogs to eat vegetables became a fetish only reliably achieved by grinding to a paste meaty bones and vegetables in what became known as the BARF (vomit) diet. The fears of bones becoming stuck became magnified in the minds of many pet owners and the craze for grinding—processing—the food of carnivores took firm hold. (Cats, we were told, should also eat their veges.)

Some well-intentioned people, and a few opportunists, saw marketing opportunities and in the ensuing scramble set up a processed raw pet food industry, distinguished from the existing artificial pet food industry in that its products are frozen not cooked. But of course, when those ground raw products thaw and are fed to carnivores, apart from any chemical inadequacies, the products do not clean the teeth and gums and thus contribute to the development of periodontal disease with resultant alarming consequences.

In fact, the situation is probably much worse.

The diet of free-living wild carnivores—whole carcasses of other animals—acts as both food and medicine. And it's the same for domestic dogs, cats and ferrets. Sick animals tend to return to health and good health prevails when pet carnivores are fed a natural diet. That's to say the diet exerts a therapeutic (treatment) effect and a disease preventative effect.

How does a natural diet treat and prevent disease?

At this stage there are too many biological pathways and too many mechanisms that await discovery. (The veterinary research industry is too busy deflecting attention from and propping up the artificial pet food industry.) However, we can say that artificial diets, whether cooked or raw, tend to poison animals in three broadly separate ways:

1. Foods that fail to clean the teeth and gums also increase the available nutrients for the oral bacteria. Bacterial overgrowth, plaque, gives rise to periodontal disease and the production of toxins which act locally and systemically to injure health. (Poisons injure health or promote early death.)

2. Inappropriate chemicals or inappropriate balance of chemicals passing through the intestines are absorbed into the blood and lymph and transported to other organs with a range of adverse effects.

3. Foods which are physically and chemically unsuitable are imperfectly digested and travel to the lower bowel where they provide nutrient supply for a host of unwelcome bacteria. Those bacteria produce toxic products, liquid and gaseous, that exert adverse effects on the bowel wall and systemic organs.

What's to be done?

First, we must publicise and talk about these things because without awareness no-one can avoid or remedy the problems inherent in cooked or raw processed diets.

Second, we can petition the 'competent authorities' and request that they take a closer look at the industries they are set up to regulate.

Third, informal and formal complaints procedures can be activated. A group of concerned pet owners in the USA are planning a series of class actions.

Fourth, do whatever it takes to improve the health of pets, the human economy and natural environment.

———

Stop press

Raw Meaty Bones, the book, is getting 'rave' reviews and just as significantly no-one has voiced any criticisms or said the thrust of the book is wrong/bad/misdirected or otherwise harmful.

Several veterinary journals are refusing to review or even discuss the book and the implications for animal health contained therein. Sometimes they give reasons but more commonly refuse to respond to correspondence.

Watch this space for names of the journals and their reasons, if any, for stifling debate.

December 2002: Keeping the veterinary record straight

Dear Reader,

How was Christmas? Good, I trust. And I hope you are looking forward to the New Year too.

Several RMB developments have come to a rapid conclusion in the run up to Christmas. One development deserves an early place on the public record, hence this last *RMB Newsletter* of 2002.

The British Veterinary Association publishes a weekly journal, the *Veterinary Record*, for its more than ten thousand members. The editor, Martin Alder, ignored letters asking him to consider *Raw Meaty Bones* for a review in the *Veterinary Record*. But in March 2002 I was able to contact him and he suggested that a copy of the book be sent to him for consideration.

Nine months later, after unanswered letters and unresolved telephone calls, Mr Alder has settled on the excuse for **not** reviewing the book. Over the nine months we have heard several excuses—'no time to look at it', 'can't find anyone to review the book', 'more important things to do' and the final choice 'not enough room in the journal'.

There are many reasons why the book *should* be reviewed in the *Veterinary Record*. First, it represents a (somewhat underhand) opportunity for critics of the book to have their say. Mr Alder pointed out that British law takes a more relaxed attitude to defamatory material published in a book review on the grounds that the 'book's author invited it'.

Second there are many positive reasons for reviewing the book (see Reviews and Veterinarians Say at www.rawmeatybones.com). Perhaps Dr Douglas Bryden sums it up with his recommendation 'every graduate and undergraduate veterinarian should read the book'.

The legitimacy of any institution or profession depends on its contribution to society. Veterinary institutions must meet a hierarchy of criteria. Decisions and actions should:

1. meet the needs of animals
2. meet the needs of animal owners
3. meet the needs of veterinarians
4. meet the needs of the institution, in this case the British Veterinary Association.

It seems that Mr Alder's decision fails on all four counts. History will judge if this apparent failure is an unfortunate mistake or whether it constitutes part of an ongoing attempt by the veterinary authorities to silence criticism and ban discussion of essential information.

The Royal College of Veterinary Surgeons, the body responsible for regulating British vets, has been kept informed and thus far has failed to act. But action will surely come against those who would ban discussion of essential information. Whether in a court room or commission of inquiry, I rather doubt Mr Alder's reasoning and defence of his employer, the British Veterinary Association, will withstand scrutiny. Criterion 4 above, under such circumstances, will be shown to fail abysmally.

Correspondence below helps to keep the British veterinary record straight.

The book review situation in the Australian veterinary journals is similarly bad and should be placed on the veterinary record. I'm hoping space will allow for a fuller description in forthcoming issues of the *RMB Newsletter*.

Wishing you a splendid New Year,
Best wishes,
Tom Lonsdale and the Raw Meaty Bones Crew

The Veterinary Record
VetRecord
VetRecord
VetRecord
VetRecord
Sorry, wrong number; you want the Honest Record

Thursday, 26 December 2002
To: Martin Alder <alder@bva-edit.co.uk>
From: Tom Lonsdale <tom@rawmeatybones.com>
Subject: Keeping the Veterinary Record Straight
Cc: AB, Alison Tyler, Bill Miller, Breck, Irene work,
Jane@rcvs.org.uk, registrar@rcvs.org.uk, bvahq@bva.co.uk

Dear Martin,

Thank you for your formal confirmation of your refusal
to review *Raw Meaty Bones* in your weekly publication *The
Veterinary Record*, journal of the British Veterinary Association. Dr Tom Hungerford OBE, grandfather of the Australian
veterinary profession, urged me:

> Tell the people who won't review their views that:
> 'The foolish and the dead never change their
> opinions.' Maybe that is an overstatement—as the
> 'brain-dead' may also refuse to revise. (Full text at
> https://rawmeatybones.com/hungerford.php[3])

In the interests of British pets, pet owners and veterinarians
I urge you and the British Veterinary Association to revise
your decision.

We must endeavour to keep faith with the community and keep the veterinary record straight. Accordingly, I
shall post this letter and the correspondence below on the
Internet.

Wishing you compliments of the Season,
Tom Lonsdale

15 July 2002
Mr Martin Alder
Editor
The Veterinary Record
7 Mansfield Street
London WIG 9NQ UK

Dear Mr Alder,

Review of *Raw Meaty Bones: Promote Health*

Further to previous correspondence on this issue I telephoned you today. You stated that you were busy and unable to discuss the matter since you were preparing to go away for two weeks. I said that I would therefore write to you.

You did say that: 'I was interested to see your line in the *Sunday Times* article,[4] the same line that you have taken in the book.'

On 28 June we discussed the issues at length. On that occasion you said: 'If we give you a good review you'll use it; if we give you a bad review you'll use it; I don't like being used.'

On 28 June you indicated that you would discuss the proposed review of the book with others at the British Veterinary Association.

It appears that rather than meet moral and ethical obligations to the membership and the wider community, the *Veterinary Record* and the British Veterinary Association are pursuing other agendas.

Please advise at the earliest if you will or will not review *Raw Meaty Bones* within the pages of the *Veterinary Record*. Please indicate the time frame for such a review or alternatively return the book and accompanying video.

Failure to resolve this issue, in my opinion, renders a considerable disservice to veterinary surgeons, pet owners and the wider community.

Please give this matter top priority.

Yours sincerely,
Tom Lonsdale
Cc. Royal College of Veterinary Surgeons

Sunday 8 December 2002
To: alder@bva-edit.co.uk
From: Tom Lonsdale <tom@rawmeatybones.com>
Subject: The Historical Record
Cc: AB, Alison Tyler, Bill Miller, Breck, Irene work, Jane Hern, press@bva.co.uk, bvahq@bva.co.uk
Bcc: Filing systemRCVS+Vet Rec,Filing systemHall of shame

Dear Martin,

Please find attached copies of letters which remain unanswered.

Alison Tyler, my US agent, informs me that on each occasion she has telephoned you that you have been evasive as to whether or not the *Veterinary Record* intends to publish a review of *Raw Meaty Bones*.

Your refusal to respond to the simplest questions has already secured you a place in the historical record.

The British Veterinary Association has an unenviable reputation as a promoter and supporter of artificial pet foods.

Raw Meaty Bones details the scandal where veterinarians promote and sell artificial pet foods and thus collude in the mass poisoning of domestic pets.

Unless British veterinary surgeons can be adequately informed, they are destined to continue their cruel and inhumane conduct.

Now through *The Veterinary Record* the BVA refuses to publish a review of *Raw Meaty Bones*, which Dr Douglas Bryden AM said[5] should be read by 'every graduate and undergraduate veterinarian'.

Please advise the names of the board of the BVA so that they may take their rightful place in the historical record.

Meanwhile it is incumbent on me to ensure that the contemporary record is maintained. Accordingly, I may publish your responses, or lack of responses, and those of other officers of the BVA, on the Internet and other places as required.

Yours sincerely
Tom Lonsdale

Monday 23 December 2002
From: alder@bva-edit.co.uk
Delivered to: lonsdale@summit.net.au
User-Agent: Microsoft-Outlook-Express-Macintosh-Edition/5.02.2022
Subject: Veterinary Record
From: Martin Alder <alder@bva-edit.co.uk>
To: tom@rawmeatybones.com

Dear Tom,

You and your agents have been pressing us to let you know whether we will be accepting your invitation [to] review your book *Raw Meaty Bones*. As I have tried to explain, other priorities mean that room for book reviews is limited, and we cannot review all the books we receive. This is to let you know that we will not be reviewing the book in the *Veterinary Record*, although we will be listing it as a 'Book Received'. As I have made clear to you and your agents, this is an editorial matter and not one in which the BVA has been involved.

Yours sincerely
Martin Alder
Editor
The Veterinary Record

3

2003: SPREADING THE WORD, FACING RESISTANCE

The campaign expands internationally, with lectures and public outreach raising awareness. However, institutional resistance stiffens, making it clear that change won't come easily.

May 2003: Raw meaty bones in New Zealand 1993 to 2003

Dear Reader,

2003 is almost half gone and no *RMB Newsletter* until now. Please accept my apologies—it's been a busy time.

How have you been? Are you still gaining the satisfaction of feeding pet carnivores on a diet close to Nature's specification? Are you spreading the good news?

In September 1993, the then dean of Massey University Veterinary School, New Zealand, Professor Peter Stockdale invited me to address the students. Recently I spent eight days in Wellington and Auckland. As the Kiwi readers of this newsletter will attest, New Zealand is a wonderful place. Visitors are made welcome and the food, scenery and Kiwi hospitality are superb. This year some journalists invited me onto their TV and radio programs.

New Zealand has a well-developed agricultural economy with many sheep, cattle and deer. Together with excellent fisheries, rabbits and possums the country, potentially, could generate a $multibillion healthy export pet food industry. I say potentially, because the veterinary establishment supports the multinational junk pet food manufacturers—and opposes the feeding of raw meaty bones.

Here's a brief account.

With best wishes,
Tom Lonsdale and the Raw Meaty Bones Crew

———

Raw meaty bones in New Zealand 1993–2003

A constant diet of junk food slowly poisons many dogs (and cats and ferrets) to death. Along the way, a plague of diseases descends on the unfortunate animals. Foul mouth-rot runs at between 70% and 100%. Liver, kidney, heart and skin diseases are common. Some animals suffer an acquired immune deficiency syndrome.

Animals can't speak about their suffering. Some become slow and sad; others become hyperactive and hard to train; some become unpredictable.

Back in 1991 the Raw Meaty Bones Lobby (Dr Alan Bennet, Dr Breck Muir and I) started to campaign within the Australian veterinary community. The essence of a carnivore diet, we reasoned, should be raw meaty bones. If pet owners get that right, then most other things fall happily into place—with good pet health and cost savings being the major benefits.

News of the Australian campaign reached New Zealand and the then Dean of Massey University Veterinary School, Professor Peter Stockdale. He contacted me and told me how he believed in the benefits, for all species, of natural food fed in a natural context and invited me to address the students. A date was set in September 1993 and I set to work on the presentation entitled 'Pet food's insidious consequences: a modern veterinary snafu'.

———

Pet food's insidious consequences: a modern veterinary snafu, 9 September 1993

Summary

A recurring theme is that both content and form of the pro-pet food argument is flawed, making invalid conclusions the rule. The euphemistic use of the term 'pet food' is deplored and the cynical manipulation of the rules of logic, mass psychology, politics and economics is described. Insidious environmental consequences are listed. Veterinary science is seen to be corrupted due to an uncritical appraisal by those responsible for animal healthcare.

The state of health is dependent upon the correct balance of quantity, quality and frequency of chemical and physical requirements provided by food intake. Examples of failure are provided with the emphasis being placed on periodontal disease. Recent case surveys and research findings are presented on foul mouth AIDS, feline eosinophilic disease complex, plasma cell pododermatitis and FLUTD.

The limitations of the clinical diagnostic pathways are shown to perpetuate the insidious process. A 'cybernetic hypothesis of periodontal disease' provides an evolutionary, ecological perspective casting the modern feeding practices in a grim light. Arising out of this dark and corrupted phase a renaissance is predicted providing beneficial insight into health and disease.

(Full transcript at Raw Meaty Bones website[1])

My lawyer cleared the paper for publication and with a video of TV segments, slide show and 100 printed copies of the lecture I headed for New Zealand. Professor Stockdale provided a warm welcome and introduced Dr Grant Guilford, who was to be my host and guide.

(Dr Guilford gained his doctorate in nutrition from the University of California.)

Some students were hostile to the natural diet message, but by and large the lecture was a success. After the lecture, over pizza and red wine, Grant Guilford and I talked until the early hours. We found common ground and areas of general agreement and when we parted Dr Guilford took the remaining printed copies for the students.

Now, ten years on, what's changed in New Zealand regarding veterinary education and attitudes to a more natural diet? Professor Stockdale has retired and Grant Guilford is now a professor and dean of the Veterinary School. Professor Guilford, so I'm informed, recommends commercial foods and opposes the raw meaty bones message.

Since the health of New Zealand pets, the education of New Zealand's future vets and the wellbeing of the agricultural economy are inextricably linked to the attitude of the dean of the Veterinary School, it might be helpful if Professor Guilford were to publish his reasons for his opposition to the raw meaty bones message.

Dog attacks in New Zealand

After a spate of dog attacks on small children, New Zealanders are concerned to deal with the issues. The government proposes to legislate that, among other things, all dogs are to be microchipped, four breeds of dogs are to be banned from importation and all properties to be fenced in such a way as to allow unimpeded access to the front door.

Governments need to be seen to be diligent, but so often they seek to restrict and prohibit activities when in fact underlying cultural problems remain to be addressed. Since a majority of dog attacks occur in the home the chief victims, New Zealand children, will be unlikely to gain increased protection and the other victims—dogs and dog owners—will be further victimised.

Journalists, aware that highly processed junk food can give rise to unpredictable behaviour in people, sought comment from me on the diet and behaviour connection in pets. First, I suggested that a culture exists, a culture promulgated by the junk pet food industry, that dogs are akin to disposable, furry toys with little in the way of maintenance necessary beyond opening a can or packet of junk food. As a result, too many unsuitable animals are kept in unsuitable conditions. A more responsible view entails accepting dogs as modified wolves with corresponding modified wolf anatomy, physiology and behaviour. People who take this responsible, realistic view may be less inclined to get a dog unless they can fully provide for its needs—including keeping it from harming small children.

Acknowledgement that the wolf gene runs through our domestic dog population leads to the acknowledgement that pet dogs need a wolf-type diet—not junk food. And of course, this is the other main area where the junk pet food industry misleads the community. Their simplistic ads persuade people to get a dog and then encourage the feeding of junk pet food at every meal—with serious health and behavioural consequences.

Dog trainers tell me that a small percentage of dogs switched from a junk food to a raw diet become more aggressive—it's as if those dogs feel more confident and can express their innate aggression. But for the majority the opposite is the case. Dogs with a range of behavioural problems—hyperactivity, disobedience, aggression—become content and tractable once fed a more natural diet. (Care should be exercised at feeding time—dogs tend to guard raw bones.)

On 24 April, *Holmes*, the main New Zealand TV current affairs program, ran a story on the adverse impact of junk pet foods and later in the evening the topic got a good airing on Kim Hill's *Face-to-Face* program. A number of radio stations covered the topic. For the future, New Zealand vets will have a big part to play in safeguarding their community against the unwelcome effects of artificial feeding. Let's hope the vets take an interest in and research the evidence.

The behavioural and neurological abnormalities passage from *Raw Meaty Bones* is reproduced below. Please circulate as you see fit.

———

Raw Meaty Bones: Promote Health, pp. 111–13

Behavioural and neurological abnormalities

Probably the most common behavioural abnormality of diet-affected pets is lassitude and prolonged sleeping. Owners do not consider this to be a nuisance, or sign of ill-health, and consequently seldom seek advice. When cats and dogs are constantly pacing, vocalising and exhibiting aggression, owners frequently take a different view. Unfortunately, anti-social behaviour often leads to the pet's early death. Each year, whether at welfare shelters or veterinary clinics, millions of unruly pets are put down by injection.

In the beginning, when I started to change animals to a natural diet, I was surprised when owners reported that previously agitated aggressive animals had become contented. (Some owners worry, unnecessarily, that pets with a taste for raw food might become savage.) On reflection one should not be surprised if artificially fed animals, in chronic pain, appear cantankerous by comparison with their naturally fed counterparts. Gnawing on bones keeps mouths healthy and pain-free. It's possible gnawing exercise releases endorphins in the carnivore brain giving rise to a natural high. In humans, evidence is being accumulated that some dietary chemicals, dubbed nutraceuticals, travel directly to the brain and thereby improve neuronal activity including ability to memorise facts. Could there be nutraceuticals in the natural food of carnivores?

Back in London in the 1970s I remember an outbreak of frenzied cats. The demented creatures would growl and hiss and race around madly as if pursued by a thousand demons. When it was discovered that not demons but benzoic acid preservative in the food was the cause, the problem subsided almost as quickly as it arose. Modern additives may be having similar if not such dramatic effects. It is now well accepted that food additives can play a part in hyperactivity and attention deficit disorder in young children. Since many pets consume still higher levels of the same additives, similar effects can be expected.

Corn (maize) is the principal ingredient in many processed foods. Tryptophan, an essential amino acid, is in short supply in corn protein and the vitamin niacin is largely unavailable. Tryptophan is a precursor of the important brain chemical serotonin and people lacking niacin suffer a disease known as pellagra, the signs of which include dementia. In 1983 Professor David Kronfeld speculated that peculiar pet behaviour may be attributable to the high corn levels in processed food. He also reported that one large pet food company was testing diets for their behaviour impact.

In 1986 the animal behaviourist Roger Mugford spoke about aggressive golden retrievers at a Waltham symposium. Some of the dogs, despite being members of a breed usually noted for docility, had inflicted serious wounds on their owners. When Mugford changed the dogs' diet from commercial to home-cooked food he observed some dramatic improvements.

This raises important questions:

- What further improvement would have been detected in the golden retrievers if Mugford had tried a natural diet?
- Since 1983, when Kronfeld said companies were researching behavioural aspects of diet, what have pet food companies discovered?
- Are pets being unnecessarily destroyed due to diet-induced aggression?
- What are the health, financial and amenity costs of food-induced aggression?

- Are manufacturers legally liable for pain, loss and suffering arising from the sale of their products?

One, admittedly isolated, example of an apparent direct connection between diet and brain function occurred when a little white shaker came into my general veterinary practice. White shakers tend to be white, for instance Maltese or West Highland white terriers, and they suffer from the uncontrollable shakes. The textbooks locate the problem in the brain but do not offer much help on an effective cure. Knowing these facts it was easy to propose a diet change for the patient—there appeared to be little to lose and everything to gain. Within a couple of days the shakes had gone. It is to be hoped that others will obtain similar good results with so little effort.

May 2003: Barbarous veterinary surgeons

Dear Reader,

The world's pets pay a high price for the veterinary profession's failings regarding the junk pet food scam.

In Britain things are especially bad. Two national vet associations ignore or suppress the diet cruelty issue whilst maintaining their contacts with the junk food producers.

Six university veterinary schools are tied to the companies by 'sponsorships' and 'research' money. A central regulatory body—the Royal College of Veterinary Surgeons—monitors the whole septic mess but does nothing to remedy it.

This *RMB Newsletter* provides a brief snapshot of recent developments.

Wishing you the best of health,
Tom Lonsdale and the Raw Meaty Bones Crew

———

Barbarous veterinary surgeons May 2003

'Promoting and sustaining confidence in veterinary medicine' proclaims the slogan at the Royal College of Veterinary Surgeons website.

Without a trace of irony they assert:

The Royal College of Veterinary Surgeons (RCVS) is the regulatory body for veterinary surgeons in the United Kingdom and ensures that standards within the veterinary profession are maintained, safeguarding the health and welfare of animals and the interests of the public.

Around 20,000 veterinary surgeons are registered with the RCVS—it's a requirement for vets wishing to practise in the UK and it's called 'being on the register'. The alternative is known as 'being struck off the register' and is the ultimate punishment the RCVS imposes on those it deems unfit to practise. Fear informs much veterinary thought and behaviour

—fear of being dragged before the RCVS and being 'struck off'.

At any time, there are usually a few veterinarians being investigated by the RCVS. Often these are the hapless individuals with alcohol, health or other social problems that get caught up in the RCVS disciplinary machinery, their alleged crime often being a single instance of purported error of judgement leading to an unwelcome outcome for a single animal. Sometimes it's a dissatisfied client who lodges a complaint, sometimes a rival veterinary practitioner.

When it comes to the mass poisoning of domestic pets by veterinary surgeons that promote and sell junk pet food, hitherto, the Royal College of Veterinary Surgeons has done little or nothing—despite their undertaking:

> The RCVS is the regulatory body for veterinary surgeons in the UK. Its role is:
>
> - To safeguard the health and welfare of animals committed to veterinary care through the regulation of the educational, ethical and clinical standards of the veterinary profession, thereby protecting the interests of those dependent on animals and assuring public health.
> - To act as an impartial source of informed opinion on animal health and welfare issues and their interaction with human health.

For the past seven years I have stood as a candidate in RCVS elections—in an attempt to draw attention to the junk-food hypocrisy and encourage the RCVS to reconsider its position and commission an independent committee of inquiry.

In most years, about 3,000 of the 20,000 veterinarians vote. And of those, about 10% cast their vote in support of appropriate action by the RCVS. This year 298 registered veterinary surgeons supported the manifesto: 'Pushers of poison or dispensers of medicine—you choose'.[2]

Old-time barber-surgeons inflicted hurt and suffering on their patients—suffering inflicted on patients, one at a time. Nowadays, I suggested:

Let's be honest, mainstream veterinary opinion and its supporting institutions pose considerable threat to the health and comfort of the world's pets. At all levels vets endorse, promote and sell artificial pet foods—the source of so much disease and ill-health.

When members of the public raise concerns about perceived, isolated instances of veterinary misconduct, the RCVS investigates. When 298 qualified and registered veterinary surgeons perceive that serious misconduct is widespread, surely the Royal College has a duty to investigate?

An open letter seeking an independent inquiry has been submitted to the journal of the British Veterinary Association.[3]

The letter draws attention to the RCVS ratification of kidney transplantation in cats.[4]

Some veterinarians expressed alarm at the apparent moral, ethical and legal implications of the RCVS ratification of kidney transplants from healthy donor cats for the questionable 'benefit' of sick, elderly animals. Prior to casting their votes, some veterinarians sought to ascertain the candidates' views. I responded:

> On the evidence available to me I am strongly opposed to kidney transplantation. Given that most cases of feline kidney disease appear to derive from an unsuitable diet (and the periodontal disease so arising) then subjecting cats to kidney transplantation amounts to one of the worst excesses of the pet food cult.

For many years the Council of the Royal College of Veterinary Surgeons has downplayed or ignored the devastating effect processed pet foods exert on the oral and overall health of pets.

But lest I be accused of bias, perhaps we should leave the last word to Waltham, the division of the Mars Corporation that makes the Pedigree line of junk food and claims to feed one third of the world's pets.

In a 2002 advertising piece, promoting their artificial bones, sent to 13,172 UK veterinary surgeons they suggest pets need to chew—

something their junk foods do not require—in order to keep teeth clean and prevent the occurrence of gum disease. They recommend that animals should clean their teeth every day because:

> Major health problems can start with gum disease. Dental problems are known to increase with age and are increasingly being linked to vital organ disease—most notably kidneys and liver.

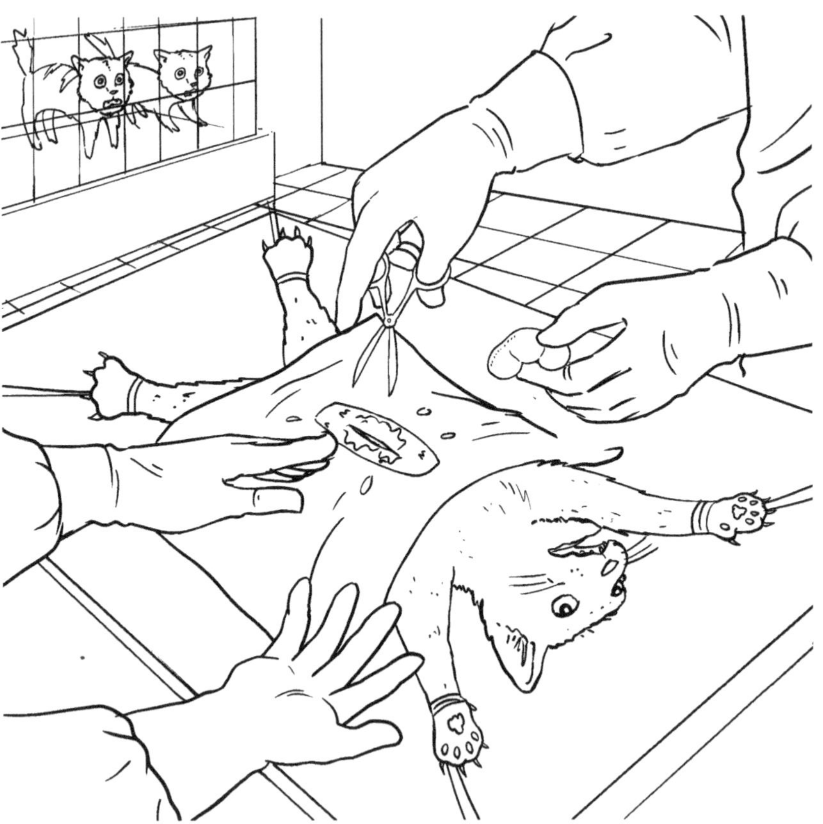

November 2003: Prescription for a healthy veterinary profession

Dear Reader,

The British Government is changing the rules for British vets.

Under the current Veterinary Surgeons Act, vets occupy 90% of the seats on the governing Council of the Royal College of Veterinary Surgeons—and as the saying goes: 'Power tends to corrupt, and absolute power corrupts absolutely.'

Now the British Government is proposing that, under the new rules, vets should control 60% of the seats. But of course, that would still give vets a permanent hold on power. Is it likely that they would behave any less corruptly?

Some excellent submissions have been sent to Paul McDonald, the government officer coordinating the review of the Act. (See below.)

Recently I spoke with Mr McDonald, who remarked that he had received 'loads of emails' from several countries and thanked us for bringing the pet food problem to his attention. It's a global problem; vets are 'living a lie' the world over. (Some animal 'welfare' organisations are also in the pocket of the pet food manufacturers.) But it is the British Government that is currently reviewing the rules—and therefore has the responsibility to ensure any new arrangements adequately deal with current and foreseeable problems.

Mr McDonald remarked that, whilst we had drawn attention to the problems, we had not recommended specific changes that we believe are necessary for the proper functioning of the veterinary profession.

If vets have complete control then the results are ruinous. They promote their own immediate self-interest—whilst pretending otherwise.

If the Government appoints a regulator then once again all power will reside with the regulator.

As imperfect as democratic arrangements may be, I suggest that the new regulatory committee overseeing the UK vets should have a limit of 50% veterinary representation. (Even 40% representation by vets would be OK.)

Under this model a sense of partnership between vets and the government and community representatives would be more likely to prevail—a realisation that their job is to serve the community not the self-interest of the vets and their pet food industry backers.

It seems to me that if the British Government gets this part right the other fine details won't matter so much. The future will be able to take care of itself. (There will likely be flow-on benefits for other countries too.)

Below I've formulated an email that you might like to copy and send to Mr McDonald. Otherwise writing your own email would possibly carry greater 'weight'. Please sign your email and indicate to Mr McDonald where you live and why you are qualified to comment.

We have until the 17 December 2003 to get *lots of* submissions to Mr McDonald.

Best wishes,
Tom Lonsdale

To: Paul.A.McDonald@defra.gsi.gov.uk
Subject: Recommendation for an improved Veterinary
Surgeons Act
Cc: tom@rawmeatybones.com

Dear Mr McDonald,

The current Veterinary Surgeons Act vests 90% control of the Royal College of Veterinary Surgeons) in the hands of veterinary surgeons.

The current proposal to reduce veterinary representation to 60% may appear to increase accountability. However, in my view this arrangement would still vest total control in the hands of veterinary surgeons.

Lord Acton remarked: 'Power tends to corrupt, and absolute power corrupts absolutely.'

The Royal College of Veterinary Surgeons' refusal to

contemplate an investigation and resolution of the pet food scandal is a prime example of power corrupting absolutely.

I suggest that power within the veterinary regulatory framework needs to be shared.

Please ensure that the new Veterinary Surgeons Act limits veterinary membership of the Council of the Royal College of Veterinary Surgeons to a maximum 50%.

In respect to the balance of the RCVS Council safeguards will need to be put in place.

I believe that manufacturers, manufacturers' organisations and 'front organisations' should be excluded from sitting on the RCVS Council.

Animal Welfare and other organisations should be required to publish their funding structure. A limit should be set, say 10%, for funding received from any one company or 20% from any one industry.

Thank you for your consideration.

Yours sincerely,
(Name, address, qualifications/experience)

Pet owner letters submitted to the Veterinary Surgeons Act review team

Dear Mr McDonald,

The following are my comments on the proposals for modernisation of the Veterinary Surgeons Act ('the Act').

In your preamble you state that the Act provides for 'regulating their professional education and professional conduct'.

My concern is primarily with the corrupting nexus between pet food manufacturers and veterinarians' professional education and ethical guidance by their professional associations.

In the 35 years since you last examined the Act, the field of pet nutrition has become almost monopolised by pet food manufacturers. These manufacturers, acting in the same way as all large commercial entities in the new capitalism, are not selling an ethical product. Rather they are more concerned with the retailing of a label to as wide a market as they can create. Their ethics are not controlled in any way by any external regulator in any part of the world and yet the veterinary profession has come to be as closely identified with processed cat and dog feed as it is with any ethically developed pharmaceutical.

I am in no doubt that the pet food companies have managed the selective release and suppression of their extensive findings on cat and dog nutrition so as to maximise their profit without regard for the welfare of the cats and dogs which consume their products. I believe this has been managed by a combination of judicious propagation of nutrition myths with just enough correct information as will ensure continued 'pushing' of their products by veterinarians.

The deleterious effects of consumption of processed pet foods are recognised and too many to detail here. They begin with an animal's dentition and cascade through digestive systems which are unsuited to dealing with carbohydrate-laden intake. They include production of excreta which adds both in bulk and hazard to the load on the urban environment. They include disease and consequent distress of a myriad poorly managed outcomes. They also include temperament and stress outcomes from as serious as dog bite to as pathetic as self-mutilation.

I am unqualified to even guess at the size of financial burdens on pet owners, but I am sure such burdens are among the effects of processed pet food.

The widespread suffering here in Australia from the feline

lower urinary tract disease epidemic in cats caused by exclusive consumption of dried pellets is alone enough reason for the pet food manufacturers to either be cut off from their cosy access to the confidence which veterinarians have from their customers or to at least be brought to account in the same ethical way as any pharmaceutical manufacturer whose product a veterinarian prescribes.

Since I doubt any government would choose to allocate already stretched revenue to the establishment of a regulatory system over cat and dog food manufacture—if indeed it had the resources to match a company the size and reach of the Mars Corporation in such a loser's game—I urge you to write into the Act the necessity for true arms-length relationships between professional veterinary bodies and pet food manufacturers and to place the relationships between the profession and those manufacturers in the same category as the relationships with pharmaceutical manufacturers.

It is easy to see that the aims of veterinarians—to heal animals and to do no harm—are at variance with manufacturers whose aims are to increase their market (and profit) above everything. Pet food manufacturers, in seeking wider markets, promote the desirability of pet ownership (mostly, I note, the kind of pet for which they manufacture a product). They are further addicting the small animal veterinarian today to the over-supply of animals as well as the manufacturers' products. So much so that attempts by responsible pet owners and welfare organisations to limit the casual abandoning or ill-treatment of pets have not even put a dent in the numbers of healthy young animals euthanised each year. How can veterinarians be objective about a problem that they are complicit in promoting and supporting?

Clearly, you will need to examine the Act's requirements for how veterinarians receive their professional education with particular reference to nutrition training. At the same time I once again urge you to examine the nexus between veterinarians' professional associations and pet food manufacturers with the aim of separating veterinary ethics from pet food manufacturers marketing plans.

I have no doubt that there is already impetus for such action in other countries.

I hope you give full consideration to my comments above, which have been hard won over around ten years of first-hand experience of many of the ill effects of processed animal foods.

I am not a veterinarian. I do not have any interest in commercial supply of any animal feed. I do not breed or care for any animals except my home companions.

I shall be pleased to supply more information if you need it.

Thank you for your consideration.

Yours faithfully,
Nancy McIntyre
Resident in Harvey, Western Australia

Address willingly supplied if requested

Dear Mr McDonald,

Thank you for the opportunity to comment on proposals for modernisation of the UK's Veterinary Surgeons Act.

I am in full agreement with Dr Tom Lonsdale that this review of the Act provides an excellent opportunity to examine the ties between the veterinary profession and the multinational companies who produce artificial diets which result in a chain of disastrous system failures for pets.

The review also presents an opportunity to examine the commercial ties between the veterinary profession and pharmaceutical companies. Unnecessary over-vaccination of pets is creating many problems for their immune systems.

Having been involved in breeding and showing purebred dogs here in Australia over three decades, I've had ample opportunity to observe the adverse impact of inappropriate nutrition and unnecessary drugs.

In my view the aforementioned alliances are little short of criminal in their effects.

Thank you for your consideration.

Yours sincerely,
Judy McMahon

Liz Hennel, RMN, RGN
3 Hanging Lees Close,
Newhey, Rochdale
OL16 3SG
Telephone 01706 846040/880209

Dear Mr McDonald,

I am writing in response to information I recently came across regarding the reform proposals for the veterinary Surgeons Act.

As a pet owner all my life, I have become increasingly concerned at the deterioration (as opposed to the improvement) in animal health over the last 10 years. Much of this I lay at the doors of the vets themselves and the pet food industry.

My reasoning goes thus: if you give any living creature an inappropriate diet then you will naturally affect its health and render it more susceptible to all forms of disease, acute and chronic. It is like trying to run a Rolls Royce car on 2-stroke fuel; it can't be done.

The 2-stroke fuel in this case is the junk food that is assertively promoted in all our information media—television and press, etc. Proprietary animal foods, packaged for our 'convenience', in both dry and wet forms are full of unnecessary ingredients that no animal in its right mind or natural state would choose to eat. These foods certainly contribute to dental problems, digestive and skin problems, and the toxic loads they create predispose to more lethal disease affecting kidneys, liver—and promoting malignancy and behavioural problems—these all have a dreadful effect on owners, emotionally—and financially. So-called science diets are formulated to make a profit and get repeat sales, to fill the animal up and not much else. Many proprietary foods are full of substances such as aromatics, as in their 'raw' state they would not be attractive food choices for the animals.

We have forgotten how to cope without great bags of dried food, or cans of pappy wet foods. Most owners are horrified when told their animal's diet has contributed to its health problems. None of us would knowingly feed toxic rubbish to our pets, but many owners don't know what else to do. This misinformation is perpetuated by the veterinary profession, promoting products only available through their practices, pooh-poohing other nutritional ideas, and further de-skilling owners. It creates a dependency culture, which given the profit bias of these practices—they are businesses first and foremost—is more than a little suspect. It actually becomes more of a fraud.

Sick animals are clearly what veterinary surgeons trained to deal with—but what if their practices are creating health problems? If this were to happen in human medicine, there would be a huge outcry. Fraudulent medicine is hunted out and ruthlessly put down, and quite rightly. But who speaks for animals? The veterinary and pet food manufacturers. But there are just so many vested interests in these two groups are they truly to be trusted? I'm afraid that I don't think so anymore.

I would also draw your attention to some other practices that I am concerned may not be in the best interests of our companion animals. Over-medication is every bit as great a problem in veterinary medicine as it is in human medicine. The rise in the use of steroidal and non-steroidal anti-inflammatory has been enormous, and antibiotic prescriptions have also risen.

One medication is accepted almost without question. Annual vaccination of cats and dogs is routine, it is drummed into us. However, there is now an increasing body of evidence both here in the UK, and overseas, to suggest that this protocol is implicated in the rise of chronic disease, including cancers. Some vets are now of the opinion that vaccination may not be required more frequently than at three- to four-year intervals, and that titre levels can be checked in between. However, there is clearly a conflict of interest here too. Vets, as already indicated, are in business and need to make a profit. Vaccinations represent a substantial profit—the mark-up on them is phenomenal. The pharmaceutical industry that supplies vets is reluctant to see a reduction in the frequency of administration—they clearly want the repeat sales, and vets are not going to promote a drop in their income.

One vet in the Midlands who charged an appropriate (lower) fee for immunisation was hounded by her professional body, to force her to comply with the rest of the profession as it was clear she was showing them up. Does this not smack of restrictive practices? Is this a body we can trust to represent our best interests when they behave in this fashion?

It is extremely difficult to make a complaint about an individual vet. The RCVS are not user friendly. They are also slow to respond. They have very restrictive methods of reporting, and they also restrict the sort of complaints that they are prepared to consider—this I know from personal experience. I would like to see much more openness and transparency in this particular respect.

I am 'just' a pet owner—I come from a nursing background, so I am well placed to be able to make some assessment of the care that my animals receive. Because I want the best for my animals I am prepared, and educated enough, to be able to do my own research, to ask questions—and sort out the misinformation from the good stuff. I have struggled to find a vet that I can have a dialogue with, rather than be patronised and patted on the head like my dogs. This profession needs to be dragged into the modern world, rather than continuing to operate in a fashion that was more acceptable some 50 years ago. This is a generalisation, and I have to say I have encountered pockets of fabulous practice too—but it is unusual.

Yours faithfully
Liz Hennel

4

———

2004: THE VET-INDUSTRIAL PET FOOD COMPLEX TIGHTENS ITS GRIP

The pet food industry's deep ties to veterinary organisations become clearer. Despite mounting evidence of harm, scientific research continues to be ignored or manipulated.

January 2004: Blindness, wilful or unwitting, it's still blindness

Dear Reader,

Here's the first *RMB Newsletter* for 2004.

How were your Christmas and New Year celebrations? Have you made New Year resolutions?

On the raw feeding front we need a resolution to collectively keep going—on the road to success.

Last year more people travelled the road and their pets are happier and healthier for it.

Discussion on the rawfeeding list continued apace.

The rawvets discussion list gained more members.

Two UK-based vets, Johan Joubert and Roger Meacock, are actively campaigning for an end to the current veterinary hypocrisy. Long term, the future belongs to the young, so it's gratifying to see the vet students on the rawvet list leading discussions. (One day, about a generation from now, they will be professors and deans of vet schools.)

To speed things up, if you know any vets or vet students, please encourage them to join the rawvet list.

But otherwise there's always lots to do. Changing the way pets are fed will not only improve the health of pets, it will also 'give the lie' to the so-called scientific methodology practised by the pet food industry/vet profession this past 100 or so years. I believe we are on the threshold of a paradigm shift which will have seismic repercussions for vet science, medicine, dentistry and science generally.

If you get time for reading, then please check out the books listed for Raw Meaty Bones seminar students.[1]

In this issue of the *RMB Newsletter* I'd like to draw attention to the wilful blindness and unwitting blindness affecting those in authority—and who thus impede progress.

Here's wishing you a successful, fun 2004,
Tom Lonsdale

———

Modernisation of the Veterinary Surgeons Act 1966

The past two newsletters were devoted to the changes in the rules governing vet conduct in the UK.

By setting up a system whereby vets have to play fair—not just give lip-service to their slogan, 'Promoting and sustaining public confidence in veterinary medicine'—we can expect major structural improvements.

Currently the rules say vets have to act honestly and fairly. But because vets control the Royal College of Veterinary Surgeons—and because we have a corrupt culture whereby the majority of vets encourage the poisoning of pets, even sell the poison—fairness and honesty are in short supply.

The Royal College of Veterinary Surgeons has consistently blocked the investigation of the mighty scientific and consumer fraud perpetrated by the vets, in conjunction with their pet food paymasters.

Now, it would seem, the British government is siding with the vets in the shameful exploitation of animals and people.

Many people wrote to Paul McDonald, the coordinator of the Veterinary Surgeons Act Team, who is reviewing the current situation with a view to an improved set of rules.

This is the standard letter Mr McDonald sent to those registering their concerns about the widespread corruption.

Letter from Veterinary Surgeons Act team

From: Paul A. McDonald (AHAW)
[mail to: Paul.A.McDonald@defra.gsi.gov.uk]
Sent: 16 December 2003
To: Sarah.Cullen@jet.uk
Subject: Review of the Veterinary Surgeons Act

Dear Ms Cullen,

Thank you for your email of 1 December, in response to the Defra consultation on the 'modernisation of the Veterinary Surgeons Act 1966'. Whilst I understand some of the issues you raise concerning the pet food industry, they are not relevant to the modernisation of the Act.

All I can suggest is that should you have any specific evidence of disgraceful misconduct against any particular veterinary surgeon in the United Kingdom, and should you wish to do so, is make an official complaint through the Royal College of Veterinary Surgeons disciplinary procedures.[2]

Should you have any specific issues you wish to raise with regard to the disciplinary procedures, the registration of veterinary surgeons, or any other points made in our consultation paper, we would be pleased to hear from you.

Paul McDonald
Animal Welfare Division
DEFRA, Area 605
1A Page Street, London SW1P 4PQ
Tel: 020 7904 6588 | Fax: 020 7904 6962

Seemingly the mass poisoning of animals by the majority of veterinary surgeons is of no concern to the Animal Welfare Division of the UK Government Department for Environment, Food and Rural Affairs.

This humbug/outrage/scandal is the more severe when one considers the first two principles of animal welfare:

- That there is a critical relationship between animal health and animal welfare.
- That the internationally recognised 'five freedoms' (freedom from hunger, thirst and malnutrition; freedom from fear and distress; freedom from physical and thermal discomfort; freedom from pain, injury and disease; and freedom to express normal patterns of behaviour) provide valuable guidance in animal welfare.

If you are shocked by the indifference of Mr McDonald's response then please let him know at Paul.A.McDonald@defra.gsi.gov.uk.

Please send a copy to tom@rawmeatybones.com for possible publication in future newsletters.

———

Evidence-based vets

So much for bureaucratic wilful blindness—now for some (likely) unwitting blindness.

Dr Trisha Greenhalgh is professor of primary healthcare at University College London. As an expert on evidence-based human medicine she was asked to lead a workshop for vet academics at the Royal Veterinary College, University of London.

That's the school that I went to 32 years ago and which is now in the grip of the pet food monster. In the RVC 2001/2 annual report, Professor Peter Bedford is listed as the grant holder for the £103,644 Waltham Lecturer and the £90,000 Ralston Purina Lecturer—money provided by Mars and Nestlé, the makers of the bulk of the poison affecting the world's pets.

Chances are that Professor Greenhalgh, when speaking with the academics at the Royal Veterinary College, had little knowledge of the guilty secret—that the entire edifice of vet teaching is founded on deceptive pretence. In her article published in the *British Medical Journal* Professor Greenhalgh casts doubts about 'jobbing vets' but she appears to be impressed that the 'elite academics didn't miss a trick'.

You can read the article at the *BMJ*.[3]

At the foot of the article there are some rapid responses.

I think it would be terrific if more rapid responses were written explaining how the 'jobbing vets' represent the leaf and branch of the corrupt culture, but the roots of the problem start with the world's vet schools and so-called 'elite academics'.

If you need help sending in a response to the *British Medical Journal* please let me know at tom@rawmeatybones.com. Similarly, it would be good to receive copies for the archives and possible future publication.

April 2004: New scientific thought, persistent vet school madness

Dear Reader,

How's 2004 treating you? Are your pets thriving, are you spreading the good health message?

Daily I receive letters from pet owners who, having switched their pets to a raw diet, confirm the good health of their pets and savings on vet bills. These benefits, if spread across the majority of the world's dog, cat and ferret owners, would make for the alleviation of cruelty on an immense scale and the dollar benefits could finance a large chunk of third world debt—and ease some of the global tensions.

That, you might say, is a mighty set of objectives and reason for us to press on with the good health message. But that's not all. The fundamental biological scientific and medical benefits waiting to be discovered and harvested add a mighty extra dimension.

This edition of the *RMB Newsletter* looks at a couple of aspects of the 'extra dimension' and concludes with comments from an oppressed veterinary student rebelling against veterinary school brainwashing.

Wishing you, your family and pets the best of good health,
Tom Lonsdale

———

Time (Australia/Pacific) cover story 23 February 2004

The secret killer
The surprising link between inflammation and heart attacks, cancer, Alzheimer's and other diseases.

What you can do to fight it

———

'Chronic inflammation may be the engine that drives many of the most feared illnesses of middle and old age.' Says *Time* magazine in its cover story.

Here are some excerpts from the article:

> This concept is so intriguing because it suggests a new and possibly much simpler way of warding off disease. Instead of different treatments for, say, heart disease, Alzheimer's and colon cancer, there might be a single, inflammation-reducing remedy that would prevent all three ...
>
> This new view of inflammation is changing the way some scientists do medical research. 'Virtually our entire R-and-D effort is [now] focused on inflammation and cancer', says Dr Robert Tepper, president of research and development at Millennium Pharmaceuticals in Cambridge, Massachusetts. In medical schools across the US, cardiologists, rheumatologists, oncologists, allergists and neurologists are all suddenly talking to one another—and they're discovering that they're looking at the same thing. The speed with which researchers are jumping on the inflammation bandwagon is breathtaking. Just a few years ago, 'nobody was interested in this stuff', says Dr Paul Ridker, a cardiologist at Brigham and Women's Hospital who has done some of the groundbreaking work in the area. 'Now the whole field of inflammation research is about to explode.'

Time reports:

> Problems begin when, for one reason or another, the inflammatory process persists and becomes chronic; the final effects are varied and depend a lot on where in the body the runaway reaction takes hold. Among the first to recognise the broader implications were heart doctors who noticed that inflammation seems to play a key role in cardiovascular disease.

Diabetes researchers have adopted the new approach.

> What they have discovered is a complex interplay between inflammation, insulin and fat—either in the diet or in large folds under the skin. (Indeed, fat cells behave a lot like immune cells, spewing out inflammatory cytokines, particularly as you gain weight.) Where inflammation fits into this scenario—as either a cause or an effect—remains unclear. But the case for a central role is getting stronger.

And the underlying inflammation, in humans as well as animals, is often considered to be periodontal disease, that chronic inflammation affecting the gums and supporting structures of the teeth.

At the end of a most illuminating article *Time* comments:

> But there is a sense that much more basic research into the nature of inflammation needs to be done before scientists understand how best to limit the damage in chronic diseases.
>
> In the meantime, there are things we all can do to dampen our inflammatory fires. Some of the advice may sound terribly familiar, but we have fresh reasons to follow through. Losing weight induces those fat cells—remember them?—to produce fewer cytokines. So does regular exercise, 30 minutes a day most days of the week. Flossing your teeth combats gum disease, another source of chronic inflammation. Fruits, vegetables and fish are full of substances that disable free radicals.

Of course, the *Time* recommendation to eat lots of fruit and vegetables refers to our (omnivorous) dietary needs. *Time* makes the point about periodontal disease and the need for dental hygiene with an illustration of dental floss being pulled from the floss dispenser. Dogs, cats and ferrets (carnivores) floss and brush as they eat their natural food. And fresh natural carnivore food provides them with the nutrients necessary to combat the chemical effects of chronic inflammation too.

———

Cybernetic hypothesis of periodontal disease in mammalian carnivores[4]

How periodontal disease inflammation might fit into the bigger picture of health, disease and population control, to my mind, is an intriguing question. The cybernetic hypothesis of periodontal disease, conceived in a dream on Christmas morning 1992, sets out a possible explanatory framework.

Last year, during the Emory University extension course, Dr Erin Mayfield found new information that appears to provide crucial support for the cybernetic hypothesis.

That information forms the basis of an article soon to be published by the University of Sydney Post Graduate Foundation in Veterinary Science.

Calculus, olfaction and cybernetics: a crucial test
University of Sydney Post Graduate Foundation in Veterinary Science, Control and Therapy No. 4516

Dr Erin Mayfield (medical doctor and gynaecologist) is: 'Horrified by the pandemic of periodontal disease, which appears to be precipitated by the artificial pet food diets'. Delighted with the tenor of an article she found on the internet, Dr Mayfield shared her find with fellow students in the Raw Meaty Bones class.[1]

Predilection to dental calculus formation in a group of dogs: influence of calculus on the sense of smell.
The tendency of some dogs to rapidly develop dental calculus is well known. A group of beagle dogs being utilised in a study of bovine estrus detection capability was found to have such a tendency. Over a period of several months it was observed that the dogs gradually lost the ability to perform the trained detection task. Subsequent examination revealed extensive tartar on the teeth of each of the dogs. Behavioural olfactometry

was used to determine the olfactory threshold. For each individual the threshold was significantly depressed from the average. The teeth were cleaned and the behavioural olfactometry repeated the following day. In each case, the olfactory threshold returned to normal. Subsequent olfactory threshold determinations were made, following the dogs for three months. The olfactory threshold was depressed in a rough correlation to the repeated development of dental calculus. This finding strongly suggests that a major factor in the efficacy of detector dogs is good dental health, and, further, that dogs with tendency to rapidly form dental calculus should be selected against within any breeding program.[2]

The author Dr Larry Myers's suggestion to use breeding programs—expensive, slow and unreliable—as a solution seems at odds with the known biology of calculus accumulation.[3] Otherwise the research appears to be a major contribution to carnivore health. Customs agencies, bomb detection units, police forces, hunters and anyone dependent on the canine nose has reason to celebrate.

The interests of pets and their owners should not be overlooked. Clearly, they need to share in the benefits too. The bigger the breakthrough, the bigger the questions that follow. What are the mechanisms? What's the purpose of a canine's ability to detect odours? And perhaps more importantly: What's the purpose of this measurable loss of olfaction correlated with an increase in calculus formation?

Dr Johan Joubert, veterinary dentist and cybernetician, and I postulate that while a good sense of smell in the carnivore is important, the rapid loss of that sense, correlated with a build-up of calculus, might in the scheme of things be equally important. Also we postulate that the vomeronasal organ (organ of Jacobson, Ludvig Jacobson 1813)[4] may be involved in this dramatic finding.

The vomeronasal organ is described as: 'Part of the olfactory sense system that consists of a pair of fleshy tubes found on the floor of the nasal cavity on either side of the nasal septum, supported by cartilage sleeve. Probably concerned with scenting and after smell of food.'[5]

Keverne says:

> The nature of stimulus access [fluids pass through an opening behind the upper incisors] suggests that the vomeronasal organ responds to non-volatile cues, leading to activation of the hypothalamus by way of the accessory olfactory bulb and amygdala. The areas of hypothalamus innervated regulate reproductive, defensive, and ingestive behavior as well as neuroendocrine secretion.[6]

If foul fluids from diseased teeth and gums gain immediate access to the vomeronasal organ and if those fluids have a negative effect on sense of smell, reproductive, defensive, ingestive and neuroendocrine functions, then we have a powerful set of determinants for the health and wellbeing of the subject animal.

Regardless of putative mechanisms, Dr Myers's work on olfaction shows that animals with periodontal disease suffer impaired ability to detect prey, competitors and enemies—a dismal prospect for the individual carnivore already conspicuous by its bad breath—but, in the scheme of things, doubly advantageous for prey animals, competitors and enemies.

And this scenario, if correct, has direct correlation with the predictions of the cybernetic hypothesis of periodontal disease in mammalian carnivores.[7]

The hypothesis explains that regulators, carnivores, need regulating—and in the absence of sufficient prey that there needs to be a feedback loop, preferably with high 'gain', leading to the rapid demise of redundant carnivores. Failing hunters become the hunted and balance is thereby maintained.

- The cybernetic hypothesis sets out a uniting paradigm of health and disease for animals—with far-reaching implications for human health too.
- If Dr Myers's work demonstrates a high-gain feedback loop, then it appears to provide a crucial test for the hypothesis.
- If the hypothesis passes the test, then elevation to accepted theory comes closer.
- If adopted as a theory, cybernetics can provide the foundation for new cures and 'miracle preventions'.[8]

Thank you Dr Myers, and thank you Dr Mayfield for bringing the information to light.

Notes

1. 'Your pet's health: nature's way', Emory University Center for Lifelong Learning, 2003.[5]
2. International Working Dog Breeding Association Conference, 5–8 October 2003.[6]
3. P. Hennet, 'Periodontal disease and oral microbiology', in D.A. Crossley and S. Penman, eds, *Manual of small animal dentistry*, British Small Animal Veterinary Association, Gloucester, 1995, pp. 105–13.
4. K.B. Doving and D. Trotier, 'Structure and function of the vomeronasal organ', *Journal of Experimental Biology*, vol. 201, 1998, pp. 2913–25.
5. D.C. Blood and V.P. Studdert, *Saunders comprehensive veterinary dictionary*, 2nd ed., 1999, W.B. Saunders, London.
6. E.B. Keverne, 'The vomeronasal organ', *Science*, vol. 286, no. 5440, 1999, pp. 716–20.
7. T. Lonsdale, 'Cybernetic hypothesis of periodontal disease in mammalian carnivores', *Journal of Veterinary Dentistry*, vol. 11, no. 1, 1994, pp. 5–8.[4]
8. T. Lonsdale, 'A cybernetic hypothesis of periodontal disease', in *Raw Meaty Bones: Promote Health*, Rivetco, Windsor, NSW, 2001, pp. 295–315.[7]

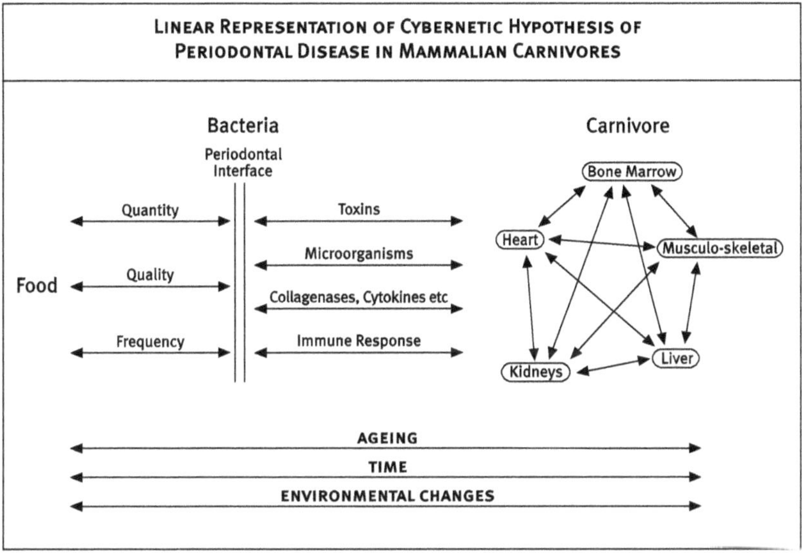

A highly stylised two-dimensional diagram used to illustrate the cybernetic hypothesis of periodontal disease.

A first-year veterinary student comments

OK, we just started Nutrition on Monday and it's already absolutely unbearable. I guess I am just hopelessly naive, but I'm not sure I actually believed until I got there, that they could think it was worth anyone's time to devote a whole class to pouring dog or cat food out of a bag and into a bowl. And that a woman who spent seventeen years of post-high-school education in veterinary nutrition studies could honestly think that commercial food is the only viable option to feed pets. She's not even making an attempt to teach us anything except how to evaluate dry foods, how to read dry food ingredient lists, how to do all these ridiculous calculations about kcal, resting energy requirement, etc.

We had two hours of it today, once at eight and once at four. I didn't go to the eight o'clock class, because every time I go, it literally ruins the rest of my day. But, two friends, one raw-feeding and the other doing her research to start, spoke to the professor at the end of the class about some things she said that they questioned or didn't agree with. They tried to pose their questions politely, but apparently the conversation degenerated pretty quickly.

One of the things they asked about was her mantra, which she regularly asks the class to chant, 'pets need nutrients, not ingredients', meaning, of course, that it doesn't matter what's in the food as long as the companies guarantee certain nutritional content. My friends brought up some non-species-specific ingredients, like corn, soy, wheat, etc., and asked if she didn't see a problem with that. Her reply was that corn gets a bad rap, that it's a perfect healthy ingredient, and that Native Americans survived on it well enough, so why not dogs? (I'm not joking.) She also told them that high cooking temps/extrusion doesn't have any affect on the health of the food at all. When they mentioned raw and some good results they'd seen with it, she said that George Burns smoked and drank every day and lived to be 100, but that didn't mean those were healthy things to do.

She also said that raw is dangerous because of food-borne pathogens, referencing an *E. coli 01:57* outbreak at a Jack in the Box as proof, even though that deals with humans eating cooked meat?!? She then told them that they're just being influenced by fad diets on the internet with no science behind them, and that she shouldn't just believe everything they hear or read. When they tried to stand up for themselves, she fell back on the 'I'm one of only 50 certified veterinary nutritionists in the country' as if that ended the argument. They were both so furious they could hardly speak when I got there.

Then, for our second hour this afternoon, she taught us the nine steps she uses to evaluate a commercial food if a client wants her opinion. See what you think of these:

1. The bag, box, or can should contain the phrase 'complete and balanced'.
2. Products that contain this claim must also follow with one of two AAFCO statements, i.e. the product was tested through feeding trials or the calculation method.
3. The label should contain a toll-free phone number so you can ask the company questions if necessary.
4. The product should have a digestibility of at least 80% (you may have to call the company to get this figure).
5. If you are feeding a dry product, it should contain a preservative (all of which are completely safe according to her).
6. Reputation of the company.
7. Cost.
8. Animals require nutrients not ingredient (this one has about three paragraphs explaining why corn, soy and other ingredients are perfectly suitable for dogs).
9. How is the pet doing while consuming the product?

That's it. Nothing about what the ingredients are, ingredient sources. As long as it fits the above criteria, it's fine in her book. The really ridiculous thing is, she keeps contradicting herself. She told us about the experiment where they made a food out of leather boots, old tires, peanut hulls, whatever, that met the pet food companies nutrient requirements, but then she stressed that she thought Purina is a really quality brand of food that has an unjustified poor reputation (she's basing this on the fact that they claim their digestibility is 84%, which is supposed to be good, I guess). She also talked about ingredient splitting and how bad it is but then showed us several labels of acceptable (to her) pet foods that had five or six split fractions of one ingredient.

I could go on with this forever, but I think this letter's

long enough already :) I just need to blow off some steam; I think I'm going to have a sneer permanently affixed to my face after a couple months of that class.

Postscript

We should not pretend that resolution of the multifaceted vet/pet food problem will be easy. But the more shoulders to the wheel the sooner it will turn.

Do your best—every little helps.

Best wishes,
Tom Lonsdale

May 2004: Food and medicine: raw meaty bones for dogs

Dear Reader,

'Let food be thy medicine', recommended Hippocrates 500 years BC. Now, two-and-a-half thousand years later, we are told we must throw the staple food—and medicine—of dogs in the bin (London newspaper article below).

How could it be that for thousands of years we ignored Hippocrates' injunction and treated food and medicine as two separate entities? For much of that two-and-a-half thousand years we did accept that dogs thrive on bones—but I don't remember seeing anywhere the suggestion that (raw meaty) bones are medicinal. Now European Union (EU) bureaucrats have decided that bones are not even a food source and should be chucked in the bin.

One day the full enormity of the blunder will be understood and the faceless faces of the men in Brussels will be covered in egg. There are parallels with the Flat Earth / Round Earth debate. Early Greeks believed the Earth to be round. But that core understanding, upon which we base modern communications, transportation, forecasting, mapping and just about the entire scientific gamut, was lost or disputed for a further one-and-a-half thousand years. But to be fair to the Brussels bureaucrats they are only responsible for the final blunder.

The rot, both actual and metaphorical, set in when we employed reductionist language—when we created two separate categories for food and medicine. And thanks to the efforts of the junk pet food industry, the veterinary schools and veterinary 'profession', bones have been labelled, not as food but as hazards. After more than fifty years of demonisation, the humble but essential bone has been defined as waste. Chances are the bureaucrats thought they were doing the logically correct thing. They probably thought that they were cleaning up a last, lingering anomaly for the betterment of the community.

If you are long-time reader of this newsletter, you know that for bones to be fully nutritious they need to be raw and meaty. That's the way dogs and other carnivores get their essential range of nutrients. For the raw meaty bones (better still whole raw carcasses) to exert their full medicinal effects, they need to be in large pieces requiring lots of ripping and tearing—and thus the cleaning of the teeth and massaging of the gums.

The alternative, either actively or passively promoted by the consortium of junk pet food makers, vets and now Brussels bureaucrats, is to feed dogs and other carnivores on factory-made concoctions. These products of the dark satanic mills are barely nutritious and definitely not medicinal—in fact they poison a majority of the world's pets.

Poisoning occurs in broadly three different ways:

1. Soft canned foods and grain-based biscuits fail to clean teeth thus giving rise to chronic oral disease and resultant production of toxins, circulating bacteria and inflammatory chemicals—all of which are triggers for systemic disease.

2. Cooked carbohydrates, proteins and fats are toxic in differing degrees. Chemical colourants, preservatives and additives are all toxic in varying degrees. Absorption into the circulation through the small intestine of this range of toxins adversely affects several body systems.

3. Poorly digested grains support a large population of colonic toxin-producing bacteria. Local reactions of the toxins on the bowel lining and absorption of the toxins affect several body systems.

Raw meaty bones, then, are the essential food and medicine of carnivores. Whilst this is clearly of interest to dogs, cats, ferrets and their owners, there are many other implications too.

Carnivores live at the extreme end of the nutritional spectrum where they use their teeth to pull down, kill and consume the carcasses of other animals—animals which may be much larger than themselves. I don't recommend that you run up to the next cow you see, sink your teeth into its leg and expect to be instantly healthy. What I do recommend, though, is for us as a society, and medical researchers in particular, to study the range of diseases that are cured and prevented in carnivores when they eat their natural diets. Once the mechanisms and the biochemical and physiological pathways are better understood we should be able to reapply that information for the betterment of people—omnivores in the middle of the nutritional spectrum. (Some of the best, most rewarding scientific research is performed at the extreme ends of spectra.)

Over the past hundred years we've seen a procession of 'miracle cures'—penicillin, corticosteroids, thalidomide and the list goes on. In fact, few of the 'cures' have come without unwanted side effects. Most have had limited curative potential and their disease prevention capabilities have been close to nil.

By contrast, in carnivores, raw meaty bones are virtually free of side effects. They can cure gum disease, skin disease, joint disease, bowel disease, and more. They can help ward off flea infestations, and raw-fed dogs are better behaved and easier to train. On the disease prevention scale, raw meaty bones and whole carcasses are peerless.

There are many miracle tales of wonder cures and miracle preventions associated with the feeding of raw carcasses and raw meaty bones. One story I heard recently can serve to illustrate. An old client of mine, with whom I'd lost contact, told me of her experiences. Fifteen years ago she was spending $1000 a month on vet bills for her kennel of rough collies. Under pressure from me, and backed up by her husband, she relented and switched her dogs to a diet based on raw meaty bones. In the ensuing fifteen years, except for two bouts of constipation in a dog fed brisket bones, the client has not needed the vet at all.

Below is the EU Bone Ban article reproduced from the London *Evening Standard* newspaper and contact details for British members of parliament and various media organisations. The EU should lift the ban and take a lead. They should provide official encouragement for butchers to supply raw meaty bones—not throw them in the bin. Please make use of all or any part of this newsletter if it helps you to persuade the relevant authorities. Butchers, journalists, doctors, farmers, teachers and a long line of professions could potentially make use of this information.

Wishing you and your pets the best of good health,
Tom Lonsdale

———

EU bans giving bones to dog owners
By Nigel Rosser, *Evening Standard*, 26 May 2004

Butchers are being threatened with fines if they give bones away to dog owners. They are being sent letters telling them that a new European directive bans the traditional practice. In future, Britain's 10,000 butchers will have to pay for the bones to be incinerated rather than hand them free to customers for their pets. The Department for the Environment, Food and Rural Affairs today confirmed the Brussels ban. It said the bones are now considered 'waste' which must be properly disposed of.

A spokesman said: 'Customers can take bones away with them when they buy the deboned meat if it is for human consumption. But if the bone is waste or for pet food then it's a byproduct—and cannot be passed to the public.' Aberystwyth butcher Aled Morgan, 35, one of the first to receive a warning letter, said: 'I just don't see where the EU is coming from. It's just going to cost butchers at least £2,000 a year.' Local dog owner Martin Swanson, 32, said: 'It seems to me to be another barmy EU directive.'

October 2004: 'Sue the bastards', lobby your MP

Dear Reader,

How are things in your neck of the woods? Things here in Australia are excellent. Last week we thought summer had arrived with the hottest Sydney October day on record: 38°C (100°F). Today, it's 14°C.

Regardless of weather fluctuations, and in countries across the globe, raw feeding continues to gain supporters. Since May, when I last wrote, I have been meeting with enthusiastic raw-feeders and, in Australia and the UK, doing battle with hostile veterinary authorities.

Best wishes,
Tom Lonsdale

Australian Veterinary Association kangaroo court 'a disgrace'

When news of the Australian Veterinary Association (AVA) kangaroo court action against me became public I received lots of messages of support. Many correspondents communicated their concerns to the AVA. Here's a brief account of the expulsion that Paul Lynch, lawyer and member of the NSW State Parliament, labelled 'a disgrace'.

Five of the eight principles of the Code of Professional Conduct for members of the Australian Veterinary Association (AVA) convey a clear message that promoting and selling processed food for dogs and cats is morally and ethically wrong.

> **Members of the Australian Veterinary Association are committed to using their skills and knowledge for the welfare of animals and society.**
>
> 1. Veterinarians shall always consider the welfare of the animal first in the provision of veterinary services.
> 2. Veterinarians should strive to improve the quality of veterinary services, and the health and the welfare of animals, at every opportunity.

3. Veterinarians should provide the best possible veterinary services to the animals under their care and to the community based on current scientific knowledge.
4. –
5. –
6. –
7. Veterinarians should continue to develop their professional knowledge and skills and share their knowledge with colleagues and other relevant professionals as appropriate.
8. Veterinarians should uphold the integrity of the veterinary profession.

Nonetheless a majority of AVA members promote and sell processed food. The governing body of the AVA operates in association with Mars, the world's leading producer of junk food, and some of its front organisations.

As responsible longstanding members of the AVA, Dr Breck Muir and I campaigned within the AVA for accountability and an end to the mass poisoning of the patients entrusted to the care of AVA members. We stood for AVA elections, usually obtaining around 10% of the vote, and tried many methods to raise awareness of the scandal. For our troubles we were vilified and our message suppressed.

Several bogus disciplinary actions were brought against me, by members of the AVA, before the Veterinary Surgeons Board of NSW.

In July 2003, after a protracted battle with a veterinary magazine, I lodged a complaint with the Veterinary Surgeons Board of NSW alleging widespread consumer and scientific fraud. But rather than investigate and report on the allegations, the Veterinary Board, either wittingly or unwittingly, passed the complaint to the AVA. The AVA then, through its kangaroo court, expelled me for blowing the whistle on widespread serious misconduct.[8]

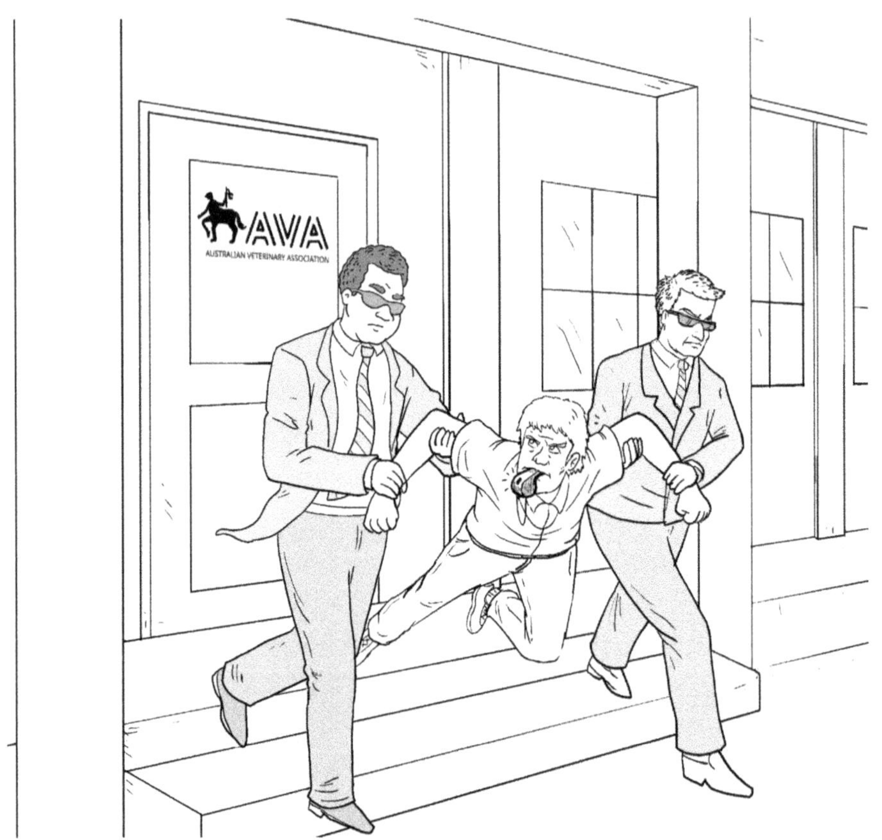

Time Magazine[9] and Channel 7 TV aired the story.[10]

Clearly the NSW state and Australian federal governments need to investigate the activities of the AVA and its partner the Mars Corporation. Members of parliament need a better understanding of the pet food consumer and scientific scam. Please consider writing to MPs.

Royal College of Veterinary Surgeons (RCVS)

In Britain, veterinary involvement in the pet food scam runs in parallel with Australia. There are about 20,000 vets registered with the RCVS and are therefore permitted to practise in the UK. A majority of British veterinarians approve of, promote or sell junk food for pets. A silent minority, about 10% of vets, disapprove.

In the 2004 elections for the council of the RCVS I received 264 votes being about 9% of the votes cast. The RCVS say:

Role of the RCVS

This can be summarised by the strapline:

> Promoting and Sustaining Public Confidence in
> Veterinary Medicine

and the mission statement:

> To safeguard the health and welfare of animals com-
> mitted to veterinary care through the regulation of
> the educational, ethical and clinical standards of the
> veterinary profession, thereby protecting the interests
> of those dependent on animals and assuring public
> health.
>
> To act as an impartial source of informed opinion on
> animal health and welfare issues and their interaction
> with human health.

In effect the RCVS is made up of three distinct organisations:

> **The college—as a statutory regulator**: undertaking
> the statutory responsibilities set out in the Veterinary
> Surgeons Act 1966—to maintain a register, regulate vet-
> erinary education and to regulate professional conduct.

> **The college—acting as a 'Royal College'**: exercising
> powers under the Royal Charter to award fellowships,
> diplomas and certificates to veterinary surgeons, vet-
> erinary nurses and others and to act as informed and
> impartial source of opinion on veterinary matters.

> **RCVS Trust—a separate charity**: established to pro-
> mote and advance the study and practice of the art and
> science of veterinary surgery and medicine—by pro-
> viding the RCVS library and information service and
> a range of grants largely to support educational and
> research activities.

That 264 veterinary surgeons supported the allegations contained in the manifesto[11] would, you might think, cause the RCVS to act promptly and diligently. But when veterinary colleague Roger Meacock and I met with the RCVS president, Professor Halliwell, on 17 June 2004, he informed us that: a hamster, if it should stand for election to the council of the Royal College, would receive as many votes.

Since the RCVS won't investigate and act on the serious allegations of widespread cruelty, scientific and consumer fraud perpetrated by veterinarians, then, it seems to me, it's time for the British government to investigate the RCVS.

Please consider writing to members of parliament and let them know how serious the situation has become and what needs to be done.

5

————

2005: HITTING WALLS: LEGAL AND INSTITUTIONAL BARRIERS

Efforts to challenge regulatory roadblocks gain momentum, but the veterinary profession openly sides with processed pet food manufacturers, intensifying opposition to RMB diets.

February 2005: EDM No. 335, Processed pet foods and vets

PROCESSED PET FOODS AND VETS

EDM (Early Day Motion)335:
tabled on 07 December 2004

Tabled in the 2004-05 session.

Dear Reader,

February here already and this is the first *RMB Newsletter* of 2005. How have you been? How was Christmas? Is 2005 shaping up as you hoped?

We venture into the unknown with expectations high. It's nice when things go well. In this newsletter I'm delighted to report on some terrific developments in the drive for a fairer deal for pets and pet owners, and transparency, honesty and accountability from vets.

In the UK the campaigners at the UK Raw Meaty Bones Support & Action Group make steady progress. Their lobbying of members of parliament gathers momentum, spurred on by the tabling of early day motion No. 335, 'Processed pet foods and vets'.[1]

Here's a brief account.

Wishing you a happy, healthy 2005,
Tom Lonsdale

Early day motion No. 335, Processed pet foods and vets

What, you may ask, is an early day motion? Is it something a dog passes first thing in the morning? Is it the motion of a person, half-asleep, rummaging in a drawer for socks? No. According to the British Parliamentary website an early day motion (EDM):

> is a colloquial term for a notice of motion given by a Member for which no date has been fixed for debate. EDMs exist to allow Members to put on record their opinion on a subject and canvass support for it from fellow Members. In effect, the primary function of an EDM is to form a kind of petition that MPs can sign.[2]

As a result of efficient campaigning by the UKRMB Group, a British member of parliament, David Taylor MP, tabled EDM No. 335 on 7 December 2004:

> That this House deeply regrets the professional endorsement of processed food for domestic dogs, cats and ferrets by some members of the veterinary profession; is concerned at the level of incidence of malodorous gum disease and associated diseases of the kidneys, liver and other organs amongst the domestic pet population; recognises that their health and welfare is best served by foods, such as raw meaty bones, that reflect the full range of nutritional need; applauds and recommends the work of veterinary surgeon Tom Lonsdale and others in this field; recognises also that vets in the UK are trusted and independent

advisers on the health of our pets; is therefore concerned by the nature of the relationship between some vets and producers of foods that cause illnesses in pets; and calls upon the Royal College of Veterinary Surgeons to make a definitive statement on the active endorsement and promotion of processed pet foods by vets.

Forty-three MPs have, at this time, signed the motion and we look forward to the Royal College of Veterinary Surgeons doing what's asked of them.

About 21,000 vets are registered with the Royal College, which states:

Role of the RCVS

This can be summarised by the strapline:

Promoting and Sustaining Public Confidence in Veterinary Medicine

and the Mission Statement:

To safeguard the health and welfare of animals committed to veterinary care through the regulation of the educational, ethical and clinical standards of the veterinary profession, thereby protecting the interests of those dependent on animals and assuring public health.

To act as an impartial source of informed opinion on animal health and welfare issues and their interaction with human health.

In effect the RCVS is made up of three distinct organisations:

The College—as a statutory regulator: undertaking the statutory responsibilities set out in the Veterinary Surgeons Act 1966—to maintain a register, regulate veterinary education and to regulate professional conduct.

> **The College—acting as a 'Royal College'**: exercising powers under the Royal Charter to award Fellowships, Diplomas and Certificates to veterinary surgeons, veterinary nurses and others and to act as informed and impartial source of opinion on veterinary matters.

> **RCVS Trust—a separate charity**: established to promote and advance the study and practice of the art and science of veterinary surgery and medicine—by providing the RCVS Library and Information Service and a range of grants largely to support educational and research activities.

Since the RCVS answers to the British Parliament, it's a 'no-brainer'. The RCVS should set the record straight, demonstrate that they know and abide by the rules, and issue a statement setting out their position—or so one might reasonably think.

But so far, nothing, not a word has been written by the Royal College, to let British vets know that they and their governing body are under scrutiny by elected representatives of the British people. The British Veterinary Association has not, to my current knowledge, published anything either. Why are vets kept in the dark, not trusted to know about matters directly affecting them? When will an official statement be forthcoming from the Royal College of Veterinary Surgeons?

When *Dog World* (24 December 2004), a leading UK dog magazine, spoke with the RCVS this is what they said:

> However, as the regulatory body for the veterinary profession, the RCVS does not exist to represent the views of vets and is not in a position to provide authoritative scientific comment on the nutritional benefits of pet foods.

> Vets are not expected to endorse products without due justification or if they might compromise the clinical care of

animals. The RCVS does, however, expect vets to make clinical decisions according to their professional judgment and based on the best available evidence at the time.

We understand that there is currently an abundance of scientific evidence available to support the use of processed pet foods for everyday feeding of companion animals, together with medicated or 'science' diets to provide advanced nutrition for animals that may be unwell, nutritionally deficient or at a certain stage in life.

Mr Lonsdale has stood in the RCVS council elections for the past eight years in order to promote his concerns. Each time he has secured the least number of votes, which would imply there is little support for his views within the veterinary profession, in which there are currently over 21,000 registered RCVS members.

We have discussed Mr Lonsdale's concerns with him on a number of occasions and have urged him to submit scientific evidence to support his claims and to publish this material in peer-reviewed (veterinary) scientific journals. We understand that Mr Lonsdale has not yet accomplished this but we would encourage him to do so.

The RCVS declare their allegiances but otherwise misrepresent the facts. Face-to-face discussion with the RCVS occurred once only. In June 2004 the then RCVS president, Professor R. Halliwell, responded to our request for a meeting and met with Roger Meacock and me. Professor Halliwell poured scorn on our submissions. Otherwise, letters to the RCVS have elicited either minimal or hostile responses that could scarcely be described as 'discussions'. The recommendation to submit material to 'scientific journals' sounds somewhat disingenuous. The RCVS are well aware of and have refused to deal with the censorship and suppression of the diet issue in the 'scientific journals'.

For the record, five eminent veterinarians have reviewed or commented on the book *Raw Meaty Bones* (including three past or present directors of the Sydney University Post Graduate Foundation in Veterinary Science[3]). *Raw Meaty Bones* thus constitutes 389 pages of peer-reviewed evidence—evidence that the Australian, NZ, UK and US 'scientific' veterinary journals refuse to consider. The following articles and papers overcame considerable obstacles and were published in so-called 'scientific' journals.

1993 'Feeding vs nutrition: have we lost the plot in small animal dietetics?' (non-reviewed opinion), *Australian Veterinary Practitioner*, vol. 23, issue 1.

1993 'Putting feline lower urinary tract disease in context' (non-reviewed letter), *Journal of Small Animal Practice*, December, vol. 34, pp. 592–3.[4]

1994 'Cybernetic hypothesis of periodontal disease in mammalian carnivores', *Journal of Veterinary Dentistry*, vol. 11, issue 1.[5]

1995 'Periodontal disease and leucopenia', *Journal of Small Animal Practice*, vol. 36, pp. 542–6.[6]

'Periodontal disease and leucopenia' found a gap in the veterinary protective cordon around the junk pet food industry. But directly after publication of the paper, the veterinary establishment moved to plug the gap. Despite the likely implications for human health in general, HIV/AIDS sufferers in particular and the foundations of veterinary science, the editor of the *Journal of Small Animal Practice* (published by the British Small Animal Veterinary Association) banned further discussion within the pages of the *Journal*. The editor also revoked written undertakings and prevented re-publication of the paper—thus stopping a wider readership from learning about and acting on the serious implications.

Research findings that have the potential to transform the lives of millions need be verified by repeated experiment. Professor Tony Buffington, a spokesperson for American veterinary teachers and researchers, on 8 August 2002 stated on National Public Radio: 'I've seen the paper. I haven't seen it reproduced by anyone anywhere else.'[7]

Now in 2005, to my knowledge, still no-one has repeated the easy-to-perform research.

Something needs to be done about the games the RCVS and international veterinary leadership play.

If you live in the UK you can help.

Please write to your MP to either thank him/her for signing EDM No. 335 or to encourage him/her to do so.

Tell your MP about the pet food industry/veterinary alliance that harms our pets whilst purporting to do the opposite.

If you live in any other country you might like to form a lobby group and start a dialogue with your political representatives. It's the politicians who delegate responsibility to the veterinary profession and it's the politicians who need to take back responsibility in the name of the people.

Stop press

In news just to hand, class actions against veterinarians are soon to be filed in Texas, California, Florida and possibly other states. The suits will be for fraud and seek refund of four years fees for unnecessary vaccinations. In Maine a bill is before the state legislature requiring vets to disclose the truth regarding vaccines.

Consider the implications if pet owners were to launch legal actions for the cost of four years supply of junk food (whether cooked or 'BARF'). And what about legislation in every nation and state requiring vets to be truthful about the devastating effects of the junk cooked and raw diets they peddle. (Actually, it's about getting existing consumer protection and truth in advertising laws enforced, but that's another story.)

In every country there are lawyers and politicians who can take aim at the pet food fraud. It's just a matter of alerting them to the scam. If you try spreading the word, you may be pleasantly surprised what happens next.

Wishing you and your pets the best of good health,
Tom Lonsdale

July 2005: A debilitating case of disinformation

Dear Reader,

Hope this edition of the *RMB Newsletter* finds you in good form, fighting the good fight.

The cover story, 'A debilitating case of disinformation', sheds some light on the emerging pet food industry/veterinary involvement with the medical profession. I hope that you can make use of the links at the bottom of the article to let the authorities know your opinions.

There's some good news from the US reported in the *Sydney Morning Herald*, 27 June 2005, which tells of pet owners suing veterinarians for malpractice:

> In Florida, for example, Adam Riff is suing a vet for alleged negligence because his sheepdog, Lucky, died after dental surgery ... The biggest damages award so far for veterinary malpractice is US$39,000 granted to Marc Bluestone by a jury in Orange County, California, last year. His sandy haired dog, Shane—bought for US$100 at a local shelter—died of liver failure following a misdiagnosis and $21,000 worth of treatment.

What penalties will courts impose on vets for promoting and selling junk pet food, the source of most dental and liver disease? What defence will vets employ in an attempt to justify injuring their patients' health and misleading their clients? I hope that you can spread the word, even launch a legal action. That way we may get some answers.

Wishing you and your animals the best of good health,
Tom Lonsdale

A debilitating case of disinformation

We can—or at least should be able to—learn from our mistakes, and the bigger the mistakes the bigger the lessons. For too long we've failed to unite the medical, dental and veterinary professions under the banner of 'one medicine' for the benefit of all Earth's inhabitants. But before embarking on such a noble cause we need to investigate and resolve a debilitating case of disinformation.

A majority of veterinarians in the western world depend on junk food-induced ill-health of pets and the sale of junk food in their waiting rooms. Veterinary schools, propped up by pet food money, program their students to ignore the origins of the dietary disease epidemics, to disparage healthy natural diets and to promote junk food at every opportunity. Veterinary associations fill their journals with pet food propaganda whilst barring healthy discussion of healthy options. Effectively, then, the veterinary profession acts as a marketing arm of the junk pet food industry.

And effective marketing it is too. The public have been duped, governments have been duped and now it seems it's the medical profession's turn to be recruited into the scam. According to a 16 April 2005 editorial in the journals of both the British Medical Association and the British Veterinary Association: 'The *BMJ* and the *Veterinary Record* plan simultaneous publication of theme issues exploring how the two professions can collaborate for mutual benefit.' After listing SARS, potential bioterrorist attack and antimicrobial resistance as subjects warranting a joint approach, the *British Medical Journal* promotes pet keeping and the Pet Food Manufacturers Association website:

> With increasing urbanisation, we can easily forget the extent to which people depend on animals. In the developing world many people rely on animals for food and transport (whether of people or goods)—and the health of those animals can mean the difference between life and death. Closer to home, livestock are important economically, but animals are also a source of companionship. Half of all households in the United Kingdom own a pet, and many pets are just as important as a family member or friend, sometimes more; for them, the same level of healthcare is expected. Cost of treatment and subsequent quality of life is an issue for the care of animals and humans.

> Doctors may not fully appreciate the importance of the relationship between owners and their animals. This may be relevant when, for example, advising immunocompromised patients of any risk from their pets, or considering the implications of taking an elderly pet owner into care in an environment where animals are banned. When advising patients about owning pets, doctors now have to weigh up the risks of developing allergies.

Following the *BMJ* exhortations, will doctors copy the vets and sell junk pet food to their patients? No, it's unlikely. If doctors collaborate with and thus endorse vets they will automatically join the protective cordon around the junk pet food industry.

- Due to concerns about possible transmission of disease from pets, many doctors express reservations about pet keeping. If medical opposition can be deflected and converted into enthusiastic acceptance then pet food sales will rise—hence the establishment of university 'research' into the human animal bond and lavish international conferences funded by the junk pet food industry.
- For many years the tobacco industry escaped scrutiny in part because the industry bought innocence by association with the medical profession. As a strategy for buying time it worked well. Huge revenue was generated before the doctors finally woke up to their involvement with disease promotion. For the junk pet food industry, with annual revenues of $30 billion, positive comments (and absence of negative comments) in medical journals are priceless.
- The veterinary profession avoids research that might reflect badly on the junk food producers. Independent medical and dental researchers, if they knew the scope and potential for new research of benefit to man and animals, could fill the void. However, if the junk food/veterinary alliance maintains the fiction that all is well and under control it's less likely that independent-minded medical researchers will venture onto veterinary turf.

- If the proposals, as published in the *BMJ*, come to fruition then research teams of vets and doctors will likely become more common—and it could be that the funds will come from confectionery giants Mars and Nestlé, the world's biggest junk pet food producers. Research funds buy silence, a precious commodity for junk food companies wanting to limit knowledge of dietary disease affecting man and animals.

As citizens, doctors can join with the rest of us in decrying the mass cruelty of forcing pets to consume products known to give rise to serious ill health and death. Doctors may be appalled at the economic costs and waste of resources, both human and environmental, which arise from the junk pet food industry. But it's in the area of human health that doctors are uniquely qualified and responsible for protecting the interests of their patients. In subtle and not so subtle ways the junk pet food industry injures human health. Let's take a look at what's known and in need of attention.

Dog bites

In the USA there are almost 5 million dog bites every year—over 13,000 every day. Extrapolated worldwide that's a considerable problem, and for individuals it can be devastating. Children are often victims and often suffer bites to the face. In almost every case the dog is fed junk food. The question arises: Was the diet the main factor influencing the dog's behaviour, a contributory factor or not a factor at all?

We can say that dogs fed junk food tend to be excitable and harder to train. One significant trial found some golden retrievers, normally a docile breed, attacked their owners when fed junk food, but became docile when fed cooked lamb and rice. How might the dogs have behaved if fed on raw natural food? Objective research is now an urgent priority; thousands of victims every day need answers.

Working dogs

Human health and welfare sometimes depends on dog health—for instance the health of assistance dogs, search and rescue dogs and bomb detection dogs. As we know, dogs fed junk food are seldom truly healthy and consequently perform below par. Researchers studied a group of beagles that, over a period of months, suffered from a progressive accumulation of dental tartar and simultaneously lost the ability to detect odours. The dogs' teeth were cleaned and within one day their odour-detecting abilities returned to normal. Imagine the consequences if a dog fed junk food, its teeth encrusted with tartar, failed to detect a terrorist bomb.

Human anxiety

The pet food industry spends lots of money on advertisements, on university departments and international symposia promoting the unqualified notion that dogs are good for human health and wellbeing.

In April 2004 the *Sydney Morning Herald* reported a study:

> Older Australians who own a pet are more likely to be depressed and in poorer physical health than people who don't own pets, according to a major new Australian study. Flying in the face of claims from the pet food industry, and others, the study shows pet ownership confers no health benefits to older people (R.A. Parslow et al., *Gerontology*, vol. 51, issue 1, 2005, pp. 40–7).

Could this compromised mental and physical health be due, at least in part, to the ill health of pets maintained on commercial diets? Could it be due to the worry associated with escalating vet bills?

Immune system depression

In 1995 the *Journal of Small Animal Practice*, journal of the British Small Animal Veterinary Association, published results of my research on dogs and cats affected by immune deficiency and diet-induced periodontal disease. By cleaning the teeth and changing the diets the animals' immune systems bounced back to a much healthier state (1995, vol. 36, pp. 542–6). The implications for immune system research in general, AIDS research in particular and wider aspects of animal and human health are immense.

Rather than promote further inquiry the editor of the *Journal of Small Animal Practice* bowed to pressure from angry veterinarians and banned discussion within the pages of the journal. The editor also revoked written undertakings and prevented re-publication of the paper—thus stopping a wider readership from learning about and acting on the implications.

The veterinary research community enjoys many privileges; they also have obligations. When published research challenges established beliefs or has the potential to transform the lives of millions, researchers need to promptly repeat the work to verify or refute the new information. In 2002, seven years after publication of the original paper, Professor Tony Buffington, a spokesperson for American veterinary researchers, stated: 'I've seen the paper. I haven't seen it reproduced by anyone anywhere else.'[7]

Dogs in medical research

New medical treatments and pharmaceuticals are often tested on dogs before use on humans. Dogs used in medical research are invariably fed junk food. I mentioned to one researcher, who was working on a new anti-inflammatory drug, that most dogs fed commercial food are suffering from gum inflammation (known to be linked to heart disease, stroke, cancer and Alzheimer's) and that my research showed that the so-called normal blood values could not be relied upon. He shrugged and said his research team used more dogs in each experiment to help compensate for statistical errors!

Unexplored opportunities

The junk pet food industry and its allies insist that dogs fed processed food are the healthiest, whereas the opposite is the case. Dogs are subject to a range of illnesses like ourselves—diabetes, arthritis, kidney disease and cancer—and often show dramatic health improvements when switched from junk food to a natural diet. Why do previously sick, debilitated animals, in the space of a few days, become 'like puppies again'? The question needs to be asked because the biological mechanisms could have dramatic implications for human diets and health.

There are enough known junk pet food issues to mobilise an army of medical and dental researchers working in collaboration with veterinarians. First, though, veterinarians must desist from their folly, they must turn their backs on their pet food paymasters and resolve to atone for past mistakes. The doctors and their journals could play a valuable part. They could help transform the health of the veterinary profession and thus provide the foundations for a medical, dental and veterinary collaboration—for the benefit of all Earth's inhabitants.

The full *British Medical Journal* 16 April 2005 article, 'Human and veterinary medicine', can be found at the *BMJ*.[8]

There's a 'Rapid Response' link that enables you to tell the *BMJ* of your experiences and concerns. To contact *BMJ* editors directly click on 'Home' and then 'Contact Us'.

British politicians are starting to take an interest in the pet food industry/veterinary shenanigans.

Tell MPs (and political representatives of any state or nation) about the pet food industry/veterinary alliance that harms our pets whilst purporting to do the opposite. Let them know about the efforts to recruit human doctors to the pet food scam.

Many thanks.

Best wishes,
Tom Lonsdale

October 2005: Five facets of the pet food fraud

Dear Reader,

Since writing in July 2005, the UK Raw Meaty Bones Support & Action group have continued their terrific work exposing the pet food industry/veterinary alliance.

They wrote to all members of the British House of Commons advising them of the *British Medical Journal* (*BMJ*) endorsement of Pet Food Manufacturers Association propaganda and how junk pet foods have serious adverse effects, whether directly or indirectly, on human health. To its credit the *BMJ* published UKRMB criticisms on the *BMJ* website.[9]

Work Wonders: Feed Your Dog Raw Meaty Bones

The new 'how to feed' book is or will soon be available in bookstores in the USA, Canada, the UK, Australia and New Zealand. See readers' comments and excerpts.[10]

Wishing you and your pets the best of good health.

Tom Lonsdale

Five facets of the pet food fraud

> 'All that is needed for evil to prosper is for people of good will to do nothing'
>
> Edmund Burke

As a reader of this newsletter, you will be well aware of the first facet of the pet food fraud. The other facets may be new to you. Let me provide some thumbnail sketches.

1. Junk-food-induced cruelty, ill-health and suffering affect a majority of the world's pets. Plentiful 'scientific' evidence, common experience and common sense confirm this fact.

2. Misuse of existing scientific paradigms and bogus administrative techniques produces a body of counterfeit science in the service of the junk pet food industry.

   The current mass poisoning of pets starts with the first lie: that processed pet food is as good as or better than the natural alternative. So-called researchers swallow the lie whole and then misuse existing scientific methods and compliant professional journals to perpetuate and bolster the lie.

3. Reliance on inadequate scientific paradigms facilitates the junk pet food fraud. The search for better options is discouraged.

   If the current methods of science can be hijacked with impunity, then perhaps there's something the matter with the so-called science. Chapter 14 of *Raw Meaty Bones* postulates a new scientific paradigm that makes use of existing paradigms without falling victim to their inadequacies. Unfortunately, the veterinary authorities have been successful in suppressing any consideration of new approaches.

4. Economic consequences can be measured in the billions of dollars. The human health and natural environmental burdens are immense.

   The junk pet food industry dark satanic mills churn out industrialised food full of dire consequences. In the Pet Food Manufacturers Association letter below they claim their industry supports

8,000 UK workers. The raw food industry is labour-intensive. Tens, perhaps hundreds, of thousands of jobs could be created by a move to more natural pet food. A full economic audit is well overdue.

5. Failure of democratic, administrative and legal systems—whether due to oversight, incompetence or corruption—facilitates the junk pet food fraud.

Jack Spratt aided by the founder of Crufts Dog Show, Charles Cruft, started the junk pet food industry in the 1860s and it's been downhill since then. We've had endless political representatives, governments have come and gone and the legal profession has been ever present. Yet despite the moral and ethical problems associated with duping people into slowly poisoning their animals and the clear illegality of such cruel treatment, our politicians and lawyers have done little or nothing.

The future does not need to mimic the past. We can make changes. In the first instance may I suggest that you contact your elected representatives and tell them of the Five Facets of the Pet Food Fraud?

Below is the British Parliament's early day motion no. 335, Processed pet foods and vets, and the British Royal College of Veterinary Surgeons (RCVS) response, which they say was produced 'in readiness for any press inquiries we might receive. We did not issue this statement proactively' ... In other words the Royal College were careful not to alarm the more than 21,000 registered vets about discussions taking place in Parliament—discussions which centred on the very essence of veterinary activity.

The RCVS confirm that their statement was: 'Based on the same scientific papers and evidence which were documented by the Pet Food Manufacturers Association in its press release dated 17 December 2004.' From which statement we can conclude that the RCVS rely on self-serving twaddle from those who slowly poison the majority of the world's pets.

The RCVS have several copies of *Raw Meaty Bones*, the 389-page fully referenced, peer-reviewed book on the pet food scam. Chapters 7 and 14 provide close detail of papers written by me and published in 'peer reviewed (veterinary) scientific journals'. Despite this they make the disingenuous claim:

> We have ... urged him to submit scientific evidence to support his claims and to publish this material in peer reviewed (veterinary) scientific journals. We understand that Mr Lonsdale has not yet accomplished this but we would encourage him to do so.

Question: Besides denying possession of compelling evidence of a multi-billion-dollar fraud, which veterinary regulator requires the whistleblower to fund and carry out research to further substantiate that evidence?

Answer: The Royal College of Veterinary Surgeons.

British Parliament, 7 December 2005, Early day motion 335

> **Processed pet foods and vets**[1]
> That this House deeply regrets the professional endorsement of processed food for domestic dogs, cats and ferrets by some members of the veterinary profession; is concerned at the level of incidence of malodorous gum disease and associated diseases of the kidneys, liver and other organs amongst the domestic pet population; recognises that their health and welfare is best served by foods, such as raw meaty bones, that reflect the full range of nutritional need; applauds and recommends the work of veterinary surgeon Tom Lonsdale and others in this field; recognises also that vets in the UK are trusted and independent advisers on the health of our pets; is therefore concerned by the nature of the relationship between some vets and producers of foods that cause illnesses in pets; and calls upon the Royal College of Veterinary Surgeons to make a definitive statement on the active endorsement and promotion of processed pet foods by vets.

Royal College of Veterinary Surgeons position paper
December 2004
Early day motion—Processed pet foods and vets
The RCVS is aware of different views within the veterinary profession concerning the feeding of processed pet foods to companion animals, not least those of Tom Lonsdale. However, as the regulatory body for the veterinary profession, the RCVS does not exist to represent the views of veterinary surgeons and is not in a position to provide authoritative scientific comment on the nutritional benefits of pet foods.

Veterinary surgeons are not expected to endorse products without due justification or it they might compromise the clinical care of animals. The RCVS does, however, expect veterinary surgeons to make clinical decisions according to their professional judgement and based on the best available evidence at the time.

We understand that there is currently an abundance of scientific evidence available to support the use of processed pet foods for everyday feeding of companion animals, together with medicated or 'science' diets to provide advanced nutrition for animals that may be unwell, nutritionally deficient or at a certain stage in life.

Mr Lonsdale has stood in the RCVS Council Elections for the past eight years in order to promote his concerns. Each time he has secured the least number of votes, which would imply there is little support for his views within the veterinary profession, of whom there are currently over 21,000 registered RCVS members.

We have discussed Mr Lonsdale's concerns with him on a number of occasions and have urged him to submit scientific evidence to support his claims and to publish this material in peer reviewed (veterinary) scientific journals. We understand that Mr Lonsdale has not yet accomplished this but we would encourage him to do so.

For further information please contact:
Ian Holloway
RCVS External Affairs Officer
T: 020 7203 0727 | F: 020 7202 0740
E: i.holloway@rcvs.org.uk

Pet Food Manufacturers Association Ltd
20 Bedford Street
Covent Garden
London WC2E 9HP

Tel: 020 7379 9009 | Fax: 020 7379 8008
Email: info@pfma.org.uk
Web: www.pfma.com
22 December 2004

Dear [Member of Parliament],

Early day motion: Processed pet foods and vets
I am writing to you on behalf of the Pet Food Manufacturers
Association. We represent over 50 UK manufacturers, directly
employing around 8,000 people. We are very concerned about
the nature of the early day motion (335) on processed pet
foods and vets. In particular there are some disturbing inaccu-
racies within the EDM, which need to be countered.

Firstly, there is simply no evidence that processed pet
food causes a higher incidence of dental problems. In fact
studies have shown that dogs fed 'natural' diets have the same
incidence of periodontal problems that are found in pets
fed commercial diets. Rather, it is the feeding of bones that
can result in chipped or broken teeth, therefore preventing
the dog from adequately chewing its food to aid digestion.
A 1997 study of foxhounds fed animal carcass showed that
older dogs had an average of 50% fractured teeth.

Secondly, it is quite wrong to claim that a diet of raw meaty bones 'reflect[s] the full range of nutritional need'. Quite the reverse, as such a diet runs a high risk of nutritional imbalance as eating only the meat and bone of a carcass does not represent a balanced diet. There are many examples of pathological fractures resulting from poor bone mineralisation and nutritional hyperparathydroidism where animals have been fed diets containing meat with inadequate calcium supplementation. Vitamins, trace minerals, potassium and essential fatty acids must be added to the diet before the diet will contain the minimum concentration of known essential nutrients.

Finally, to imply that pet food manufacturers produce food that 'causes illness in pets' is false, and to suggest that a number of veterinary surgeons are party to this is wrong. Our members take the responsibility of feeding the nation's pets very seriously. They have spent decades understanding the nutritional requirements of pets to develop products that provide optimum nutrition and promote the health and wellbeing of the UK pet population. Industry has done this work often in concert with a number of dedicated veterinarians. Their expertise on the physiology of pet animals ensures we are providing the optimum nutrition for the pets' needs. As a result, knowledge has advanced beyond recognition, and it is now widely recognised by veterinarians that pets are leading longer and healthier lives.

I attach some further background. Please don't hesitate to contact me if you require any additional information.

Yours sincerely,
Michael Bellingham
PFMA Chief Executive

FDF a member of the Food & Drink Federation
Registered Office: 15 High Street, Brackley, Northants,
NN13 7DH
Registered No: 3139685

November 2005: British Veterinary Association policy brief

Dear Reader,

Sometimes I write to you as a researcher, sometimes a foot soldier and sometimes a war correspondent. This time I'm a war correspondent reporting on the latest battle in the paper war with the junk pet food industry/veterinary alliance. The massed battalions of the British Veterinary Association (BVA), British Small Animal Veterinary Association (BSAVA) and the Pet Food Manufacturers Association (PFMA) have opened up a new front.

In their 12 October 'policy brief' the BVA–BSAVA–PFMA alliance deliver a salvo of unsubstantiated, misleading or false statements under the heading 'Key Facts'. Their opening line 'An ongoing debate within the veterinary profession' suggests an honest profession engaged in vigorous debate in earnest pursuit of the truth. It's a cruel joke.

My files contain numerous documents detailing the efforts of the BVA and BSAVA to suppress and censor debate on how pets can and should be fed healthy diets. Accounts of the confrontations, dating back to the mid-1990s, appear in *Raw Meaty Bones*. When, in 2002, I asked the BVA and BSAVA to review the book and thus to get an informed discussion going, they refused. Now in 2005 they maintain their hostile rejection of natural feeding. They make no effort to conceal their affiliations; they stand in company with the Pet Food Manufacturers Association in a monstrous show of force.

But with the bodies falling, the bodies of millions of dogs, cats and ferrets, poisoned by the disgusting industrial 'food' they are compelled to consume, we cannot give up. The UKRMB Support and Action Group are doing a fine job, but they should not be left to fight the fight alone. Please consider joining UKRMB and please give them generous financial support—the costs of the war are high.

Please also consider opening discussion with your legal and political representatives. The more loudly we complain the sooner something will be done to investigate the pet food industry/veterinary alliance.

Please find below the BVA policy brief and rebuttal statements (pages 124–6). There's a separate annotated document in colour.[11]

Best wishes, Tom Lonsdale

BVA Policy Brief

Page 1 of 1

Raw Meaty Bones Lobby

An ongoing debate within the veterinary profession. A small lobby group proposes that pet dogs and cats should be fed a 'natural diet' of raw meat and bones rather than commercially prepared diets. The group is active in their criticism of the commercial manufacturers of pet foods. This criticism has recently been extended to the university veterinary schools, which have been accused of teaching undergraduate veterinary nutrition in a biased fashion in return for financial support for research and clinical work within the schools.

Key facts:

- Dogs are omnivorous animals whilst cats are obligate carnivores. Both species require a balance of essential dietary nutrients (e.g. vitamins, minerals and essential fatty acids) for optimal health and longevity.

- Commercially prepared pet foods have been scientifically formulated to contain the optimum balance of essential dietary nutrients for each species. Some commercial pet foods have been designed to satisfy the requirements of specific breeds or the specialised dietary needs of animals with a range of illnesses. The use of such diets over the past decades likely accounts for the increased health and longevity of companion animals.

- These commercial diets are based on extensive research, performed both 'in-house' and in collaboration with veterinary schools. Much of this research is published in the peer-reviewed scientific literature. By contra st, there is no scientific evidence base to support the benefits of feeding raw meat and bones.

- Dogs and cats may be fed with home-prepared 'natural diets', but it is difficult to achieve the optimum balance of requisite nutrients in this fashion.

- The feeding of raw meat and bones to companion animals carries particular risks, including infection with pathogenic bacteria associated with uncooked meats (e.g. Salmonella, Campylobacter) and injury (e.g. intestinal perforation) caused by bone fragments. The BSAVA (the BVA's relevant specialist division) advises against the feeding of raw meat or bones to companion animals for this reason.

- The RMB lobby proposes that the feeding of bones is beneficial to oral health (teeth and gums). Similar benefits may be achieved by feeding of purpose designed kibble food or dental chews, without the attendant risk of damage (e.g. fractures) of the teeth.

Main Contacts

BVA: Dr Freda Scott-Park
BSAVA: Mark Johnston

PFMA: Nicole Harrison
20 Bedford Street, London, WC2E 9HP
Tel: (020 7379 9009)
Fax: (020 7379 8008)
Email: nicole@pfma.org.uk

BVA Press Office:
Chrissie Nicholls
E: chrissien@bva.co.uk
Nadin Sajakow
E: nadins@bva.co.uk
Helena Cotton
E: helenac@bva.co.uk
T: 0207 636 6541
Out of hours: 07810 433 730
                     07929 620 325

Additional Resources

- Pet Food Manufacturers Association Information Paper on Raw Meat and Bones Discussions. PFMA, January 2005.

Date last edited: 11 October 2005

Rebuttal of British Veterinary Association policy brief

When vets unwittingly, accidentally injure the patients under their care it's regrettable but, because vets are human, it's mostly forgivable. When vets conspire with the manufacturers of junk food to promote the mass consumption of products known to maim and kill a majority of the world's pets then forgiveness is no longer an option.

The organisations:

- The British Veterinary Association (BVA) is the main UK veterinary association, with over 10,000 members.[12]
- The British Small Animal Veterinary Association (BSAVA) claims to 'foster high scientific and educational standards of small animal medicine and surgery in practice, teaching and research' and represents over 5,500 members.[13]
- The Pet Food Manufacturers Association (PFMA) represents 50 small, medium and giant junk pet food companies doing business in the UK.[14]

BVA ASSERTIONS	TOM LONSDALE REBUTTALS
An ongoing debate within the veterinary profession.	**False**: Apathy rules within the veterinary profession and the veterinary authorities censor and suppress attempts to raise awareness of the junk pet food scam.
A small lobby group proposes that pet dogs and cats should be fed a 'natural diet' of raw meat and bones rather than commercially prepared diets. The group is active in their criticism of the commercial manufacturers of pet foods.	**True**: The UKRMB Support and Action Group (www.ukrmb.co.uk) promotes the feeding of a diet based on whole carcasses or raw, meaty bones and a few table scraps. UKRMB accuses the junk pet food industry of producing products that injure the health of a majority of the world's pets.
This criticism has recently been extended to the university veterinary schools, which have been accused of teaching undergraduate veterinary nutrition in a biased fashion in return for financial support for research and clinical work within the schools.	**True**: It's a multi-million-pound scandal. The vet schools are propped up by junk pet food company funds; they grovel to the companies; teach from company-produced textbooks and consciously, deliberately exclude the provision of natural dietary information. Young vets emerge from the vet schools brimful of counterfeit science, clueless about natural feeding but well versed in junk petfood company factoids and falsehoods.
Key facts	Pet food industry inspired factoids and falsehoods.
Dogs are omnivorous animals	**False**: Dogs are carnivores like their wolf ancestors.

Cats are obligate carnivores.	**True**: That's why cats catch birds and small mammals — unless forced to consume cooked, pulverised grain.
Both species require a balance of essential dietary nutrients (e.g. vitamins, minerals and essential fatty acids) for optimal health and longevity.	**Pseudoscientific gobbledygook**: Air, water and food are all essential and well defined and provided for by nature.
Commercially prepared pet foods have been scientifically formulated to contain the optimum balance of essential dietary nutrients for each species.	**False**: Companies formulate their products to maximise profits and to minimise or disguise the adverse health consequences. Nature determines the optimum balance of essential nutrients.
Some commercial pet foods have been designed to satisfy the requirements of specific breeds or the specialised dietary needs of animals with a range of illnesses.	Marketing scam: should be investigated.
The use of such diets over the past decades likely accounts for the increased health and longevity of companion animals.	**False and absurd.** No evidence that there is increased longevity (save for the control of infectious diseases). Junk food known to impair health and shorten life.
These commercial diets are based on extensive research, performed both 'in-house' and in collaboration with veterinary schools.	**True**: Veterinary profession little more than R&D and marketing arm of the junk pet food industry.
Much of this research is published in the peer-reviewed scientific literature.	**Disinformation**: The 'scientific' journals are crammed with biased research endorsed by the anonymous peer-review process that the editor of the *Lancet*, Richard Horton, labelled: 'Biased, unjust, unaccountable, incomplete, easily fixed, often insulting, usually ignorant, occasionally foolish and frequently wrong.' Journal peer reviewers don't sign their reviews; they operate in secrecy, and the so-called scientists, whose papers are reviewed, mostly come from the same pool of pet food company servants.
By contrast, there is no scientific evidence base to support the benefits of feeding raw meat and bones.	**False**: The medical, dental and veterinary literature is replete with hard scientific evidence. Common sense and common experience confirm that Nature got it right. *Raw Meaty Bones: Promote Health* comprises 389 pages of referenced evidence, fully endorsed by five veterinary peer-reviewers who signed their reviews.
Dogs and cats may be fed with home-prepared 'natural diets', but it is difficult to achieve the optimum balance of requisite nutrients in this fashion.	**Egregious nonsense**: Dogs and cats have been fed by humans for thousands of years. The junk pet food industry is less than 150 years old.
The feeding of raw meat and bones to companion animals carries particular risks, including infection with pathogenic bacteria associated with uncooked meats (e.g. salmonella, campylobacter) and injury (e.g. intestinal perforation) caused by bone fragments.	**Scaremongering disinformation**: Negligible risks compared with the widespread ill-health and injury associated with junk foods. (See *Raw Meaty Bones*.)
The BSAVA (the BVA's relevant specialist division) advises against the feeding of raw meat or bones to companion animals for this reason.	**Disgraceful: The BSAVA should be investigated.**

The RMB lobby proposes that the feeding of bones is beneficial to oral health (teeth and gums).	**True**: Raw meaty bones are essential for oral health and to ward off many fatal diseases.
Similar benefits may be achieved by feeding of purpose-designed kibble food or dental chews, without the attendant risk of damage (e.g. fractures) of the teeth.	**False**: Reckless scaremongering and commercially inspired disinformation.
Main contacts: BVA: Dr Freda Scott-Park BSAVA: Mark Johnston PFMA: Nicole Harrison 20 Bedford Street, London, WC2E 9HP Tel: (020 7379 9009) Fax: (020 7379 8008) Email: nicole@pfma.org.uk	**Disgraceful: The BVA, BSAVA and PFMA should be investigated by several arms of government.**
BVA Press Office: Chrissie Nicholls E: chrissien@bva.co.uk Nadin Sajakow E: nadins@bva.co.uk Helena Cotton E: helenac@bva.co.uk T: 0207 636 6541 Out of hours: 07810 433 730 07929 620 325	**Disgraceful: Why are the BVA, BSAVA and PFMA so desperate to present their disinformation day and night? Who pays for this outrage?**
Additional resources Pet Food Manufacturers Association Information Paper on Raw Meat and Bones Discussions. PFMA, January 2005.	**Disgraceful: The PFMA calls the tune; the BVA and BSAVA march in step singing in harmony.** **What about the animals? When will this cruel alliance be made accountable?**

November 2005: EDM 1003: Raw Meaty Bones Group

Dear Reader,

Amazing good news—the hard work by the UKRMB Group has resulted in a second early day motion in the British parliament.

Do you remember back in February this year I wrote about the first early day motion, 'Processed pet foods and vets'?[1]

According to the UK Parliament website:

> An Early Day Motion, or EDM, is a motion put down ('tabled') by Members of Parliament calling for a debate on a particular subject. In practice, there is rarely time to debate EDMs nowadays and their true modern-day purpose is to enable MPs to draw attention to an issue and to canvass support for their views by inviting other Members to add their signatures in support of the motion.

The two MPs who tabled the recent motion, Mr David Lepper MP and Dr Rudi Vis MP, encapsulated the essence of the RMB Campaign. They've provided a stable foundation upon which to build a healthful, secure future free of the junk pet food scourge. Please take a moment to study what the MPs wrote.[15]

> **EDM 1003: Raw Meaty Bones Group 11 November 2005**
> That this House notes the controversy surrounding the promotion and sale of processed pet foods by veterinary surgeons; acknowledges the evidence and analysis in the book *Raw Meaty Bones* by Tom Lonsdale; commends the UK Raw Meaty Bones Group's public awareness campaign; and calls for a wide-ranging inquiry into that group's serious concerns relating to human and pet health, the economy and the environment and the adequacy of the current veterinary regulatory system to investigate these issues.

Until now the UK veterinary authorities have consolidated their alliance with the junk pet food makers and together have maintained implacable opposition to an inquiry. But with allegations of incompetence and corruption swirling around, then the best way for them to clear their name is to welcome an open inquiry.

So what needs to be done from here? How can you help get an official inquiry established?

In the first instance, the more MPs who know about early day motion 1003 and the more who add their signatures to the list the better.

Please, I urge you write to MPs and ask them to sign EDM 1003 Raw Meaty Bones Group.

6

―――

2006: CONFIDENCE TRICKSTERS AND CENSORSHIP

Internal conflicts within the raw feeding community become a contentious issue, as opportunists push misleading diet models for profit. Meanwhile, the British Veterinary Association and the Royal College of Veterinary Surgeons actively suppress and censor RMB advocacy.

April 2006: Raw Meaty Bones campaign update

Dear Reader,

Welcome to the first *RMB Newsletter* of 2006.

How have you been? Making good progress I trust.

In October 2001 *RMB Newsletter* 1:1 opened with the statement:

> With a majority of the world's pets suffering the effects of an artificial diet and a majority of the veterinary profession—the pet healthcare professionals—endorsing these diets, there's a huge job to be done. But we must start somewhere, and where better to start than by staking a claim to freedom of speech?— the subject of this first *RMB Newsletter*.

Five years on and without the internet freedom of speech would be a rare event. Occasionally pet magazines provide a watered-down version of what should go in the dog's bowl. Once in a while a TV station or radio program partially lifts the lid—and quickly closes it again with self-serving celebrity vet shows promoting junk pet food and needless veterinary services.

Recent experience liaising with a top journalist is par for the course. Four months were spent researching the story. Photos were taken, even the page layout was completed and the publication day set. On the eve of publication and without explanation four months of commitment and a deepening understanding was tossed aside. The editor ruled that the massive pet food/veterinary/faux animal welfare fraud should be left undisturbed.

So, it seems, it's up to us to use the internet in ever more effective ways. Please check out the links in this newsletter and spread the electronic word.

Best wishes,
Tom Lonsdale

Raw Meaty Bones Diet Sheet

For a quick three-page summary to download and print please go to the Raw Meaty Bones website.[1]

Work Wonders: Feed Your Dog Raw Meaty Bones

Please consider ordering bound copies for your family, friends and vet and thus help fund the RMB campaign.

You can read *Work Wonders* in Spanish, Dutch and French, located under the national flags at the Raw Meaty Bones website.[2] Please join with me in acknowledging the terrific work done by the translators.

Do you have the time and skill to translate *Work Wonders* into any of the 5,000 world languages? Please contact tom@rawmeatybones.com.[3]

Raw Meaty Bones in the veterinary profession

Once again the Royal College of Veterinary Surgeons elections are underway. You can find ten years of election statements urging the vets to clean up their act.[4]

About 21,000 vets are registered with the UK vet regulator, the Royal College of Veterinary Surgeons. Only a small proportion of the total number vote and, in previous years, only one tenth of voters voted for reform. What will be the veterinary verdict this year?

In their policy brief entitled 'Raw Meaty Bones Lobby' the British Veterinary Association in conjunction with the Pet Food Manufacturers Association referred to 'an ongoing debate in the veterinary profession'.[5]

Veterinary associations worldwide have not encouraged debate. They actively stifle debate. But, in a spirit of optimism, the UKRMB Group wrote to seven UK veterinary schools and seventeen European veterinary schools inquiring if they would like to host 'an evening talk, whole day seminar or other discussion'. All of those veterinary schools are enmeshed with the junk food poisoners and not one of those schools accepted the offer to talk about a natural diet.

Veterinary students are deliberately dumbed down and disadvantaged by the policies of their veterinary schools. Eventually we can expect some young veterinarians to seek legal redress. The junk pet food industry pays the universities now. But who will pay the universities' legal fees and compensation awards when aggrieved former students win class actions?

Raw Meaty Bones in the medical profession

In *RMB Newsletter* 5:2 we looked at some of the human medical implications of the pet food fraud and how the medical profession is itself becoming enmeshed in the scam.

For a short time the *British Medical Journal* (*BMJ*) permitted limited discussion, and Jackie Marriott of UKRMB contributed an excellent letter to the *BMJ* online.[6]

UKRMB sent the *BMJ* several copies of *Raw Meaty Bones: Promote Health* and asked the journal to open up discussion on the full extent of the medical implications of the pet food fraud. The *BMJ* editors simply stopped replying to correspondence. The editors are aware of but nonetheless stifle discussion of major issues affecting the health of the British people.

June 2006: BARFmania: The junk raw pet food scam

Dear Reader,

How's 2006 treating you? Well, I trust.

Here in Australia the days race by with ever new information to chew and digest. Changing the way dogs, cats and ferrets (and zoo animals) are fed is a big task needing many shoulders to the wheel. Initially we need to look after our own animals. With our domestic arrangements in place, it's then a case of tackling the triple plague of the junk pet food industry and their veterinary and faux animal welfare allies.

Although the junk pet food alliance is the main scourge there is perhaps a more immediate obstacle to feeding our pet carnivores as Nature intended. In the mid-nineties BARF (vomit) mania swept across North America and much of Europe too. Pet owners were conned into believing that dogs are omnivores, not carnivores, and need lashings of vegetables and bottled supplements.

Here in Australia BARFmania has not taken hold to the same extent. But wherever it spreads it does harm. If we want to take decisive action against the junk cooked pet food alliance I believe we first need to tackle the BARFmaniacs and their raw junk pet food scam.

Best wishes,
Tom Lonsdale

BARFmania: the junk raw pet food scam

We humans are an odd lot. We can put a man on the moon, but we can't agree on how to feed a dog. How crazy is that?

Having lived with this conundrum for a few years now, I still find it disturbing. And in my opinion both the problem and the solution lie with the veterinary profession.

Where understanding and certainty exists, the room for debate and chatter shrinks almost to zero. That's how it is regarding the moon's orbit, rocket fuel technology, electrical conduction and differential calculus, the necessary building blocks of a successful moon landing. Experts agree about these things. Universities teach the subjects and the population at large is satisfied that genuine experts are in control.

When it comes to feeding pets, the community can have no such confidence. The self-appointed but non-genuine experts in this field, veterinarians, are variously cowed or incompetent and in notable instances corrupt. It's largely by default that veterinarians have been given authority over pet diets. Vets are supposed to know about health and disease and an assumption is made they will be trained to put prevention first—in keeping with the first rule of medicine 'First do no harm'.

Young vets start their induction in kindergarten. They watch their parents feeding pets out of the can and packet; they watch the TV ads and the celebrity vets feeding junk food too. By the time they have come top of their class, passed their exams and been admitted to vet school the young vet students are filled with misplaced assumptions about the world, their position in it and that pets should be raised and maintained on junk food. Doing harm for most budding vets is a way of life.

Nothing at vet school tells them otherwise. In fact, nutrition courses are frequently taught by pet food company guest lecturers and the textbook, if there is one, will likely have been supplied by a pet food company. Courses in medicine and surgery are taught by lecturers receiving pet food company research money, or by lecturers eyeing the money and hoping their turn will soon come.

In the final years at vet school, diagnosis and treatment of disease is the priority focus. Assumptions about diet continue and little or no time is spent thinking about preventive medicine. A raw diet, where it is discussed, is used as an object of ridicule to warn the students of the alleged risks of bacterial disease, parasitic disease, broken teeth, and choked, obstructed and constipated dogs. With the preventive benefits of natural feeding up-ended and replaced with scaremongering, the students dutifully absorb the diagnosis and treatment options in readiness for the final exams.

I pity the new graduates. I was one once. The first weeks in practice are, for many young vets, a nightmare experience. Attempting to recall diagnosis and treatment options from the textbooks and fit them to real life patients is a scary business with pitfalls at every turn. Small wonder prevention never gets a moment's consideration. And thus the scene is set for a professional life spent treating animals that are fed the canned and packet junk food displayed in the vet's waiting room.

There are other nuances, but you get the idea. Vets live in a culture that puts them in charge of pet healthcare, but they generally know nothing and care little about the benefits of a natural diet. Governments innocently bequeath self-regulatory status on the veterinary profession meaning that vets themselves decide what is and what isn't good practice. The veterinary leadership, veterinary schools and veterinary research establishments decided long ago to accept junk food as the norm—it's what defines the culture. (You and I know it also makes the vets a lot of money treating the diet-affected animals.)

Once a culture is established it's really hard to divert or change it. Where vets are put in charge of identifying, researching and communicating good preventive options, but where they abrogate their responsibilities, a vacuum develops. And as the saying goes: 'Nature abhors a vacuum.' This brings us to the predicament we now face—a cacophony of voices filling the vacuum with their pronouncements about the dog's bowl and what should go in it.

It's a free for all where the well-meaning jostle with the naive and the devious—where those with nothing to sell spread confusion and others exploit the confusion to sell junk raw food and bottled supplements. The major aspects of the junk pet food fraud amounting to 95% of the issues we face don't get a mention or, worse still, are specifically frowned upon by the self-styled experts in pet nutrition.

Principal among the junk raw food merchants are the BARFers who contend that dogs are omnivores not carnivores. Without protection from a competent veterinary profession many people fall victim to the BARF absurdity. Trouble is the victims all too often become victimisers. They victimise their own pets and then seek to spread the BARF nonsense to other defenceless pet owners who get caught in a web of confusion as illustrated by the following commentary.

I decided when I started this the best thing for us was to follow some kind of recipe and grind it together in some sort of patty and go that route until we all were more experienced. I followed Dr Billinghurst's recipe in his book for canine patties. The last time we made it we made a huge batch and if you don't mind me going on and on here's what we put in it: 80 lb chicken necks and backs, 40 lb chicken wings, 10 lb beef liver, 10 lb beef heart and kidney, 30 lb various veggies, 10 lb various fruits, 6 lb yogurt, 6 lb ground flax seed, 30 oz kelp and 16 oz garlic.

We grind this all together and freeze it in daily amounts. I guess my question is ... is this adequate? Does it sound like a fairly good recipe to be feeding daily? We do occasionally give [our two dogs] chicken wings whole; beef rib bones and larger beef bones they can't totally eat. The pup eats everything. Grimly (2 years old) is not eating this new batch very well at all. Is garlic necessary? It makes the mixture smell horrible. Any suggestions?

In reaction to BARFmania a new strand of thought says that instead of a recipe for minced meat, vegetables and supplements pet owners need a recipe for different organs. 'Prey-model' is the term applied and imposes strictures on the amount of meat, bone and certain organs that should be fed to a pet. Head, hide and guts are left out of the reckoning. To my way of thinking, although well meaning, 'prey model' is another piece of jargon and best avoided.

What we can be sure of is that Nature has had lots of practice and practice makes perfect. If we feed our pets according to Nature's model we'll get the best available health, vitality and longevity. Whole carcasses of other animals set the standard in canine cuisine. Next, I suggest, comes a diet based on raw meaty bones. It's the physical side of ripping, tearing and chewing meat from bone that is central to the needs of a carnivore diet. By all means include whole carcasses as often as possible; include meaty bones and offal from a range of fish, mammals and birds. For fuller practical details on feeding dogs please see *Work Wonders: Feed Your Dog Raw Meaty Bones*. For a fuller exposition on diet disease and the five facets of the pet food fraud please see *Raw Meaty Bones: Promote Health*.

Australian College of Veterinary Scientists (ACVS) award nomination

Back in 2003 I complained to Dr Richard Malik that he had not read *Raw Meaty Bones*. Fortunately, he was not offended by my remarks and continued to listen as I told him of efforts to get the book reviewed by veterinary journals. The journals of the American Veterinary Medical Association and the American Animal Hospitals Association had simply ignored all correspondence. Other journals refused to review the book, some giving excuses and some not.

Richard is well liked, respected and in the top tier of vets in Australia, possibly the world. When he offered to review the book and then seek publication of the review I was delighted, especially given that two Australian journals said they were unable to find anyone to do the job.

After some months a letter arrived from Richard and a quick glance informed me that he was no longer planning to review the book.

Imagine my disappointment—that quickly turned to joy! Richard went on to say: 'I have taken the initiative ... and thought of something that may achieve the same end. I have taken the liberty of putting you forward for the College Prize of the ACVS.'[7]

Dr Douglas Bryden, former president of the ACVS, seconded the nomination and together two of the most eminent veterinarians in Australia wrote magnificent nomination statements that fill me with pride.

The nomination stood for three years, 2004 to 2006, and was unsuccessful each year, including in 2005 when there were no other candidates. Now at the conclusion of the nomination period the statements are available for public scrutiny.[7]

Royal College of Veterinary Surgeons elections 2006

Followers of the Raw Meaty Bones campaign know that each year at around this time I report on the Royal College of Veterinary Surgeons elections. As ever I came a distant last with 263 votes (ten fewer than last year).

The quantity of votes may be low, but the quality is high and I received some terrific messages of support. However, at 7.4% of the votes cast it's not nearly enough to bring about the sought-for reform—hence the need for committed political and legal action that vets cannot ignore.

July 2006: Bad to worse

Dear Reader,

How are you? Hope this finds you wonderfully well and fighting the good fight against the junk pet food monster.

This last couple of weeks it's been hot here in England. Near record temperatures were reached in London. Record and sometimes heated discussions were held on three separate days with UK members of parliament about the pet food industry/veterinary alliance's callous indifference to animal cruelty. By the next newsletter I hope to have some details.

The main item in this newsletter focuses on the British Veterinary Association and Royal College of Veterinary Surgeons going from bad to worse.

Have fun and much success too.

Tom Lonsdale

BVA and RCVS going from bad to worse

Part of the Raw Meaty Bones campaign involves standing for the council of the Royal College of Veterinary Surgeons (RCVS). The RCVS is the regulatory body for veterinary surgeons in the UK whose function it is:

- To safeguard the health and welfare of animals committed to veterinary care through the regulation of the educational, ethical and clinical standards of the veterinary profession, thereby protecting the interests of those dependent on animals and assuring public health.
- To act as an impartial source of informed opinion on animal health and welfare issues and their interaction with human health.

Effectively, then, the RCVS is the body responsible for the parlous state of the veterinary profession in the UK. By standing for election there is just a chance other vets will get to read about the issues and start to take notice. In each of the past nine years I received around 9% or 10% of the votes cast. This year the figure slipped to 7.5%. No other candidates mention the pet food fraud, so it seems UK vets are becoming less interested in putting their house in order.

When thanking the voters in a letter I sent to the *Veterinary Record*, journal of the British Veterinary Association, I also mentioned the RMB U-turn briefings for members of Parliament:

Dear Editor,

RCVS Election

Thank you to all supporters at the 2006 Royal College of Veterinary Surgeons election—the tenth election highlighting the junk pet food superstitions gripping the veterinary profession.

Eventually we shall win through. We must never give up. In the words of the late great J. K. Galbraith:

> In all life one should comfort the afflicted but verily, also, one should afflict the comfortable, especially when they are comfortably, contentedly, even happily wrong.

In October 2005 the British Veterinary Association, speaking about raw meaty bones, stated that there is 'an ongoing debate within the veterinary profession'. In March 2006 the UK Raw Meaty Bones Group invited seven British veterinary schools to give validity to the notion of an 'ongoing debate' and host discussions on the nutritional and medicinal benefits of natural foods for domestic and wild carnivores. Not one veterinary school accepted the invitation.

Undaunted the UKRMB Group press on because, unlike

the veterinary authorities, many Members of Parliament have indicated their willingness to discuss the five facets of the pet food fraud. On Wednesday 12 July 2006 there is to be a two-hour briefing for Members of both Houses of Parliament. Please, for the benefit of pets, pet owners and the wider community, encourage your MP to attend the briefing.

I welcome your comments and shall be pleased to meet colleagues during the European 2006 Raw Meaty Bones U-turn Tour.

Unfortunately, the British Veterinary Association appears contemptuous of parliament, its members and the wider community. Martin Alder, editor of the *Veterinary Record*, wrote:

Dear Tom,

Thank you for sending us your letter.

Traditionally, we publish 'thank you' letters from candidates standing in the RCVS Council elections as a courtesy to those candidates. However, with space being limited, and having already published the manifestos, we need to keep them short. As for a number of other candidates, we will therefore be shortening your letter, and plan to publish the first two paragraphs only.

... I trust you will find this acceptable.

Yours sincerely,
Martin

President of the British Veterinary Association, Dr Freda Scott-Park, and the president of the Royal College of Veterinary Surgeons supported the *Veterinary Record* decision to keep British vets in the dark.

Letter from the president of British Veterinary Association, 30 June 2006

Dear Mr Lonsdale,

Thank you for your letter of 29 May 2006.

As with all previous BVA presidents, I do not seek to influence the content of the *Veterinary Record*, which is rightly the responsibility of the Editor.

BVA members and other veterinary surgeons can obtain news of developments from various sources, including other veterinary publications, more general publications such as magazines and newspapers and parliamentary websites.

Provided the nutritional needs of the individual animal are identified and addressed and provided health and safety protocols, e.g. food hygiene guidelines are followed, we as a profession have no objections if owners wish to provide their pets with alternative diets.

Yours sincerely,
Dr Freda Scott-Park

Letter from the president of the Royal College of Veterinary Surgeons, 2 June 2006

Dear Mr Lonsdale,

I write in reply to your letter of 29 May 2006 which I received by fax on 1 June 2006. I am also aware of email correspondence which you have copied to the College in recent weeks in connection with the way in which the Editor of the *Veterinary Record* has responded to a letter you have submitted for publication. The decisions of the Editor are not matters for the College and it would be wholly inappropriate for the RCVS to seek to influence them in any way.

Members of the BVA and the profession generally may receive information about developments at Westminster:

through a variety of media sources, including veterinary journals (other than the *Veterinary Record*), national newspapers and magazines.

Yours sincerely
Mrs Lynne V. Hill MVB MBA MRCVS
President

Censorship and suppression are only part of the British Veterinary Association/Royal College of Veterinary Surgeons endeavour. They either facilitate or encourage British vets to capitalise on the epidemic of junk food induced disease:

Off the Record, News from the British Veterinary Association, vol. 5, issue 7, July–August 2006

How can Pet Smile Month benefit your practice?
Pet Smile Month can benefit both pets and veterinary practices according to Bob Partridge, the event's organiser [Member of the Council of the RCVS]. This year a £1 million TV advertising campaign is planned to get the healthcare message out to the pet-owning public. Pet Smile Month is excellent PR for the veterinary profession but, he says, you have to take part to benefit.

The promotional activity will encourage pet owners to visit local participating practices to receive a free dental health check for their pets, by either a vet or trained member of staff. In addition to providing recommendations on dental treatment, preventative health will be discussed and the client will go home with a free dental-health goody bag, containing helpful leaflets and samples of products that can help to reduce dental disease.

Benefits

So why should you give your time for free? The advertising allows the Pet Smile message to be spread across a wide range of pet owners. Signing up could bring new and lapsed clients back into your practice.

Since 80% of cats and dogs over the age of three have dental disease, all practices should benefit from the increase in dental work required. Other long-term benefits will include being able to offer this new pool of clients other preventative healthcare measures, such as vaccinations, wormers and flea treatment.

As in other areas of veterinary medicine, prevention is better than cure and Pet Smile Check-Ups are a fantastic opportunity for you to discuss preventative dental care. If your staff can successfully communicate the importance of tooth brushing, dental chews and specialist dental diets, this could be a new long-term source of revenue for your business.

Chance to win a new dental unit

Hopefully your 'ops' list will be brimming with dental work but you may be wondering how your old scaler will cope with the increased workload. Well, it may not have to. Pet Smile Month has teamed up with Kruuse (UK) to offer a prize of a high-tech dental unit worth £3,000 to one lucky practice. Every Pet Smile Check-Up survey form returned will be placed in the draw. To make things easier, survey forms can be submitted online this year.

How to register

Return your registration form, or download details from the vet area at www.PetSmile.org. Demand will be high and early registrants will receive priority in the allocation of goody bags.

August 2006: Spin doctors

Dear Reader,

How's things with you? Good I trust.

These last few weeks on the RMB U-Turn Tour there has been action aplenty. Debbie Hill did a fine job hosting the Wisbech, Cambridge seminar on 6 August. A well-known UK vet attended, as did a couple of representatives from the local Nestlé-Purina factory. Jackie Marriott, UKRMB convenor, made the journey up from Brighton. Thank you, Debbie, for hard work and generous hospitality coping with three extra house guests. We much enjoyed the rural charm and meeting your dogs, pigs, goats, ducks and chickens.

Natural health seminar, Victoria, Australia

On 10 September the Victorian Canine Association are convening a seminar in Skye, Victoria.

Online seminar

Jeannie Thomason and Kim Bloomer have put together The First Online Dog Expo, 22–24 September. The 'virtual' system holds immense potential. Congratulations to Jeannie and Kim on their initiative.

In the Raw Meaty Bones segment introduction, I say:

> For too long the junk pet food industry/veterinary alliance has exploited pets, pet owners and the global community. A majority of the world's pets are sick and dying of diet-induced diseases. We need to identify the issues, increase our understanding and fight back. The Virtual Dog Exposition provides a fine opportunity to do all three.

Here's hoping to meet you there.

Excellent movie

As I write this, I'm in Guangzhou, China, the last stop on the way home to Australia. Whilst sitting high above the clouds on the night flight from London to China, and unusual for me, I actually watched a movie. *Thank You for Smoking* follows tobacco spin doctor Nick Naylor as he spins and twists the English language to better serve Big Tobacco because, as he says, he 'needs to pay the mortgage'.

In this newsletter we take a brief look at some junk pet food spin doctors. For now, the written word must suffice. Ideally though, we need the movie. Anyone know a Hollywood director or two?

Best wishes,
Tom Lonsdale

Junk pet food industry spin doctors

Mars Corporation

Don't know what motivates the junk pet food spin doctors—some of them must have mighty big mortgages. For instance, the Mars heirs, Forrest, Jacqueline and John, are reputed to be worth $10 billion each. With money like that they could fund massive anti-cruelty, good-health initiatives—instead they are the biggest junk pet food makers on the planet.

Take a look at their company website.[8]

Nancy McIntyre comments:

> From the spiel on 'responsibility' you get a lovely double-think: 'Communication and teamwork turning common business goals into shared aspirations'.

> But

> 'Respect for the individual is at the heart of the Responsibility principle.'

> (Pause for a quiet vomit.)

> But the visual represents the underlying aim of disinformation perfectly: it's circular, unpredictable, mazelike and it ***spins*** Ha!

Dr Ian Billinghurst

Recently UK magazine *Dogs Today* published a two-part evaluation of Billinghurst's 'BARF' diet as compared with a diet based on raw meaty bones.

Author Hsin-Yi Cohen and publisher Beverley Cuddy are to be congratulated on their extensive coverage. Journalists have a strict code, at least early on in a debate, of leaving readers to draw their own conclusions. Mind you, the caricature of spin doctor Billinghurst with his BARF machine disgorging dollar and pound signs makes a telling statement enhanced by Billinghurst's comment:

> The bottom line is, for those owners who either can't or don't want to feed whole bones, the patties on their own provide a perfect solution. While dogs which do not get to gnaw on whole bones will miss out on the physical and psychological benefits this brings, they at least benefit from the enormous nutritional benefits.

It's a far cry from the early 1990s when Dr Billinghurst applied to join the Raw Meaty Bones Lobby of concerned veterinarians. We were a small group of Sydney veterinarians who, as the name implied, stressed the pivotal role of raw meaty bones in carnivore biology. We were dedicated to:

A. Affirming that first and foremost domestic dogs, cats and ferrets are **carnivores**, and that providing people feed raw meaty bones then most other things fall neatly into place.
B. Raising awareness of the ravages of periodontal disease (mouth rot) in domestic pets—not only as a foul-smelling and painful affliction of the mouth but also the origin of a range of diseases including diseases of the kidney, heart, liver, and immune system. A diet of predominantly raw meaty bones was (and is) the simple preventative for a vast array of problems.
C. Informing the veterinary profession of the perils of junk pet food—easily offset by a diet based on raw meaty bones.

D. Campaigning, both within and without the veterinary profession, against the corrupt junk pet food industry/veterinary profession alliance.

At the time we welcomed Dr Billinghurst into the lobby group and shared with him our findings about the essential nature of raw meaty bones. Judging by his 1993 statement published in the Sydney University Post Graduate Foundation in Veterinary Science newsletter he appeared to understand and accept our advice:

> Tom Londale has started the ball rolling. He has been a lone voice, crying in the wilderness. Now is the time for the profession to get behind this man and share his vision. Have a good look at what Tom is seeing.
>
> At the moment he is seeing a [veterinary] profession that is blinkered, may be blinded and possibly hoodwinked into promoting products that are not worthy of our professional approval.
>
> He is seeing that we are doing our clients a disservice every time we advise them to feed their pets commercial pet food. He is seeing the importance of feeding an animal a diet which matches the one it evolved upon. In the case of cats and dogs, that means a diet based on raw, meaty bones.
>
> He is looking into the future and seeing a veterinary profession with a clear vision and a clear conscience, advising their clients as only true professionals can, with honesty and understanding.
>
> That understanding includes the very simple healthy and cost-effective way to feed cats and dogs ... without using commercial pet foods.

Nowadays Billinghurst forgets the essential vision of the Raw Meaty Bones Lobby; he turns fundamental scientific concepts, English usage and common sense on their collective head and insists that 'both dogs and wolves are omnivores'.

The Dogs Today article showcases Billinghurst-style spin:

> Apparently, carnivores in zoos fed a diet of ground-up raw food show no periodontal disease, implying that the chemical nature of raw foods plays a role in the prevention of gum disease, even if the physical cleaning benefits (from gnawing bones) are missing.

Susan Chrissy, director of nutrition services, Brookfield Zoo, Chicago, when attempting to defend the use of ground-up raw food in zoos torpedoed the Billinghurst spin when she admitted:

> Well, the raw meat usually comes like the consistency of hamburger, and so therefore, we get plaque build-up and we get dental problems unless there is some way that we can make sure that that plaque isn't built up. Sometimes it's tranquilising the animal and actually doing a teeth cleaning, which we don't like to do at all, but if it has more of a crunchy diet that would certainly help in that respect.

And on the internet you can find a whole website run by veterinary dentists and dedicated to Sir Frank Colyer, past president of the British Dental Association, who in 1947 wrote 'cats and dogs which lead a freer life and obtain a diet more nearly approaching their natural food, are practically free from [periodontal] disease'.

Although nominally a member of the Raw Meaty Bones Lobby Group, Billinghurst was more a passenger rather than a driver. In 1997, at the height of the battle with veterinary and pet food industry forces he resigned abruptly. In his letter of resignation, he wrote:

> Worldwide my credibility is rising... I am here to educate whoever will listen. Pet owners, vets and even pet food companies —if they are interested. It is not necessary; in fact, it is counterproductive for me to participate in the politics of this debate.

> If I am to be of use, I need to be seen as outside the political arena. Someone who has the respect of the profession, whilst retaining strong views and unequivocal beliefs—supported of course by good evidence. My aim is to make a positive difference in this debate and continue to make a living.

Spin mesmerises and confuses. Spin doctors assign new meanings to old words or—a cunning trick—fabricate new terms to suit hidden agendas. And so it was with BARF, a contraction of Born Again Raw Feeders, first coined by Debbie Tripp. Being synonymous with vomit, BARF was a faintly amusing term that meant different things to different people. Various self-styled experts latched onto the term, bending it to suit their agendas. Sales of meat and vegetable grinding machines soared. Niche marketers raced to grab a share of the junk raw pet food market.

In December 2001, four years after resigning from the Raw Meaty Bones Lobby, spin doctor Billinghurst published his *BARF Diet* recipe book and subsequently took out trademark protection on the word 'BARF'. Nowadays Billinghurst produces a line of junk raw pet food—presumably to 'make a living', even to 'pay the mortgage'.

References
1. Hsin-Yi Cohen, 'Bones of contention', *Dogs Today*, September 2006, pp. 38–44.
2. I. Billinghurst, 'Commercial dog food vs bones: myth or science', *University of Sydney Post Graduate Foundation in Veterinary Science Control and Therapy*, vol. 174, no. 3443, 1993.
3. 'Public interest with Kojo Nnamdi', *National Public Radio*, 8 August 2002.[9]

BARFer Spin Award (BS Award)

Announcing the BARFer Spin Award. Here's your chance to win a copy of *Work Wonders: Feed Your Dog Raw Meaty Bones*. Over the coming months we shall be publishing examples of BARFer spin ranging from the mad to the barking mad. If you know the whereabouts of standout BS please do send it to us, verifying source and date. Ideally you should include your name and address for publication. However, if you prefer to remain anonymous we shall respect that wish.

December 2006: Three-part test

Dear Reader,

Time flies when you're having fun. Now back in Australia and still catching up on the pile of waiting correspondence after the trip to Europe and China.

On 10 September the Victorian Canine Association, guided by Lorraine Cossart-Walsh and Heather Simpson, put on a fine seminar. We met lots of interested and interesting people. Thank you everyone who helped make our weekend most enjoyable.

Jeannie Thomason and Kim Bloomer hosted a wonderful Virtual Dog Exposition on the weekend of 22–24 September and then followed up with a lively online interview broadcast on 14 November 2006. Thanks Jeannie, thanks Kim. Looking forward to the next chat in May 2007.

Back in 1995 Mara Cvejic at the Dental School, Westmead Hospital, University of Sydney, helped me obtain some scanning electron microscope images of dental calculus. We've been friends and allies ever since and it's thanks to Mara that the 'The pet food debacle: dental and medical research perspectives' lecture took place 17 October 2006. Videos, transcript and slides are available on YouTube.[10] Thanks also to Associate Professor Hans Zoellner and Professor Neil Hunter for making the event possible.

In this newsletter I 'grasp the nettle' with an airing of the Three-Part Test. For too long I've observed pet owners fall prey to false prophets, whether those prophets were simply well-meaning but misguided, or more cynical and calculating. By broaching a difficult and challenging subject I believe we can better serve the needs of the majority of animals and their owners.

Wishing you and yours the most wonderful Christmas and New Year.

Best wishes,
Tom Lonsdale

The Three-Part Test

All that is necessary for the triumph of evil is that good men do nothing.

Edmund Burke, Irish orator, philosopher
and politician (1729–1797)

How perverse that the global community permits giant corporations, Mars, Nestlé, Colgate, Procter & Gamble and others, to mass-produce junk pet food and thus to injure the health of a majority of the world's pets.

How obscene that the organised veterinary profession colludes in this mighty junk pet food industry consumer and scientific fraud.

Surely then it's incumbent on those of us 'in the know' to do something about it. Recently I've been giving this matter some thought and would like to suggest a new and objective approach and would appreciate your thoughts on the matter.

Here's what I propose.

As a starting point I believe we need to invoke two fundamentals of carnivore biology—the two imperatives that drive carnivores to do what they do. Carnivores need to:

1. seek out, pursue and consume whole carcasses of prey animals (or parts of animals and table scraps offering nutrients in similar formulation), and
2. spend considerable time and energy gnawing, ripping and tearing and thereby 'brushing' and 'flossing' their teeth.

If we are to be true friends to our carnivore companions then invoking the two points above should, I believe, be our starting point. By reaffirming the biological basis of our beliefs, we stay in touch with Nature and ensure validity to our approach.

But clearly that's not enough in the face of the junk pet food/veterinary alliance. We need to keep to the fore how powerful, how determined the alliance is and we need to constantly work to defeat it by all means at our disposal. Anything less fails our carnivore companions and their dependent owners.

Unfortunately, these days, there's a multiplicity of quacks, opportunists, niche marketers and false prophets seeking to turn a buck and gain kudos peddling nonsensical gibberish and weird incantations that do little to help companion carnivores in their time of need. How can we spot the well-meaning and ill-informed and those with more cynical intent? How can we protect ourselves and our pets against slick presentations and marketing hype?

Maybe it's not so difficult. Maybe by applying the Three-Part Test false prophets can be identified and thus resisted.

Here's the test:

Does the speaker/proponent/prophet affirm and invoke the need for:

1. Carnivores to have a regular full belly of whole prey or something akin to the same [chemical nutrients]?
2. Carnivores to maintain a pearly white set of teeth and salmon pink gums [dependent on the physical form of the food]?
3. Every effort to overturn the junk pet food industry/veterinary alliance?

Check out the articles, the websites, the books and the sly rhetoric of a multiplicity of BARFers, herbalists and pushers of supplements and quack cures. Do they pass one, two or three parts of the Three-Part Test? Or do they fail abysmally?

To my mind we've got a massive job to do, if we are to combat the junk pet food/veterinary alliance and restore pets to rightful good health. We don't need opportunists and false prophets deflecting the issues and making the job more difficult. Let's invoke first principles, stick to first principles and advance the cause of animals, people and the planet.

It would be real good to hear your thoughts on the introduction and application of the Three-Part Test.

Papers

In May 1955 the *Journal of the American Veterinary Medical Association* (*JAVMA*) published a paper entitled: 'Kennel construction and management in relation to longevity studies in the dog'. The researchers were keen to 'provide optimum conditions for normal life in a number of dogs'. Under 'Nutritional regimen' they report:

> The diet consists of raw beef and compounded ration. Once or twice weekly, each animal receives between ¾ to 1 lb of fresh frozen beef obtained directly from a local abattoir and consisting of cheeks, hearts and oxtails. Oxtail, besides being a food, is excellent for de-tartaring and keeping the teeth and gums in good condition.

In 1968 a paper entitled 'Control of dental calculus in experimental beagles' published in *Laboratory Animal Care* cited the *JAVMA* paper as a reference. Brown and Park, the researchers, stated:

> The test confirmed the feasibility of preventing the accumulation of dental calculus in experimental beagle dogs by regular weekly feedings of oxtails.

and

> No harmful effects of feeding oxtails have been observed in the colony of 200 dogs after more than 6 years.

These days *JAVMA* publishes no papers on the extensive benefits of raw food but does publish scare stories about minor and imagined dangers of raw food. A few years ago we tried to engage *JAVMA* editor-in-chief, Dr Janis H. Audin, in correspondence with nil result. Her address is:

Dr Janis H. Audin
Editor-in-Chief JAVMA
1931 N Meacham Rd, Suite 100
Schaumburg, IL 60173-4360, USA

If perchance you manage to write to Dr Audin and obtain any useful information we shall be pleased to publish it in the *RMB Newsletter*.

Good luck.

Confidence tricks

Some of the richest people on the planet engage in some of the most deceptive conduct. The Mars Corporation is a family-owned business responsible for thousands of tons of candy and thousands of tons of junk pet food.

Whilst the Mars family is conning people into believing bone-shaped junk food is good for dogs, Pfizer Inc. is pushing its gum disease vaccine 'Periovac'. Pfizer has spent a reported $15 million working with vet dentists to develop a vaccine that according to Professor Colin Harvey is: 'A marketing challenge—the value to a particular patient will never be demonstrable to an owner.'

Professor Harvey appears to be a willing participant in the Pfizer scheme although in his 1993 book the professor tells readers:

> The diet of the wild carnivore has a plaque-retarding effect. In rigidly controlling and optimising the nutritional content, palatability to the pet, and acceptance of commercially available dog foods, by the pet-owning public, we have created materials that in gross form do not closely resemble the natural diet of wild carnivores.

But at the Periovac launch in New Zealand, he posed the rhetorical and ridiculous question: 'Does a vaccine make sense for something that is best prevented with a toothbrush?'

If you fancy dropping Professor Harvey a line to inquire as to his doublespeak and why he rides to work on the Pfizer gravy train you can find him at:

Professor Colin E Harvey FRCVS
Department of Clinical Studies
3900 Delancey Street

School of Veterinary Medicine
University of Pennsylvania
Philadelphia, PA 19104-6010
USA

UK struggles

In 1992–1993 the UK veterinary authorities were provided with ample evidence of the junk pet food fraud. At last, fourteen years too late, the Royal College of Veterinary Surgeons makes a response.

Pet nutrition

Over the last few years we have received considerable correspondence on pet nutrition. This interest perhaps mirrors a growing preoccupation with healthy eating at large, whether in the form of improved school dinners or initiatives to reduce trans fats, salt and other additives in human diets. During discussions with MPs and other individuals, questions have been raised about veterinary surgeons' responsibilities for pet nutrition. The Pet Food Manufacturers Association has recently launched a new website to provide better information, and individual pet food companies have called for more focus on pet nutrition at undergraduate level.

Meanwhile, an action group called UKRMB (United Kingdom Raw Meaty Bones) has proclaimed its mission: '… to draw attention to the harm that feeding processed pet food causes our pet dogs and cats, and the continuing refusal by the veterinary authorities to acknowledge this.' We have indicated to this group and others that there is no current evidence to support the allegation that processed pet food causes harm to cats and dogs. We have also suggested that other views should be submitted for peer-reviewed publication in the usual way.

Nevertheless, it is worth reminding members that while the responsibility for pet food sold out of practice premises may be limited to that of a retailer, if specific advice is given on pet nutrition, or particular products recommended, then this is part of professional practice. Veterinary surgeons should be aware that many clients buying pet food from them in either context will assume it carries some veterinary endorsement.

If you have time and energy, please drop the RCVS a line to let them know your thoughts on their false and misleading statement. We shall be delighted to see their reply.

Good luck.

Best wishes, Merry Christmas,
Tom Lonsdale

7

———

2007: FEEDING FADS AND FALSE PROPHETS

The pet food industry, BARFers and prey model promoters exploit pet owners with misleading diets. Pseudoscience and marketing gimmicks cloud the raw meaty bones message.

May 2007: Open secret: giant USA corporations poison pets

Dear Reader,

Welcome to the first *RMB Newsletter* of 2007.

How are you and how have you been?

Most North American and South African readers know about the contaminated pet food recall. If you live in any other country, then you may have missed the news about pets dying of acute renal failure and the subsequent recall of canned and packaged junk pet food.

If you lost a pet as a result of the contaminated 'food', I extend my sympathies and wish you solace in your time of grief.

If you are one of the many who are now searching for helpful, healthful advice in the wake of the pet food recall I welcome you to the newsletter.

The Raw Meaty Bones Lobby Group of veterinarians first came into being in Sydney, Australia in the early 1990s. Having tumbled to the reality that most of our patients were sick and dying as a result of their junk food diet, we set about trying to communicate the message.

I say 'trying to communicate the message' because on the evidence, few in positions of responsibility have heeded the warnings.

Take the *New York Times* for instance—the subject of this edition of the newsletter. They publish provocative headlines about Chinese adulteration of animal foods whilst steadfastly ignoring the open secret concerning the devastating effects of junk pet food—junk food sold in most countries of the world by giant USA-based corporations.

Please read on.

Best wishes,
Tom Lonsdale

Open secret: giant USA corporations poison pets

First some background information.

On 16 March 2007, junk pet food manufacturer Menu Foods issued a press release.

> **Menu Foods Income Fund announces precautionary dog and cat food recall**
>
> Attention: Business/Financial Editors
>
> Menu Foods Income Fund (the 'Fund') (TSX:MEW.UN) today announced the precautionary recall of a portion of the dog and cat food it manufactured between 3 December 2006 and 6 March 2007. The recall is limited to 'cuts and gravy'-style pet food in cans and pouches manufactured at two of the Fund's United States facilities. These products are both manufactured and sold under private label and are contract-manufactured for some national brands.

As a result of the recall, we gained a peek into the contract-manufacturing practices of several junk pet food companies including Mars, Nestlé, Colgate-Palmolive and Procter & Gamble. Far from offering premium products it appears they simply affix different (misleading or false) labels to substantially the same toxic brew from the same manufacturing vats. By 23 March the ABC News reported that aminopterin, a rat poison, may have been the toxic agent responsible for the cases of acute kidney disease.

Melamine is now the contaminant suspected of triggering the acute kidney disease outbreak as is reported at the Pet Connection website.

> More than 5,500 pet food products, house brands and name brands alike, are now on the FDA's recall list. The first recall was the largest, of more than 60 million containers of 'cuts and gravy' canned or pouched food that turned out to have wheat gluten tainted with melamine, which is used in the manufacture of plastic countertops, cleaning agents, glue and fertiliser. Those products were all made by Menu Foods, under almost 100 different brand names.

The *New York Times* has been following the story and on 30 April 2007, carried the banner headline 'Filler in animal feed is open secret in China'.

> **Filler in animal feed is open secret in China**
> Zhangqiu, China, 28 April—As American food safety regulators head to China to investigate how a chemical made from coal found its way into pet food that killed dogs and cats in the United States, workers in this heavily polluted northern city openly admit that the substance is routinely added to animal feed as a fake protein.
>
> For years, producers of animal feed all over China have secretly supplemented their feed with the substance, called melamine, a cheap additive that looks like protein in tests, even though it does not provide any nutritional benefits, according to melamine scrap traders and agricultural workers here.
>
> 'Many companies buy melamine scrap to make animal feed, such as fish feed', said Ji Denghui, general manager of the Fujian Sanming Dinghui Chemical Company, which sells melamine.
>
> 'I don't know if there's a regulation on it. Probably not. No law or regulation says, "don't do it", so everyone's doing it. The laws in China are like that, aren't they? If there's no accident, there won't be any regulation.'
>
> Melamine is at the centre of a recall of 60 million packages of pet food, after the chemical was found in wheat gluten linked this month to the deaths of at least 16 pets and the illness of possibly thousands of pets in the United States.

If we follow the *NYT* line of reasoning, and alas many people will, then the lawless Chinese are the culprits and the American manufacturers are innocent victims. But not so fast. For sure adulteration of any foodstuff should be condemned and, hopefully, if those responsible can be found they will receive appropriate penalties.

Of much greater concern is that this current, albeit, significant issue should serve as a distraction, as a smoke-screen to the main game; that the junk petfood manufacturers should once again turn adversity into advantage; that they should continue to cheat the public whilst killing a majority of the world's pets, sometimes quickly but mostly slowly as a result of diet-induced chronic kidney disease, cancer and a host of other painful diseases.

Mass deception of such magnitude depends on other individuals and institutions that are either part of the scam or turning a blind eye. In this regard we can identify the organised veterinary profession, so-called animal welfare bodies, Food and Drug Administration and numerous commentators who, either passively or actively, stay mute.

The *NYT* remark: 'But, by using the melamine additive, the feed seller makes a heftier profit because melamine scrap is much cheaper than soy, wheat or corn protein.' They don't, however, mention the open secret that soy, wheat or corn protein has little or no place in a carnivore's diet. The junk pet food companies know that; the vets know that, but they also know that vegetable protein is cheaper and returns a bigger profit than protein of animal origin.

As one pet food manufacturer commented about turning cheap waste products into pet food:

Give me a tyre, an old leather shoe and a quart of oil and I can meet the specification for the NRC diet.

Vet Bill Miller puts it another way:

It's all about least-cost formulation ... using some fairly sophisticated algorithms (based on a technique called linear programming) which allow a least-cost (actually maximum-profit) ration to be formulated from a wide variety of ingredients (some of which are pretty unconventional for carnivores). The 'constraints' are things that get printed on the label e.g. crude protein, fat and fibre ... how you get there and what gets included are 'open season' ... this is how low-quality wheat gluten ... which is a by-product of some other manufacturing process ... gets included.

Of course, the companies are aware that by keeping their costs down they impose a massive cost burden on pet owners who first pay for the harmful products and then endure the emotional and financial costs of their pets' veterinary treatment. Pets obliged to consume these products slowly, sometimes quickly, pay with their lives.

These days there's a 389-page peer-reviewed book, *Raw Meaty Bones: Promote Health*, which tells the whole sorry story of graft and corruption in the junk pet food/veterinary/faux animal welfare alliance.[1]

Since 2002, the *New York Times* along with many other USA media institutions have been informed by letter and email about the junk pet food scandal. Editors and journalists have hard copies of *Raw Meaty Bones* and, if not, can read the book for free online.

What, I wonder, will it take to get them to take notice and inform their vulnerable and dependent readership?

From 1993 to 1995 I corresponded with the Food and Drug Administration (FDA). On 1 February 1995, I wrote:

> Please advise as to the FDA's current attitude to the now widespread confirmed and suspected adverse consequences of feeding carnivores on chemically and physically unnatural products.
>
> It is my impression that manufacturers are generally aware that their products are associated with periodontal and a range of degenerative diseases in carnivores. They do, nonetheless, advertise their products as being 'complete and balanced' and generally beneficial for health and longevity. This appears to be deliberate deception.
>
> Does the FDA agree that this conduct represents deliberate deception? Does the FDA have a policy towards such conduct in the marketplace?

Please advise the FDA's attitude to the misappropriation and use of the word 'food' without qualification in the labelling of artificial products designed for consumption by small domestic carnivores.

What, I wonder, will it take to get the FDA to take notice and take action in accordance with their responsibilities? Will they perform the function they are paid for, or will they continue to 'run interference' on behalf of the junk pet food industry/veterinary/faux animal welfare alliance?

Sydney Morning Herald

The *Sydney Morning Herald* gains attention and commands respect here in Australia. In January 2007 health writer Paula Goodyer posed the question: Dog's breakfast—so what's a dog really meant to eat?

There were answers from BARF and RMB points of view.

Here's one piece of Aussie wisdom to raise a smile:

I got my first puppy a few months ago, and just about the first thing I discovered is that *no smart person* discusses what they feed their dog. It's a worse minefield than breastfeeding (at least there's broad agreement that breast is best). So I'm not telling what my dog eats. Can we talk about something safer, like abortion, religion, politics, racism ... ?

May 2007: Raw Meaty Bones Diet and Campaign

Dear Reader,

How are things in your part of the world? I hope your 2007 goes well.

The Raw Meaty Bones Diet and Campaign commenced in December 1991. From the outset the Campaign was about helping individual pets and pet owners whilst doing the utmost to combat the system controlled by the junk pet food industry/veterinary/faux animal welfare alliance. Explaining that to pet owners is relatively easy and there's a mass of information at the Raw Meaty Bones website.[2]

Complications arise when people contact me who mistakenly believe that 'BARF' (vomit) recipes or 'prey model' menus are somehow akin to a Raw Meaty Bones Diet.

This edition of the *RMB Newsletter* provides some background on how the original RMB Diet and Campaign was usurped and corrupted leading to the creation of 'BARF', which subsequently mutated to become 'prey model' and why neither ideology serves the interests of pets, pet owners or the wider community.

Best wishes,
Tom Lonsdale

Raw Meaty Bones Diet and Campaign

Three principles built on firm foundations
In the 1860s when Jack Spratt and his sidekick Charles Cruft hit on their scheme to turn wheat and beef blood into dog biscuits, they set in train a disgraceful and escalating chain of events.

Nowadays we have a junk-pet-food-controlled culture where pet dogs (modified wolves), cats (modified desert predators) and ferrets (modified polecats) are deemed a necessary adornment of every modern household. 'Never mind the biology, never mind the science', the ads seem to say. 'Get a pet carnivore and your life will be enhanced. Naturally you will want to feed it the convenient, complete and balanced ration we've provided in the brightly coloured packet.'

As a young person exposed to the junk pet food culture I didn't think much about it; nor at the vet school; nor during the first 15 years of veterinary practice. As far as I was aware, junk pet food was the norm and the litany of diseases—whether minor, major, acute or chronic—affecting my patients were an inevitable fact of life.

Insulated and unaware of alternative views, I had never heard of Sir Frank Colyer, the president of the British Dental Association who, in 1947, described the dental diseases affecting carnivores fed a processed diet. Neither was I aware of Juliette de Bairacli Levy who recommended more natural feeding in her 1950 book *The Complete Herbal Handbook for the Dog and Cat.*

Gradually in the late 1980s things began to change. The epidemic of periodontal disease was at full tilt. Dogs, cats and ferrets fed junk food were almost certain to be suffering from the disease. Gradually the Raw Meaty Bones Lobby of concerned veterinarians—Breck Muir, Alan Bennet and me—woke up to the problems. In 1991 we commenced our campaign for better pet health and an end to the veterinary and junk petfood scam whereby our pets were condemned to lifelong diet-induced ill health.[3]

The RMB Lobby was founded on the need to:

A. Actively 'unlearn' the pet food industry/veterinary dogma and indoctrination.
B. Actively stop doing harm—stop feeding junk food.

Upon these firm foundations we erected the three principles of our campaign.

1. The chemical ingredients of a diet, the nutrients, should be as close to a diet of wild animals as is reasonable in a modern world.
2. The physical form of the food should be as close as possible to the tough chewy diet of wild animals and thus ensure optimum dental health. Dental examination and treatment should be initiated at the outset and not left to chance.
3. Every effort should be expended to combat the junk pet food

industry/veterinary/faux animal welfare alliance and thus bring about the necessary change in the junk pet food dominated culture.

Billinghurst's BARF (vomit) influence

Dr Ian Billinghurst, who had previously been promoting the de Bair-acli Levy and Pitcairn recipes, saw the importance of the RMB diet and campaign, and applied to join the RMB Lobby Group. Ever keen to spread the word we welcomed Billinghurst and shared our findings with him. For a time, he was a signatory to our campaigning efforts. But we were in for the first of a series of shocks.

In 1993 Billinghurst published a book, *Give Your Dog a Bone*, in which he advised against feeding junk cooked food and made much use of RMB Lobby information—a good thing. Otherwise, the book was founded on fallacies, for instance:

- Because dogs are omnivores, vegetables, particularly green leafy vegetables should form a substantial part of the diet.
- Cereals are useful to feed in winter.

Billinghurst told pet owners that, over a two-to-three-week period, dogs should be fed:

10 bone meals combined with 4 green leafy vegetable meals, 1 starchy meal, 1 grain and legume meal, 1 purely meat meal, 2 milk meals and 1 or 2 offal meals.

Ironically, at the front of his book, Billinghurst wrote thanking:

Dr Tom Lonsdale for sharing your vision and having the courage to continue pushing for honesty, integrity and truth in our profession, in the face of strong opposition.

Although nominally a member of the RMB Lobby Group, Dr Billinghurst was more a passenger than a driver. In 1997, at the height of the RMB Lobby battle with veterinary and pet food industry forces, he resigned abruptly giving the following reasons.

Worldwide my credibility is rising ... I am here to educate whoever will listen. Pet owners, vets and even pet food companies—if they are interested. It is not necessary; in fact, it is counterproductive for me to participate in the politics of this debate.

If I am to be of use, I need to be seen as outside the political arena. Someone who has the respect of the profession, whilst retaining strong views and unequivocal beliefs—supported of course by good evidence. My aim is to make a positive difference in this debate and continue to make a living.

In the same year, 1997, pet owners who had swallowed the Billinghurst misinformation began to refer to themselves as Born Again Raw Feeders, hence the acronym BARF, 'vomit' in American slang. BARF/vomit/puke was to become a widespread and malignant influence, helped along by a series of websites and discussion lists established by Jane Anderson (formerly Jane Johnson) and others. Here Jane Anderson explains her purpose for the websites:

Welcome to the BARF (Bones and Raw Food) Web Ring. This ring was put together on 15 February 1999, specifically to link BARF sites together, and to allow BARF surfers a good link path to similar sites. If you would like to join the ring, please fill in the table below.

The criteria for joining the webring is that you feed your dog or cat a diet of bones and raw food, and that you talk about it on your page. This sort of diet is explained in books written by Billinghurst, de Levy, Pitcairn, and the like. You must not feed your dog or cat any commercial dog foods.

If you do feed your dog/cat a BARF diet mixed with commercial foods, please feel free to join the ring, once you have switched completed over to a BARF diet.

As of November 2001, this is what Jane Anderson had to say about her main BARF discussion list:

> This is a list for dog and cat lovers who either already feed BARF or want to learn more about the BARF diet. BARF—Bones and Raw Food. The BARF list is a community, and we treasure the non-flaming approach on the list. We have lots of great discussions, share our stories, and develop great relationships between ourselves. Topics for discussion include (but not limited to) diet, breeding, whelping, puppies, aged dogs, your stories, etc. This will be appropriate for those who have read Billinghurst, Pitcairn, Levy, Shulze, or those who just want to know the facts.
>
> We also aim to find and discuss reports that have been done giving empirical evidence on the goodness of BARF particularly when compared with commercial animal foods. The list archives are well worth looking at to learn more. You'll find the discussion informative, and we pride ourselves on our learning environment and friendliness.

With amazing religiosity, the BARFers proclaimed the superiority of their 'omnivore' diet for dogs, which by this time often meant a ground concoction of minced meat, vegetables and bottled supplements. Dogs denied proper teeth cleaning were supposed to gain benefit from the occasional inclusion of 'recreational bones', meaning large beef leg bones devoid of meat and tendon.

Erasing the BARF stains

However, in December 2001 or thereabouts, Billinghurst pulled a swift one on the BARFers that soon had them in a state of open warfare. Apparently without notification he registered the trademark 'BARF' and used it to promote his newly established 'BARF in a bag' line of processed products. The BARF banner, cherished by Jane Anderson and fellow BARFers, was no longer theirs to wave.

Five months earlier, in August 2001, *Raw Meaty Bones: Promote Health* first appeared. In 389 pages the essential foundations, history and three defining principles of the Raw Meaty Bones Diet and Campaign were clearly articulated—and as a by-product the book exploded the absurd 'omnivore' BARF/vomit fiction.

As a new author I was invited onto the BARF list as a guest speaker. Jane Anderson advised members on 1 December 2001:

> I can't stress enough how important it is that you educate your-self further by ensuring you have read [Dr Lonsdale's] book. I finished reading it on Friday, and will start reading it again later today.

Four days later on 5 December 2001, and newly attuned to the RMB Diet and Campaign information, Jane Anderson registered the name 'RMB Lobby' on Yahoo Groups.

> Let's feed raw now!
> The RMB Lobby Group is for people who want to work together to help our vets, vet schools, and general public be better educated about the most appropriate diet for our domestic animals.

Previously and for ten years 'RMB Lobby' had been the distinguish-ing name of a dedicated band of veterinarians, but now at a stroke belonged to Jane Anderson. Theoretically, at least, Anderson could have used her influence to galvanise fellow BARFers into action. That, unfortunately, remains a forlorn hope. The Yahoo RMB Lobby Group is an empty shell.

Dietary advice dispensed on the various Anderson-owned BARF lists also underwent change—to reflect the carnivore diet advice con-tained in *Raw Meaty Bones*.

The following month, January 2002, Anderson launched her CARD list.

> CARD is a new acronym meaning Canine/Cat Appropriate Raw Diet. This has been formerly known as BARF—Bones and

Raw Food. The new acronym removes the displeasure that some felt in the alternative meaning of the term. Interestingly, for some people even the thought of having to refer to it as the 'BARF' diet, put them off trying it.

Initially Jane Anderson operated her BARF and CARD lists in parallel. However, six months later in July 2002 she closed her main BARF list and moved discussions to her new list under the name 'rawfeeding'.

> Feeding a dog or cat an appropriate natural diet is now known as 'raw feeding'.
>
> Some people used to call it 'BARF' and a small number of people still do. Now that's a term that really is 'so last century' now.
>
> On this list, we only use the term 'raw feeding'. It's a simple generic term, and we don't have to then spend a lot of time explaining an acronym that most people find distasteful and some even associate with vomit.

Stains of a BARF past were being erased.

Nowadays the 'rawfeeding' entry page carries the following information:

> **Let's feed raw now!**
> There's an awesome amount of knowledge out there about how to successfully feed a raw diet. There are also some wonderful people who give up hour after hour of their time for free to assist people.
>
> This list will give you access to an amazing amount of knowledge from people who own just one dog, to those who feed a raw diet to in excess of 30 dogs. There are people on this list with pet dogs (of all breeds), the tiniest dogs, to the largest! We also have a huge number of people with top show

dogs, through to racing dogs (professional greyhounds), lure coursing dogs, working dogs, and dogs who provide special assistance to people. Whatever your type of dog, there is sure to be someone here just like yourself.

The good news is you don't have to be a genius to work out how to feed a raw diet. You will need to do a bit of reading, and learn new ways of doing things, but in the general health of your dog or cat, it should well be worth it. I hope you get as much fun out of being on the list as is possible. We will try to keep on topic though!

This list has been established for the discussion of raw feeding, not the politics of raw feeding. If you would like to discuss that the RMB Lobby group has been established for such discussion.

Please help us to maintain a friendly list environment, creating a free learning community of likeminded people.

Did you notice that, unlike the 2001 BARF list introduction, there are no recommended books or sources of information? On the outside there's no mention of 'prey model' jargon either. That surprise awaits those who venture inside.

Prey model jargon

In 1925 scientists introduced the term 'carnivore prey model' as technical jargon to describe predator–prey population dynamics.[4]

BARFers, I suspect unwittingly, misappropriated and misused the term 'prey model' for some (but not all) body parts in the carcass of a dead animal. And then in a further twist they used the misappropriated jargon as their name for the Raw Meaty Bones Diet.[5]

With the passage of time prey modellers began to differentiate 'their' diet from the Raw Meaty Bones original. They don't mention table scraps; neither do they include the head, guts, gut contents nor hide of a prey animal. In their arbitrary scheme they set great store by selected menu ingredients. Their mantra became:

80% meat, 10% edible bone, 10% offal.

Of course, there's not an animal on the planet that returns those sorts of figures.

However, armed with their magic formula the former BARFers turned prey modellers tell folks with unshakable certainty that theirs is the only way to feed carnivorous pets. Rawfeeding (prey model) group moderators declare that there are no suitable raw diet books and instead pet owners should comb the list archives for the moderators' own (mis)pronouncements concerning details of the pet's bowl. Discussion aimed at combating the pet food industry exploitation of the majority of pet owners is prohibited.

In March 2006, I attempted to draw attention to the contradictions and inadequacies of the misappropriated prey model jargon in discussions on the RawVet List. An outraged prey modeller took serious offence. Jane Anderson, the list owner, intervened and banned discussion.[6]

October 2007: *Nexus* magazine

Dear Reader,

Welcome to the 29th edition of the *RMB Newsletter*. It's always a pleasure to write to you. It's finding the time that's difficult. Do you need more time in your day too?

Three guiding principles underpin the RMB approach. Carnivores, be they pets or wild predators:

- need a diet that provides the correct balance of nutrients
- need food in large, tough, chewy lumps that scrape, scrub and squeegee the teeth and gums clean at every meal
- need an end to the corrupt system dominated by junk pet food companies in alliance with the veterinary profession and fake animal welfare groups.

Progress is slow. But I do believe that progress is being made in small and unexpected ways that often depend on the media. That's somewhat paradoxical, given that it's the media that shares responsibility for the current mess. Modern newspapers, radio, TV and the internet grew up supporting the junk pet food industry, vets and fake animal welfare groups. The media gains its income servicing the *status quo* with ads, advertorials and uncritical articles extolling the alleged benefits of pet ownership for the masses, junk food, vet services and the fiction that animal welfare groups put animal health and wellbeing first.

Nevertheless, here and there, the media airs information contrary to the interests of the pet food industry alliance. *Nexus* magazine in particular concentrates on 'suppressed information'. When in August 2006 *Nexus* editor Duncan Roads asked for '5,000 words, with footnotes and references' I was delighted to accept but slow to act. Finally, in August this year I submitted a draft article and the published version appears in the October–November 2007 edition. On the cover in bold type *Nexus* says: 'Junk pet food: recipe for cruelty and disease'.

I would like to take this opportunity to thank Duncan Roads and his team for their courage and leadership. I also take this opportunity to thank a number of *Nexus* readers who have now subscribed to the *RMB Newsletter*. Together we become a stronger force.

Wishing you good reading and good health,

Tom Lonsdale

Nexus, vol. 14, no. 6, 'Junk pet food and the damage done'

See endnotes for the unabridged and published versions of the *Nexus* article.[7]

Prominent on the *Nexus* homepage is the famous quote:

> One night, probably in 1880, John Swinton, then the pre-eminent New York journalist, was the guest of honour at a banquet given him by the leaders of his craft. Someone who knew neither the press nor Swinton offered a toast to the independent press. Swinton outraged his colleagues by replying:
>
> > There is no such thing, at this date of the world's history, in America, as an independent press. You know it and I know it. There is not one of you who dares to write your honest opinions, and if you did, you know beforehand that it would never appear in print. I am paid weekly for keeping my honest opinion out of the paper I am connected with. Others of you are paid similar salaries for similar things, and any of you who would be so foolish as to write honest opinions would be out on the streets looking for another job. If I allowed my honest opinions to appear in one issue of my paper, before twenty-four hours my occupation would be gone.
> >
> > The business of the journalists is to destroy the truth, to lie outright, to pervert, to vilify, to fawn at the feet of mammon, and to sell his country and his race for his daily bread.
> >
> > You know it and I know it, and what folly is this

toasting an independent press?

We are the tools and vassals of rich men behind the scenes. We are the jumping jacks; they pull the strings and we dance. Our talents, our possibilities and our lives are all the property of other men. We are intellectual prostitutes.

(Source: *Labor's Untold Story*, by Richard O. Boyer and Herbert M. Morais, published by United Electrical, Radio & Machine Workers of America, NY, 1955/1979.)

Too often the quote is true and hence the domination of the mass media by the junk pet food industry/vet/fake animal welfare alliance.

There are notable exceptions. One such article appeared in the *Sunday Age* newspaper. http://www.rawmeatybones.com/presscoverings.php. William Birnbauer, the author of the piece, is the first journalist to give credence to the 'cybernetic hypothesis':

He buttresses his views on the beneficial qualities of a bone diet with a Gaia-like theory which takes anyone listening on a journey to the very beginnings of time and the role of anaerobic bacteria in regulating a world dominated by mammals. Carnivores live by the tooth and die by the tooth, he maintains.

For 65 million years during the age of mammals, the dry land on planet Earth has been colonised by mammals. And, until relatively recently, we can assume that mammalian carnivores ruled supreme as regulators of other terrestrial animals. Leastways, that was the case until mankind overran the planet.

Nowadays carnivores are in retreat, the environment is in serious decline and global warming is on the rise. Surely, we ought to give some consideration to how the planet was once regulated by carnivores and, importantly, give some consideration to how the regulators were regulated. This could provide a foundation for our discussions of biological mechanisms, medical issues and climate change.

For more information on these aspects please see 'Cybernetic hypothesis of periodontal disease in mammalian carnivores' at: http://www.rawmeatybones.com/pdf/periodontal-cyber.pdf with expanded information in *Raw Meaty Bones*, Chapter 14.

And now from the sublime to the sinister, we lurch off in another direction.

William Birnbauer's last paragraph in his *Sunday Age* article states:

> Of course, the last word should go to the grand poobah of all things pet, Dr Hugh Wirth. The RSPCA president says the 'compromise attitude' of veterinary associations in Britain and Australia is that raw meaty bones should be fed to pets a minimum of three times a week for dental health.

Not knowing the meaning of 'grand poobah' I looked it up on the net:

> Grand Poobah is a term derived from the name of the haughty character Pooh-Bah in Gilbert and Sullivan's *The Mikado*. In this comic opera, Pooh-Bah holds numerous exalted offices, including Lord Chief Justice, Chancellor of the Exchequer, Master of the Buckhounds, Lord High Auditor, Groom of the Back Stairs, and Lord High Everything Else. The name has come to be used as a mocking title for someone self-important or high-ranking and who exhibits an inflated self-regard.

'Spot-on' I thought. 'That's the Wirth I know.' Hugh Wirth's suggestion that the 'compromise attitude' of veterinary associations in Britain and Australia is that raw meaty bones should be fed to pets a minimum of three times a week for dental health is simply not true. And neither is it true for the RSPCA, who collaborate in a cross-promotional scam with Hill's junk pet food company.

Other publications

Shona Whaite has worked wonders renovating the Raw Meaty Bones website. On a new page we have posted some articles from outside sources.[8]

The wellbeing of Australians—owning a pet
Australian Unity Wellbeing Index
Survey 9 Report 9.0 February 2004
Rigorous article that debunks the pet food industry false claims regarding alleged medical and social benefits of pets.[9]

Overconsumption of pet food in Australia
R. Denniss
Australia Institute, July 2004
Read how pet owners are controlled by the junk pet food industry. See how an affluent society, instead of dealing with fundamental social issues, is 'directed towards solving new "problems" such as the need to clean dogs' teeth'![10]

Feeding cats for health and longevity—an idiosyncratic perspective
R. Malik
Australian College of Veterinary Scientists, 2007 Science Week Proceedings
Highly esteemed veterinarian Dr Richard Malik is arguably the first veterinary academic to publish forthright criticism of the junk pet food industry.[11]

Rats reveal risks of 'junk food' during pregnancy
The Veterinary Record, 18 August 2007
We always knew that veterinary schools are infested with rats working with and for the junk pet food industry. This *Veterinary Record* article shows a group of veterinary school rats not obscuring but revealing the risks of junk food.[12]

It's all the more ironic given that the *Veterinary Record* is published by the British Veterinary Association, collaborator with the junk pet food industry.[13]

Other links

They eat what we are

New York Times, 2 September 2007

Frederick Kaufman

Long article looking behind the scenes of the junk pet food industry and their ghoulish labs. Sanitised and made palatable by typical *New York Times* treatment. Where's the rage? Where's the revulsion?[14]

Brushing your cat's teeth

Cornell University College of Veterinary Medicine

Video evidence of end-stage intellectual prostitution. Guaranteed to enrage.[15]

'Raw feeding'

See the Wikipedia entry that seeks to rewrite history. Or as an article in *Nexus* (vol. 14, no. 6) says: 'Welcome to WikiWorld, a realm where inconvenient truths can easily be removed, while erroneous information—convenient lies and disinformation—can be entered in the encyclopaedia.'[16]

Dog food salmonella outbreak linked to Mars Petcare's Pennsylvania factory

Useful information on the perils of industrial food.[17]

Burns Pet Nutrition fined £13,000

UKPets

Thursday 24 November 2005

Vet John Burns and his junk pet food company Burns Pet Nutrition were prosecuted for making illegal health claims.[18]

December 2007: Veterinary students debate pet diets

Dear Reader,

As I write 2008 is but a few hours away. Where did 2007 go? It's true that time flies when you're having fun. It flies by when you get older too.

In December 2006 the Three-Part Test edition of the *RMB Newsletter* was published. A year on I reckon it's just as relevant. Do take a look if you get chance. (See p. 150.)

Given that junk pet food is the single most important trigger for the epidemics of disease affecting our pet carnivores, a visitor from Mars (the planet) might reasonably expect that pet health and welfare professionals would give the matter top priority. How might we explain to our Martian visitor that the diet scandal is definitely not top priority and seldom on the agenda?

Occasionally, though, the subject of diets for carnivores gets an airing in the veterinary arena. You have to be quick, and you have to be in the right place to hear what's said.

In this edition of the *RMB Newsletter* I mention the recent vet student debate about pet diets and the subsequent *Veterinary Record* coverage and non-coverage. This way, at least we have a benchmark against which we can judge future progress.

I also take this opportunity to thank all those who have sent me their observations and kind words throughout this past year. Thank you for your wonderful support.

There's much to be done and it's so good to see so many putting their shoulders to the wheel.

Wishing you and yours a wonderful, healthy,
Happy New Year,
Tom Lonsdale

Veterinary students debate pet diets

Congratulations to UK vets Roger Meacock, Richard Allport and Tom Harcourt-Brown for scoring good points that clearly influenced the vet student audience.

'Know thine enemy.' Accordingly I encourage you to listen to the vet academic, the past president of the British Small Animal Veterinary Association and the animal welfare group vet spinning their disinformation in support of junk pet food.

If we are to counter these people, we need to hear and understand how they misuse language, distort information and abuse their positions of power and trust.

Veterinary Record report

The Veterinary Record, journal of the British Veterinary Association, reported on the debate in the 3 November 2007 edition.

Diets on the menu for AVS debate

'This house believes vets should advocate feeding manufactured pet foods.'

This was the motion debated at a meeting organised by the Association of Veterinary Students (AVS) at Cambridge University on 24 October. Explaining what had prompted the debate, the AVS's Cambridge representative, Mr Alex Corbishley, said that the relationship between veterinary surgeons and pet food manufacturers was receiving increasing public attention. He said that although it was the opinion of the AVS that pet food nutrition teaching in the veterinary schools was excellent and unbiased, sponsorship in this area by pet food manufacturers had left nutritional teaching open to accusations of bias.

Three speakers were scheduled to speak in support of the motion and three against. Those opposing the motion argued that a nutritionally sound alternative to commercial pet food was provided by raw meaty bones, home-prepared meals or plant material.

Arguments for

Giving a presentation in support of the motion on behalf of Dr Marge Chandler, who was unable to attend, Mr Chris Laurence, veterinary director of the Dogs Trust, said that, unlike the situation with commercial pet food, there had been no controlled feeding research trials performed for home-made diets. While it was possible to make a home-made diet that was complete and balanced, many did not meet the published nutritional requirements that had been formulated through decades of research. In two published studies by independent researchers, who were unconnected to the pet food industry, home-made diets did not meet official requirements for, among others, calcium and phosphorus, and had low levels of nutrients such as zinc, iron and manganese; other diets had excessive levels of vitamin D, manganese and zinc.

Commercial food helped to reduce the incidence of food poisoning; raw food had a higher risk of containing bacterial toxins and pathogenic protozoa. Studies had shown that 69% of cats fed a raw meat diet were seropositive for Toxoplasma species, compared with just over 19% of those fed commercial or cooked food. Pets shedding these organisms could provide a health risk to humans. With a raw meaty bones diet there was also the risk of bones obstructing and perforating the intestinal tract.

Also arguing in support of the motion, Mr Mike Jessop, a practitioner from Merthyr Tydfil, said that the increasing use of commercial diets had been a major advance in improving general animal health. He strongly believed that abandoning commercial foods would significantly increase the incidence of gastrointestinal disease, salmonella and broken teeth. 'From a veterinary business aspect that has some plus points, but from a welfare aspect it's appalling.'

He argued that even if there were ready supplies of food to feed the nation's pets, modern society did not have the time to spend preparing nutritionally balanced meals for its pets. He also argued that the high quality of modern pet food was extending the lifespan of pets. 'We see longer-living healthy pets', he said. One could regulate food intake much more easily with a commercial diet, which helped to control obesity. He added that there was a spectrum of quality in the commercial diet range and this was reflected in the price banding. He said that the veterinary profession should be behind the super-premium end of the market as this would encourage science and evolution and raise the standards of all commercial pet food.

Giving his own views in support of the motion, Mr

Laurence looked at how the argument was influenced by the provisions of the new Animal Welfare Act 2006, which imposes a duty of care on all animal owners and the need to provide a 'suitable diet'. It was impractical to expect that the average owner could perform any sort of analysis on unprepared food; for example, how much fat and protein was in a piece of meat. Furthermore, feeding an animal an unbalanced diet that resulted in a nutritional disease might result in an offence of causing 'unnecessary suffering' being committed.

The Dogs Trust used prepared food as it was practical, consistent and reduced the incidence of nutritionally induced diarrhoea. Logistically, he said, the trust could not feed raw meat to dogs, as it would be unable to guarantee to trustees that the dogs were being fed a nutritionally balanced diet.

Arguments against

Arguing against the motion, Mr Roger Meacock, a referral veterinary surgeon based in Swindon, said that cats and dogs should be fed raw meaty bones as they were carnivores and not, as generally thought, omnivores. He pointed to the dogs' dentition, mastication action and lack of a fermentation area for plant material as evidence of its carnivore status.

He was not advocating a 'willy-nilly' diet—it should be appropriate to the species and comparable to what the animal would have in the wild. What dogs and cats needed was a wide variety of foods, for example, chicken one week and rabbit the next. Dogs were also able to dissolve bones in their stomachs.

What did a raw meaty bone diet offer a cat or dog that a commercial diet did not? He said that it helped clean their teeth much more effectively than kibble, chews or any toothbrush. Animals also gained satisfaction from chewing and crunching their food, which led to better behaviour. It also resulted in defecation being slightly more difficult, which helped to squeeze the anal glands and thus reduced anal gland problems.

Mr Richard Allport, from a referral practice based in Potter's Bar, argued that the pet food industry was motivated largely by money. He also argued that commercial cat and dog pet foods contained too much carbohydrate because this tended to be cheaper. Why did manufacturers not produce more high-protein diets? A study had shown that diabetic cats were significantly more likely to revert to a non-insulin-dependent state when given low-carbohydrate, low-fibre foods.

Also speaking against the motion, Mr Tom Harcourt-Brown, a resident at Cambridge veterinary school, focused on rabbits where, he said, the arguments 'are pretty clear cut'. He said that most rabbit problems seen in practice were dental related. Research dating from the mid-1990s had shown that dental problems were largely caused by an inappropriate diet, and that low calcium and vitamin D levels led to dental disease. Rabbits were adapted to eat high volumes of low-quality food and, in the past, low volumes of high-quality food provided by pet food manufacturers had led to behavioural and dental problems.

Grass and other vegetation growing at the side of the road provided rabbits with all their nutritional needs. There were arguments not to feed grass, mainly convenience: people did not want to pick their rabbits' food. Another argument was that there was no money to be made from grass. However, he said: 'There is only evidence to say that we shouldn't be feeding them manufactured food.'

After the debate, a vote was taken by a show of hands among those present; the motion was carried by a small majority.

Letter for publication

Seeing the apparent willingness of the *Veterinary Record* and *Veterinary Times* to send reporters to cover the Cambridge University debate and given that past president of the Royal College of Veterinary Surgeons, Professor Sheila Crispin, had attended the debate, I thought it worth attempting to widen discussion.

On 5 November 2007 I submitted a letter for publication in the *Veterinary Record* and *Veterinary Times*. Full credit to the *Veterinary Times*, the commercial, independent publication; they published the letter in the 3 December 2007 edition.

As is their custom, the *Veterinary Record* did not publish the letter. Mr Martin Alder, the editor, was on holiday when I rang to ask why yet again the journal of the British Veterinary Association had suppressed information.

Dear Editor,

Open letter to presidents of RCVS and BVA

In 1991 the Raw Meaty Bones Lobby of concerned veterinarians blew the whistle on the gathering pet food crisis.[1] The global veterinary authorities refused to hear the allegations. Ten years later in 2001 *Raw Meaty Bones: Promote Health*, the fully referenced, evidence-based exposition was published but widely suppressed.[2] In 2004 the House of Commons early day motion, 'Processed pet foods and vets', gained 55 signatures.[3] In October 2007, in the absence of leadership from the veterinary authorities, the Association of Veterinary Students of Great Britain and Ireland took the initiative and debated the motion that: 'This House believes vets should advocate feeding manufactured pet food.'[4] (Perhaps young doctors will advocate the feeding of manufactured diets too!)

Incongruous as it may be, after 65 million years' evolution during the Age of Mammals, some vets were prepared to stand up and argue for the motion. Without offering a shred of evidence Mr Mike Jessop suggested that 'the high quality of modern pet food was extending the lifespan of pets'. Mr Chris Laurence sought to rattle his complete and balanced manufactured sabre by invoking the Animal Welfare Act in support of manufactured diets. He emphasised that under the Act dogs, cats and rabbits have three essential needs:

1. To be provided with a suitable diet.
2. To be protected from pain, injury, suffering and disease.
3. To express normal behaviour patterns.

Of course, the Raw Meaty Bones Lobby provides extensive evidence to demonstrate those needs can only be satisfactorily met by feeding a natural diet.[2] Mr Laurence rather helpfully suggested in respect to the need to express normal behaviour:

> Now normal behaviour patterns for dogs and cats includes chewing. And I don't think any commercial manufacturer would suggest that all you should ever feed is their commercial food—that you shouldn't give them something to chew and to exercise their gums and teeth on because that's the need to express natural behaviour.

Are we about to see Mr Laurence fall on his sabre? Perhaps he will be an early casualty when the prosecutions begin against those who disregard the Animal Welfare Act and force defenceless pets to consume junk food and force defenceless veterinary students to swallow hogwash.

Professor Sheila Crispin, an invited guest, abstained during voting. She stressed that she was speaking in a private capacity on behalf of her dogs and 'that her dogs are fed a mixture of commercial and home prepared food and that she would like to see more research that compared both commercially prepared and natural diets.'

Manufactured pet food has not been trialled for suitability and safety (unless covertly in pet food company marketing and research establishments) by comparison with the 65 million year established natural standard. Until advocates of manufactured pet food can present independent data confirming suitability and safety then all those engaged in the promotion and sale of artificial products do so without a shred of evidence.

Unfortunately, as Mr Roger Meacock pointed out during the Cambridge debate, when the truth about manufactured pet foods is finally known it will be the veterinary profession, not the manufacturers, who become the 'fall guys'.

But is it fair that the sons should pay for the sins of the fathers? In the veterinary context I think not and accordingly ask the president of the Royal College of Veterinary Surgeons and president of the British Veterinary Association to open up debate and hasten a solution to the pet food crisis.

Notes
1. T. Lonsdale, 'Junk pet food and the damage done', *Nexus*, vol. 14, no. 6, pp. 31–5, October–November 2007.[19]
2. T. Lonsdale, *Raw meaty bones: promote health*, Rivetco, 2001.
3. D. Taylor, House of Commons early day motion 335.[20]
4. Association of Veterinary Students of Great Britain and Ireland. 'Should vets advocate feeding manufactured pet food?' Report of debate held at Robinson College, University of Cambridge, 24 October 2007.

Researchers grind whole rabbits with disastrous consequences

A group of University of California researchers published a paper entitled 'Role of diet in the health of the feline intestinal tract and in inflammatory bowel disease'. Although influenced by the BARF/

vomit madness, in some ways they represent a welcome change from the typical hidebound researchers. They say:

> It is reasonable to speculate that cats fed a 'natural diet' are less likely to develop IBD than cats fed 'unnatural diets'. The natural diet of cats does not contain wheat, milk, soybean, egg or many other ingredients commonly used. Nor does the natural diet of cats contain additives and preservatives such as guar and xanthan gums as food stabilisers, propionic acid and sorbic acids as preservatives, or carrageenan (made from seaweed and shown to cause intestinal inflammation in certain circumstances) (Strombeck, 1999). These ingredients, and many others, are added to commercial diets to improve their appearance to the pet owners and palatability to pets, but may result in an adverse reaction. The natural diet of cats is primarily small mammals, with a lesser proportion of insects, reptiles and birds. There is an obvious need for a 'gold standard diet' against which to compare and study all 'unnatural diets'. Such a diet should be complete and balanced, relatively cheap, easily obtained and may need to mimic the diet consumed by cats during their evolution. The task to develop and validate such a diet was given to Dr Angie Glasgow.

Despite apparent good intentions, Dr Glasgow failed in her task—even though she fed her research cats on whole rabbit.

> Since cats eat most parts of their prey and essential nutrients are concentrated in different organs, the rabbits were not skinned, dressed or cleaned, but rather ground in their entirety. The ground whole rabbit diet was frozen in smaller batches and thawed prior to feeding.

Note the misplaced emphasis on so-called 'essential nutrients' without any concern for the equally 'essential' physical form of natural food.

Chewing on raw whole carcasses provides fundamental psychological benefits and 'essential' physical cleaning of teeth and gums. Besides predisposing her cats to periodontal and a host of other chronic diseases, it seems that somehow by grinding and freezing the rabbits the taurine was destroyed too. (There may be other explanations for the reported outcomes but for now we have Dr Glasgow's report only.)

Avoiding disastrous consequences should not be difficult providing researchers pay attention to basic biological principles and the requirements of the Animal Welfare Act. Perhaps Dr Glasgow and her colleagues might like to check out the Three-Part Test. (Please see p. 150.)

8

2008: SMOKESCREENS AND RED HERRINGS

The veterinary profession remains wilfully blind to widespread diet-related disease in pets. The profession's deep ties to the pet food industry continue to drive misinformation and neglect.

February 2008: WSAVA

Dear Reader,

As a *RMB Newsletter* subscriber you know that junk pet food is the single biggest threat to the health and welfare of pets.

Front, centre and conspiring in the back rooms, large segments of the veterinary profession feed off the junk pet food fraud. So much so that we can say that the veterinary profession is the single biggest obstacle to resolution of the problem.

Unfortunately, rank and file vets frequently have no idea of the nature and scale of their involvement. The junk pet food manufacturers and veterinary authorities ensure that the majority of vets stay ignorant and in the dark.

In an attempt to shed light and help resolve the immense and growing crisis, I submitted three papers for inclusion in the 2007 World Small Animal Veterinary Association (WSAVA) Congress. Alas, as is usually the case, light was not permitted, darkness prevailed.

Thanks to the internet we can at least place information on the record. Perhaps one day we may obtain resolution of the mighty fraud.

Abstracts of the rejected papers are listed below.

Here's hoping that this finds you and your pets in top condition.

Best wishes,
Tom Lonsdale

WSAVA

RIDGEON. We're not a profession: we're a conspiracy.
SIR PATRICK. All professions are conspiracies against the laity.

The Doctor's Dilemma
George Bernard Shaw, 1906

One hundred years on, and judging by the articles in the *International Journal of Epidemiology*[1] and the *Medical Journal of Australia*,[2] there are medical doctors who are prepared to give some credence to George Bernard Shaw's contention that the medical profession is a 'conspiracy' and that 'the medical service of the community, as at present provided for, is a murderous absurdity'.

Had Shaw lived to see the current state of the global veterinary profession, what would he say? Had he attended the WSAVA Congress in Sydney in August 2007 he would have seen 'conspiracy' and 'murderous absurdity' writ large.

Even the bunting on the lampposts approaching the conference hall proclaimed the link between vets and Hill's, the Colgate-Palmolive junk pet food makers. As main 'sponsor', the Hill's stand dominated the entrance to the event. When Royal Canin, a division of the Mars Corporation, had the temerity to raise its banner higher than Hill's they were told to lower it forthwith.

It gives you an idea of the pet food titans jousting to capture the hearts and minds of impressionable vets lured by the 'free' coffee and the goody bags emblazoned with junk pet food slogans. Gathering in groups or strolling jauntily to their next lecture, the vets had not the faintest idea that they were pawns in a massive fraud. Little did they realise that the junk pet food goody bags marked them as walking adverts for the abandonment of thought and the mass poisoning of pets. According to their website:

The World Small Animal Veterinary Association (WSAVA) is an 'association of associations'. Its membership is made up of veterinary organisations from all over the world, which are concerned with small companion animals such as cats, dogs, rabbits, guinea pigs etc. Currently there are 76 member and affiliate associations, representing over 70,000 individual veterinarians from around the globe.[3]

Many of the vets at the congress were flown in by the junk pet food companies. The man on the Royal Canin stand told me that the company sponsored several vets from South Korea, all tickets and accommodation paid for. Others were flown in from India and China, the burgeoning new markets targeted by the pet food titans. For the companies it's money well spent. The hapless, helpless vets become junk pet food salesmen and women for life.

The WSAVA boasts that:

... 2,048 delegates representing 67 countries [attended] ... the 32nd WSAVA Congress held from 19 to 23 August 2007. The top five countries of attendee origin were Australia, South Korea, New Zealand, the United Kingdom and the USA. The continuing education (CE) program was comprised of over 240 lectures (including four state-of-the-art lectures or SOTALs) accommodated into eight streams with over 23 disciplines presented by 70 speakers from 10 different countries. This was complemented by 95 oral or poster abstract presentations.

Be amazed at the nonsense and impenetrable jargon dished up as 'continuing education'.[4]

The September 2007 edition of *The Veterinarian* tells us that:

The scientific program was put together by former Sydney University faculty Jill Madison, now Director of Professional Development at the Royal Veterinary College (RVC), [London

University] and David Church, Professor of Small Animal Medicine and Head of the RVC's Department of Veterinary Clinical Sciences.

What else do we know about these two Australian vet academics besides that they are a married couple who now live and work in the UK?

See Jill Madison, in 1997, proclaiming on TV how she's a pet food company 'consultant'.[5]

In April 2005 the RVC were 'able to supply only limited details of current grants, for reasons of commercial sensitivity'. However, they did disclose that Professor David Church received a grant of £132,000 (US$260,000) from Hill's Pet Nutrition.

You might be tempted to think that the Dr Madison and Professor Church may be unaware of the junk pet food issues—except that they were both in attendance at the 1992 presentation of 'Pandemic of periodontal disease: a malodorous condition'[6]—and were both perched at the back of the lecture theatre during the 1993 Veterinary Dental Conference presentation.[7]

On another occasion the director of the Sydney University Post Graduate Foundation in Veterinary Science, Dr Douglas Bryden, handed Dr Church (in the days before he became a professor) a copy of the Dental Conference proceedings and suggested that he make a point of reading the chapter on preventative dentistry.[8]

About the same time, in a crowded Sydney University lecture theatre, I asked David Church to comment on the Mars corporation junk diets labelled as 'Professional Formula'. Dr Church admitted that it was 'incongruous' that dogs should be fed rice-based food and cats be fed corn-based food. A hardnosed Jill Madison simply refused to answer my questions—at which her sycophantic audience erupted in spontaneous applause.

Against this admittedly dismal backdrop, I thought it nonetheless worth submitting three abstracts for consideration by Dr Madison and Professor Church for inclusion in the oral presentation sessions of the WSAVA Congress.

Permitting myself a ray of optimism, I hoped that they might take the opportunity to add an element of 'balance' to their lopsided and largely irrelevant program. But after 17 years spent grappling with a deaf, dumb and blind veterinary establishment, I should know better. Three rejection notices arrived by email.

Please see the abstracts reproduced below that were not 'selected for presentation in the Congress Program'. For fuller information on each of the topics please see *Raw Meaty Bones: Promote Health*.

Raw Meaty Bones: past, present, future

Context

In London in the 1860s Jack Spratt established the world's first processed pet food company. Charles Cruft joined Spratt and started pedigree dog shows as a pet food marketing scheme. Now in 2007 pets everywhere, pedigree or cross-bred, are fed from the manufacturers' can or packet.

In the 1980s a group of Sydney veterinarians, Raw Meaty Bones Lobby (RMB Lobby), noted the correlation between diet and ill-health, in particular dental disease, affecting their patients. A diet of raw meaty bones and a few table scraps acted as both cure and prevention.

Objectives

To show:

- how the early RMB lobbyists gained awareness of the diet and disease connection
- history of the debate within the Australian veterinary community
- the current levels of diet and disease awareness
- future plans and prospects.

Key messages

1. Processed pet foods injure the health of pet carnivores.
2. A more natural diet acts as both treatment and preventative.

3. Processed pet foods are associated with ill-health, economic loss and environmental damage.

Conclusion

Veterinarians can readily obtain a historical perspective and scientific understanding leading to changes in clinical practice. Administrative and political changes at the professional level will take a considerable act of will. Better that a start is soon made.

References

1. T. Lonsdale, 'Preventative dentistry in veterinary dentistry', University of Sydney, PGFVS, Proceedings 212, 1993, pp. 235–44.
2. T. Lonsdale, *Raw Meaty Bones: Promote Health*, Rivetco (www.rawmeaty bones.com).
3. R. Malik and D.I. Bryden, ACVS Nomination Statements, 2004.[9]

Haematological assessment of dogs and cats undergoing dental treatment

Background

Early reports suggested a link between periodontal disease and systemic disease in elderly animals. In human medicine considerable research efforts focus on the connections between periodontal inflammatory disease and systemic diseases affecting the heart, kidneys, liver and including cancer, Alzheimer's disease and premature births.

In our small animal practice we were familiar with the clinical improvement in patients undergoing dental treatment. We were also aware that a more natural diet served as an ideal preventative of periodontal disease.

Aims

In an area of conflicting opinions but absence of hard data, it was decided to obtain some haematological data pre and post dental treatment.

Methods

Six dogs and two cats undergoing dental treatment for advanced periodontal disease and showing low or very low white cell counts were selected for follow-up testing after dental treatment.

Results

White blood cell counts increased between 37% and 150% with an average of 78%. Six animals had red blood cell changes which averaged 23% increase. All animals showed marked clinical improvement in condition with owners reporting marked increase in vitality.

Prior to dental treatment several of the animals had blood values within reference ranges.

Conclusion

Common reference haematological reference values may be too wide allowing patients with severe disease to go undetected.

Lowered white cell counts and anaemia are associated with periodontal disease.

More work is necessary to further quantify and qualify these findings for the benefit of animal and human patients.

References

T. Lonsdale, 'Periodontal disease and leucopenia', *Journal of Small Animal Practice*, vol. 36, 1993, pp. 543–6.[10]

Cybernetic hypothesis of periodontal disease in mammalian carnivores

Context

Throughout 65 million years of the Cenozoic Era, mammals have played an intrinsic part in the ecology of the Earth. All life forms are coevolved and carnivores at the top of the food chain have an important regulatory role. In contrast to their importance, it seemed odd that carnivores, both wild and domestic, should suffer 'weakness' and be susceptible to periodontal disease.

Objective
In the early 1990s periodontal disease was a subject of hot debate in the Australian veterinary profession. In an attempt to better understand the anomalies, the pathogenesis and natural ecology of the condition research got underway.

Key messages
Mistakes frequently lead to re-evaluation of our circumstances and, if we're lucky, provide us with new insights. So it was with the pandemic of periodontal disease affecting domestic carnivores. Instead of blaming bacteria or a failure of the immune system we saw that the relationship between carnivores and their tough 'chewy' diet was the defining characteristic.

A cybernetic system based on the 'benefits' of periodontal disease was conceived with strong explanatory and predictive powers. Germ theory and Darwinian evolutionary concepts, already weakened, are further attenuated and subsumed into the new hypothesis.

Conclusion
In an age of global warming new insights into our planet's regulatory systems are essential—better still if those insights lead to a new theory of health and disease.

Reference
T. Lonsdale, 'Cybernetic hypothesis of periodontal disease in mammalian carnivores', *Journal of Veterinary Dentistry*, vol. 11, issue, pp. 5–8.[11]

Postscript

Of all the links listed above, if there is one that thoroughly deserves your attention, it's George Bernard Shaw's scathing analysis of the medical conspiracy—with the obvious veterinary parallels.[12]

June 2008: Pet food scourge

Dear Reader,

How's your year going? Hope things progress well.

Here in Sydney, Australia, the days are sunny and good for working, with nights that are cold and good for sleeping. Already it's mid-year and time for the second *RMB Newsletter* of 2008.

In this newsletter I'd like to welcome new subscribers and thank subscribers who have provided support since publication of the first *RMB Newsletter* in 2001

Did you check out George Bernard Shaw's 1906 preface to the *Doctor's Dilemma* mentioned in the last newsletter? Please take a look.[12] The old genius was definitely onto something when he said that 'All professions are conspiracies against the laity.'

Loosely speaking, we're all members of professions or clubs of one sort or another. So in reality, Shaw was speaking about the human condition: that when we form into groups we tend to place our perceived group interests above those of the wider community.

Groucho Marx put group behaviour in context when he quipped: 'I refuse to join any club that would have me as a member'.

As both hunters and hunted, cunning and devious, humans have a long history of putting the interests of their group/club/profession ahead of the interests of the wider community. We're genetically programmed to overlook the shortcomings of ourselves and our peers as we push our luck promoting our group interests.

We can generalise that many, perhaps most, vets conspire against their clients and injure the health of their carnivore patients. Figuratively, if not literally, the vet profession gets away with murder. Why is this so and what's to be done about it?

To my way of thinking, it's to do with the honest vets being too timid to speak up and pet owners being too accepting of the mass poisoning of pets. Dogs, cats, ferrets and captive wild carnivores deserve better.

In this newsletter we take another look at the dismal state of things with a view to sparking debate and a resolution of the pet food scourge.

Best wishes,
Tom Lonsdale

2008 Royal College of Veterinary Surgeons elections

Each year since 1997 I've contested elections to the Royal College of Veterinary Surgeons (RCVS) Council.[13] It's been the best, effectively the only way, to communicate with the over 21,000 vets registered to practise in the UK.

The RCVS sends candidates' manifestos out to voters. And with a measly quota of 300 words, only brief information about the benefits of natural food/medicine gets placed before the voters. It's a mere drop in the ocean when you consider the TV ads, magazine ads, vet school propaganda, vet conference humbug and endless 'learned' papers that swamp the global community with disinformation.

As in past years Roger Meacock and longstanding Raw Meaty Bones ally, Alan Bennet, nominated me for the election.

> ### RCVS 2008 manifesto
>
> Another year slips by as the veterinary profession slips deeper into the junk pet food mire. Thousands more pets are forced to consume junk food by a profession that either does know or should know better. Hundreds more school leavers enter veterinary schools to begin their programming in diagnosis and treatment, but not prevention, of the pandemic of junk pet food induced diseases.
>
> In 1995, past president of the RCVS, Henry Carter wrote:
>
> > For 45 years I have observed Pedigree Petfoods (and its predecessor, Chappie Ltd) seeking to influence veterinary students and practitioners.

> For over 25 years I have observed Pedigree Petfoods and other pet food manufacturers exerting what some may consider to be undue influence on the BSAVA. ...
>
> As a former editor of the *Journal of Small Animal Practice*, I believe that your letter 'Revitalising veterinary science'[14] should have been published ... If the board of management had overturned my decision as editor, I would have resigned on the spot. I believe in open government and free debate in the veterinary press.
>
> You may use these comments in any way you choose.

Ignoring professed standards and suppressing core issues seems to be a strategy favoured by the veterinary authorities.

In October 2007, veterinary students, betrayed by their universities and caught in the junk pet food mire, attempted to make sense of their situation by convening a debate. (See page 179.)

If 'self-regulation' holds any meaning then veterinary institutions and those at the helm must be held morally, politically and legally accountable. We need—our clients and their animals need—urgent resolution of the junk pet food debacle, the most important issue facing the veterinary profession in the 21st century. I have the experience, am ready to serve and seek your vote. Thank you.

Now for the good news: 359 vets voted in support of the manifesto. If assembled in one room that would be a sizable crowd of vets who want a better life for pets, pet owners and a more honourable vet profession.

The not such good news is that once again I trailed the poll coming a distant last: 3,378 votes were cast for the other candidates.

Worse news still is that a total of 21,693 UK registered vets could have voted, but only 1.6% chose to support proposals to do something about the junk pet food scourge, 'the most important issue facing the veterinary profession in the 21st century'.

Perverse incentives for vets

'Is it wonder nutrition or a modern scourge?' asks journalist Wendy Knowler in the South African newspaper *The Star*.

Posing the question in such a way provokes interesting answers from the junk food exponents. None of them claim their junk is 'wonder nutrition'. They dissemble, cheat and lie as per usual.

Wendy Knowler tells us about 'perverse incentives', a term that's new to me.

> In South Africa, most vets have packets of pellets piled high in the reception area of the practice.
>
> I'm told that the receptionists are treated to lavish lunches and other 'spoils' by the pet food companies, and vets routinely attend training seminars at luxury locations, also hosted by the industry.
>
> The (human) medical profession has a name for such perks: perverse incentives.
>
> Medical reps used to give doctors expensive gifts; doctors were invited to lavish 'speaker functions' with their spouses, as well as fully paid medical conferences, often overseas.
>
> But thanks to the Perverse Incentives Policy—implemented as part of the Medicines Control Act's Marketing Code in 2004—the drug company freebies are now extremely limited.
>
> Apparently, no such limitations hamper the pet food companies in their quest to sell as much of their product from veterinary practices as possible.

What's your opinion? Might this be a way to get governments and regulators to take a look at the pet food scourge?

First, get some perverse incentives policies operational in respect to the kickbacks and drug company freebies that the vets currently enjoy. Then when the spotlight is on the vets' shonky business practices broaden the focus to take in the main issue—junk pet food poisoning of pets and the inherent vet corruption.

Perverse incentives for retailers

Of course, making the vets accountable for harming their patients will only be a starting point. Supermarkets, pet shops and the monster pet food manufacturers need to be made legally accountable for duping pet owners and poisoning pets.

Unfortunately, whilst they have a clear run, the pet food manufacturers bind their retailers with perverse incentives and thus present a united front.

International Ferret Congress Australia

In early May 2008 the International Ferret Congress Australia was held in Melbourne. I was privileged to present a paper and partake of a delightful weekend in the company of a band of enthusiastic ferret supporters.

My admiration and thanks go to Shirley Hewett, Shona Whaite and their team of helpers for wonderful organisation and fine hospitality. Shirley spoke about diet logistics and her ferret Jaikoy demonstrated diet logistics by devouring whole mice in full view of the audience and flashing cameras.

Whilst the weekend provided an excellent opportunity to deal with the big issues affecting ferret health, in particular disease prevention, the vets who spoke dished up heavy doses of vet diagnostic and treatment protocols—for diseases that mostly afflict ferrets fed a junk food diet. These same vets, when asked what to feed ferrets, recommended junk food. One American vet (or was he a pet food salesman?) pushed the brand names of his preferred junk products!

Zooarchaeologist Bob Church is known for his passion 'not only for ferrets but also for Hawaiian shirts'. Mr Church showed pictures of skulls and teeth of domestic ferrets devastated by junk food—teeth ground to the pulp cavity by abrasive kibble, broken teeth, missing teeth, rampant periodontal disease, osteomyelitis, jaw bone abscesses and infection tracking throughout the skulls. By contrast his examinations of skulls from ferrets that had lived in the wild revealed little or no pathology. Dried, bleached ferret skulls can't tell the whole sorry story—but they add information to that well known from reliable veterinary, medical, dental and nutritional sources.

Unfortunately, Bob Church disregards existing sources of information and jumps to absurd conclusions far removed from his own data—data that, when accurately interpreted, reveals the ravages of junk pet food and the connivance of an incompetent veterinary profession. Here's a summary of his 'Recommendations' from the 2007 edition of *Ferret Husbandry, Medicine and Surgery*:

> Ferrets require regular tooth brushing with a non-fluoridated dentifrice, with periodic inspection with probing, cleaning and polishing by a qualified veterinarian or veterinary technician. Cages should be modified to prevent a ferret from using their teeth [*sic*] in an attempt to escape. If a softer diet cannot be provided, kibble should be softened to minimise its abrasive effect on the teeth. If a ferret consistently desires to chew fabrics, they [*sic*] should be removed (shredded paper is a good substitute for cloth bedding). Ferrets with bad breath, facial swellings, loose teeth and bleeding, red or puffy gums should have dental X-rays made to check for abscesses, bad teeth and bone loss. Veterinarians should start regarding periodontal disease as a serious threat to a ferret's long-term health, rather than assuming it is just a minor problem that does not need to be aggressively addressed. Commercially available chewing treats, such as gelatin chews or edible sticks, should be provided for stimulating the gums and satisfying the urge to chew. Research needs to be done on the impact of periodontal disease on ferret health, including its involvement in other organ diseases.

That Mr Church intersperses elements of truth along with nonsensical 'recommendations' worsens the impact. How can pet owners distinguish truth from falsehood, what to accept and what to reject? That Bob Church's 'recommendations' are now printed and bound in a textbook ensures that they will circulate and do harm for years to come.

The animals have suffered long enough, they deserve better. It's up to us to speak on their behalf—expose and root out the nonsense peddled by pet food companies, vets and assorted self-styled experts.

Wishing you courage and strength in the mighty struggles ahead,

Tom Lonsdale

August 2008: Straight questions: crooked answers

Dear Reader,

How have you been? How's your family?

Norma Hiller in Pennsylvania first wrote to me in 2001 and has been a raw meaty bones enthusiast ever since. Norma recently sent an update on her 'family':

> Hi Tom ... hope this finds you well and enjoying the summer months ... my eight furkids continue to thrive on the raw diet ... I brought all four cats in for the required rabies shots a few months ago and the vet checked them out one by one, ears, teeth, skin, etc., then he looked me straight in the eyes and said 'Norma, you're going to put me out of business—your cats are *too* healthy!' ... I love it! Thanks again for everything!

At least Norma's vet managed to joke about the health benefits of a raw diet. Most pet owners are not so lucky. Their smiling vet's demeanour changes to a hostile grimace the moment a raw diet is mentioned.

No vet relishes the thought of going out of business. But therein lies the vets' difficulty—they are under oath; they have an obligation to place the interests of their patients and their clients before their own. No other participants in the pet food fraud have the same burden of responsibility. As far as truck drivers are concerned, they are merely doing a job delivering goods. The supermarket shelf stacker doesn't consider the fatal consequences of his actions—fatal for the pets that is. The slick advertising executive doesn't care, and there are no sanctions, when he fabricates elaborate lies to be repeated over and over again on prime-time TV.

But all vets face this dilemma. Mostly they dissemble, cheat and ultimately lie—to themselves and their clients. Of course, it's more than their business that the vets are protecting. It's the corrupt nexus of junk pet food companies, veterinary profession and fake animal welfare groups. As the authority figures, the arbiters of good medicine, good nutrition and good animal welfare, the vets' pronouncements provide a protective cordon around a massive scam costing the community billions of dollars.

But as easy as it is to blame the vets, it does not stop there. Whether in a western-style democracy or in communist China, vets are given privileges, rights and responsibilities by politicians who are elected or appointed to serve the community interest. When an industry is corrupt, regulators or politicians are supposed to step in and take control.

Let's take a look at what's happening in the UK.

Best wishes,
Tom Lonsdale

Straight questions, crooked answers at EFRACom hearings

In the UK the Veterinary Surgeons Act 1966 provides the rules by which the veterinary profession is governed. The British government, aware that the Act is out of date, is developing a new one. Earlier this year, as part of that process, members of parliament on the Environment, Food and Rural Affairs Committee (EFRACom) interviewed leaders of the UK veterinary profession and then submitted recommendations to the UK government.[15]

Actually, it's all part of a big charade. The UK government already has plenty of information on the veterinary profession's Faustian pact with junk pet food manufacturers. There's no escaping the fact that a majority of the world's pets will experience sickness due to a diet of junk food, often recommended and sold by vets who take the oath: 'To pursue the work of my profession with uprightness of conduct and that my constant endeavour will be to ensure the welfare of the animals committed to my care.'

Unfortunately, the UK government and most MPs avoid tackling the issues. They don't want a showdown with the vets and their powerful pet food industry backers. By tiptoeing around the issues, the government hopes for a miracle when they say there is a 'need for the veterinary profession to work together to establish a greater consensus on the way forward.'[16]

As you can see from EFRACom member Mr David Taylor's straight questions and the crooked answers of the vets, the prospect of consensus in the vet profession is a long way off.

EFRACom examination of Royal College of Veterinary Surgeons witnesses, 18 February 2008

Mr Bob Moore, president, Professor Sheila Crispin, senior vice-president, and Ms Jane Hern, registrar

> **Q87 David Taylor**: I think I just heard Sheila Crispin talk about the concerns the RCVS has about the growth of non-veterinary practice, and she included the example of pet food manufacturers. Can you elaborate on that very quickly?

> **Professor Crispin**: I think anyone who owns an animal is very aware that when they go into veterinary practice these days there is a lot of advertising of pet foods, and some practices are now set up within pet food companies; you can go and have an animal looked at in that type of situation, but it is something that is changing and yet the legislation is not there to deal with the change.

> **Q88 David Taylor**: The Association of Veterinary Students of Great Britain and Ireland recently debated a motion that vets should advocate feeding a manufactured pet food, did they not? (Page 179.)

> **Professor Crispin**: Yes, I was there.

> **Q89 David Taylor**: You were a guest at that debate, were you not?

> **Professor Crispin**: Yes, I was.

> **Q90 David Taylor**: You declined to vote on that.

Professor Crispin: I was there on an evening off; I was not there in any official capacity, so I spoke on behalf of my dogs because I thought that was the safest thing to do. But my views are quite well known: I think that we probably require a rather pragmatic approach to what we feed our animals, and that it may well in the case of my dogs include commercial and non-commercial food.

Q91 David Taylor: There are good numbers of vets, are there not, that believe—I can quote one to you: 'As varied as my patients were in size, species, age, sex and breed, the one common uniting feature was their junk food diet.' Do you recognise the author of that?

Professor Crispin: I think so, yes.

Q92 David Taylor: But he speaks on behalf of growing numbers of not just vets but companion-animal owners, does he not? There is a real growing concern about the junk that we push down our pets, is there not?

Professor Crispin: I am not sure that you should equate being vociferous with speaking on behalf of large numbers. It is worth remembering that the pet food manufacturers removed bovine products from pet food before we did for humans. It is not a black-and-white situation.

Q93 David Taylor: It never is, but the veterinary profession, particularly the RCVS, has been very reluctant to be involved in this for a long period of years. That is true, is it not?

Professor Crispin: I do not think that is true. If I can now go back to my time as president, I spent a lot of time dealing very politely with the many letters that the president gets on this topic.

Q94 David Taylor: No-one denies the politeness.

Professor Crispin: No, but the line I took was to speak as president, as a scientist and as an owner of animals, and actually doing it like that, hopefully, you got a rather balanced view.

Q95 David Taylor: Do you see the thrust of the vets' professional standards being the treatment of or prevention of disease?

Professor Crispin: I think very much the prevention. Indeed, one of the aims of the new Veterinary Surgeons Act is to be proactive rather than reactive. I think that is crucial. And, yes, the debate has made me look very carefully at what I feed my dogs, and it has modified what I feed my dogs, but I have not gone so far as to go entirely for raw meaty bones.

Q96 David Taylor: It is not intended to be an approach on you; it also involves your colleagues as well. The concern that people have is that the curriculum of the veterinary colleges contains relatively little about the nutrition of companion animals. Is that a fair comment?

Professor Crispin: Actually, there is quite a lot on the nutrition of companion animals. The people like Tom Lonsdale, who you quoted, would say that it is very much weighted in terms of feeding commercial foods.

Q97 David Taylor: Is that partly because the mega pet food manufacturers have a very large slice and a captive market in every sense? They have ingratiated themselves with the profession and with the veterinary colleges, have they not? They sponsor various chairs of veterinary science, do they not? You are not going to bite the hand that feeds you!

Professor Crispin: Lectureships, I think. I do not think it is quite—

Q98 David Taylor: Professionally, you are not going to bite the hand that feeds you, are you? Mr Moore, it is not aimed at you.

Professor Crispin: No.

Ms Hern: It does not say a lot for the impartiality of the profession that they would be swayed by that sort of thing.

Q99 David Taylor: But it is something that has grown up over a long period of years with relatively few people that have questioned the given wisdom that somehow pet food manufacturers are there to promote the health of the many millions of companion animals in this country and elsewhere. Do you accept that given wisdom—that it should not be examined and should not be criticised and that we should not instigate some research into the comparative diets, which, as Sheila Crispin said, at the debate which I mentioned—you would have liked to have seen some research. Why is the RCVS not banging the drum on this?

Ms Hern: Because it is not a scientific body in that sense: we are here to regulate the profession and maintain—

Q100 David Taylor: Against professional standards, against expectations, against whether or not you are trying to prevent ill-health or merely treat it.

Ms Hern: But we do not prescribe how—

Q101 David Taylor: You should be part of it though, surely?

Ms Hern: We do not tell veterinary surgeons how they should exercise their professional judgement.

Q102 David Taylor: Ah, you say you are just packing up; you are just walking by on the other side?

Ms Hern: No, but they have to exercise their professional judgement in relation to the animal and the client in front of them, and we do not go down the road of being prescriptive in all of those contexts.

EFRACom examination of British Veterinary Association witnesses, 3 March 2008

Mr Nick Blayney, president, and Ms Nicky Paull, president-elect.

Q158 David Taylor: Whilst no pet food manufacturers own any practices, what proportion of the income of some of your practices would you say is derived from the promotion or sale of pet food?

Mr Blayney: I cannot give you that statistic off the top of my head, but I am sure we would be glad to research it and provide it to you at a later date.

Q159 David Taylor: Would it be a substantial amount in some practices?

Mr Blayney: I am not prepared to answer that without some data in front of me, other than to say that most veterinary practices do sell pet food. The reason they do it is because veterinary practices supply goods and services to their clients, goods and services that presumably they have judged to be useful to their clients. The goods we supply include a lot of medications and food. There is no doubt that the arrival of commercial pet foods has improved the quality of life and wellbeing of a lot of pets because it provides well prepared, scientifically based, nutritionally acceptable diets.

Q160 David Taylor: What evidence do you have that it has improved the quality of life and indeed the longevity of companion animals?

Ms Paull: This is more of a clinical discussion. We could look at ready-made meals at Marks and Spencer that people eat. They might be better for them than eating bags of crisps and biscuits because they do not have time to cook. It is trying to balance sensibly what clients are available to do for their animals. For instance, an owner could get together a nutritionally balanced diet or could opt for purchasing one, but I think that is a decision that has to be made between the veterinary surgeon and the client. The pros and cons of each diet can be discussed.

To insinuate that because we happen to have dog food available for sale in the practice means that we are going to force this down our clients' pets' throats is not the case. Nick is right. Some practices do sell pet food but equally many do not. It is a commercial decision as to whether that is something that we are going to supply to our clients just the same as we might offer pet collars or something like that.

Q161 David Taylor: Are you aware that out there amongst the millions of owners there are companion animal owners—dogs and cats in particular—and there is a fairly significant lobby that argues that vets are promoting the sale and sometimes selling the pet foods which create the illnesses which keep you in business?

Mr Blayney: This is complete nonsense.

Q162 David Taylor: You are aware of the lobby?

Mr Blayney: Very much so. It is quite a dangerous lobby because it is seriously misinformed and very good at lobbying. The reason that vets choose to use foods is because they have been scientifically convinced that these foods are of value.

Q163 David Taylor: By whom?

Mr Blayney: By the data that has been produced by the manufacturers in the same way—

Q164 David Taylor: Would these be the same manufacturers who sponsor good numbers of the chairs of veterinary science at universities in the UK?

Mr Blayney: They do contribute to education. If the government funding was higher then perhaps the universities would not have to look elsewhere for funding.

Ms Paull: You could argue the same with pharmaceutical companies as well that give CPD lectures to us and so on. At the end of the day, it is the responsibility of the veterinary surgeon to make a clinical decision with the owner of the animal as to what is the best thing for that animal. To say that because a pharmaceutical company sponsors a course, automatically we are going to supply lots of their product and sell it out to an owner where it is not required, I would take offence at.

Mr Blayney: Vets are very good at seeing the wood for the trees in much the same way that I am sure, when MPs are entertained by various lobbying groups, you can see right through what their mission is. What we are exercised by is good science. The pet food manufacturers have invested a lot of money in this, and it is up to veterinary surgeons, judging by their own levels of professional integrity, to decide whether this is appropriate for their animals in the respect that they do absolutely everything else for the good of the animals under their care.

Afterword

What did you make of the vets' answers? Were you, like me, suitably outraged?

After many years observing the vet establishment serve up red herrings in a smokescreen of misinformation, I'm still taken aback by their apparent disregard for the animals under their care.

If pets and pet owners are to be protected from an unbending veterinary profession, something needs to be done and this is where you can help.

If you live in the UK, please contact your MP and let him or her know about the massive pet food fraud in our midst and ask that the matter receive the highest priority. Tell your personal story and why action is long overdue.

Please also contact EFRACom at:

Clerk of the Environment, Food and Rural Affairs Committee
House of Commons
7 Millbank
London SW1P 3JA
UK
Telephone: 020 7219 5774
Email: efracom@parliament.uk

Individually written letters sent to the postal address would be best and are more likely to receive a reply.

However, wherever you live, please send an email to: efracom@parliament.uk

If EFRACom receive emails from residents of every continent and many countries, they will get an idea of the seriousness of this global issue and consider holding an inquiry into the relationship between vets and pet food manufacturers. No need to comment at length (unless you want to). Just a line telling EFRACom why you object to the vets' promotion and sale of junk food would be enough.

If you can enlist friends and relatives to help that would be terrific and contacting your local newspaper, TV or radio station would be worth a try. (Eventually the media will need to treat this matter seriously.)

Unless and until we speak up, those with the crooked answers will continue to hold sway. The junk pet food fraud is now on the agenda in the UK Parliament. If we can make progress there, then that will create a basis for change in other countries too.

Good luck and best wishes,
Tom Lonsdale

PS Please send copies of any letters and responses received to tom@rawmeatybones.com. I'll keep a record with a view to future publication.

November 2008: Partners in crime

Dear Reader,

Here's the 2008 Christmas edition of the *RMB Newsletter*. What a year it's been!

Global warming, the US presidential election and the Global Financial Crisis fill the headlines. I wonder what 2009 has in store. Hopefully there'll be a period of calm where the world and its people can spend time addressing the issues affecting our tenure of the planet, repairing frayed nerves and shaky finances.

In a crisis-ridden world it's easy to see how the issue of pets and the diet they're fed gets pushed off the agenda. That's not to say the issues are unimportant—just the opposite. The junk pet food industry is said to be worth $30 billion annually. Who knows what the veterinary profession extracts from the community? The UK Royal College of Veterinary Surgeons (RCVS) reported that 70.1% of UK veterinary endeavour is spent treating pets. They omitted to mention that the majority of pets need the vet due to the effects of their modern junk pet food diet.

Ignore the maker's instructions and put adulterated fuel in your motor car and soon you'll need a mechanic. Forget to put oil in your sump and your engine, lacking essential lubrication, will seize. Pets need the right fuel and lubrication too. Fill them up with junk food and you overload their system with harmful chemicals. Forget to give carnivore pets a regular supply of raw meaty bones and their teeth become tartar encrusted and their gums rot—leading to an array of further health problems.

We know these things. The world's veterinary authorities know these things—at least since 1992 when all English-speaking veterinary schools and veterinary associations and the RCVS were circulated the paper 'Pandemic of periodontal disease: a malodorous condition'.[17]

In 1993 two more monographs were mailed to each veterinary school, association and RCVS.[18]

But, as we know, arrogant, hard-faced veterinary officials carried on regardless. The junk pet food industry increased its research efforts and spent even more dollars (dollars expropriated from unwitting pet owners) to bribe and corrupt veterinary schools, veterinary associations and rank and file vets in their practices.

In the previous *RMB Newsletter* 'Straight questions: crooked answers' we looked at how the UK veterinary authorities were less than honest when being quizzed by a panel of MPs about the junk pet food/veterinary conspiracy. (See page 206.)

Thank you to all those who wrote to MPs and to the Environment, Food and Rural Affairs Committee. Official replies forwarded to me were condescending and intended to fob off the correspondents. Hopefully we shall return to this matter in a future newsletter.

Recently the UK Government Department of Environment, Food and Rural Affairs (DEFRA) announced its consultation process on codes of practice supporting the Animal Welfare Act. There are details at the end of the newsletter.

My thanks to Carol Auld who provides the prime topic for this newsletter. Carol obtained Freedom of Information documents from the Ontario Veterinary College regarding their partnership with Royal Canin, a division of the Mars Corporation.

Wishing you, your family and animals a relaxing, restful and happy Christmas and hoping 2009 ushers in the changes we all want and need,

Tom Lonsdale

Partners in crime

Down south Mexico way there's a crippling drug war. The army has been deployed because many police officers act with and for the drug cartels.

Time magazine reports:

In Mexico's drug war, bad cops are a mounting problem. Few rituals are more futile than the 'housecleaning' of Mexico's police forces. So deep, broad and brazen is cop corruption south of the border that removing it makes eradicating rats from landfills look easy ...[19]

To the north, Canadian Mounties retain a good reputation; it's the veterinary authorities that are the problem. So flagrant, so brazen is their abuse of power that they crow about their partnership with the junk pet food cartels.

Imagine if a police academy in Mexico or anywhere else took millions of dollars from the drug barons, the money to be used for training police to promote and sell drugs in the community. I know it's a bit far-fetched, but would the criminal conspirators announce their deal by press release? Would they describe their drug cartel/police partnership as having a 'beneficial impact'?

Have a look at the press release below and then the contract entered into by the University of Guelph, Ontario Veterinary College (OVC). You'll likely need to reach for the vomit bag.

When you've regained composure, please consider contacting Ontario members of parliament to let them know your thoughts.

It's not just the OVC that enters into dirty deals. Virtually the entire global veterinary 'education' industry is operated of, by and for the junk pet food industry. They are inseparable. The pet food cartels poison the pets, which keeps the vets in business. The vets use junk pet food money to inculcate their students in junk pet food propaganda to keep the cartels in business.

Please, if you've got a moment, conduct a Freedom of Information (FOI) inquiry at your local veterinary school concerning its collusion with the junk pet food industry. It's usually a straightforward process. Just phone the switchboard and ask to be put in touch with the FOI officer who will then describe the process.

Please send through any documents obtained under FOI. We can assemble a file to help establish our case for change. Let's try open debate supported by hard evidence. Mind you, from past experience, it's going to be tough. We should consider legal actions against those who defraud the community on a grand scale. Let's hope good sense prevails before the army needs to be deployed!

Press release

Royal Canin Canada commits $3 million for OVC[20]
22 April 2008: news release

The University of Guelph today received a $3 million commitment from Royal Canin Canada Company to establish the Royal Canin Veterinary Diet Endowed Chair in Canine and Feline Clinical Nutrition and support independent research and graduate scholarships at the Ontario Veterinary College (OVC).

This first-of-its-kind chair will be held by a faculty member in OVC's Department of Clinical Studies and the University will conduct an international search for the first chair holder.

'This generous gift is a wonderful example of the importance of private sector–university partnerships', said UofG president Alastair Summerlee. 'Royal Canin Canada's investment in an endowed chair allows us to develop the area of feline and canine nutrition.'

The Royal Canin Veterinary Diet Chair is also an important part of a strategic initiative by UofG to establish new teaching and research chairs across the spectrum of the University's disciplines.

'The application of nutrition in both optimising health and in the prevention of and management of specific clinical conditions is increasingly important in veterinary practice. As a pet first company we know this investment will have a beneficial impact on the health of dogs and cats', said Xavier Unkovic, CEO of Royal Canin Canada Company.

'We are extremely proud of the contribution that

Medi-Cal / Royal Canin Veterinary Diet has made to the veterinary profession in Canada', said Dr Brent Matthew, veterinary division director, Royal Canin Canada Company. 'Our partnership with the University of Guelph represents a dramatic new commitment to clinical nutrition in Canada.'

OVC Dean Elizabeth Stone said innovative nutritional research is essential to maintain and improve the health of dogs and cats. 'We are excited that this innovative new faculty position will help us find answers to important questions about how we should feed our feline and canine companions. In addition, this gift enables us to start a new graduate program in this area.'

Royal Canin is a worldwide manufacturer and supplier of high quality, specialised dog and cat foods in the veterinary, pet specialty, and breeder channels. Its headquarters are in France and production operations exist in 10 countries around the world, including a new Canadian plant opening in Guelph in 2008. The company has a comprehensive veterinary exclusive line of diets under the Medi-Cal / Royal Canin Veterinary Diet brand name.

Media contacts
Royal Canin:
Jennifer Brown
613 230-2220, ext. 227 (office)
613 614-2894 (mobile)

University of Guelph:
Lori Bona Hunt
519 824-4120, ext. 53338

Royal Canin, OVC contract

University of Guelph
Ontario Veterinary College
Office of the Dean
Terms of Reference

Royal Canin Veterinary Diet Endowed Chair in Canine and Feline Clinical Nutrition at the Ontario Veterinary College, University of Guelph

1. The Royal Canin Veterinary Diet Chair in Canine and Feline Clinical Nutrition was established through a gift commitment of $2,500,000 ('Endowment') made to the University of Guelph ('UofG') by Royal Canin Canada Company ('Royal Canin').

2. It is agreed that the purpose of this Endowment is as follows: To establish the Royal Canin Veterinary Diet Endowed Chair in Canine and Feline Clinical Nutrition (the 'Chair'). The Chair will be filled by a canine and feline clinical nutritionist, who will be hired as a regular full-time tenure-track faculty member at the Ontario Veterinary College ('OVC'), for the purpose of veterinary and graduate student teaching and research in canine and feline clinical nutrition.

3. The expendable income from the Endowment should be sufficient to pay the appointee's full initial term and prospective reappointment salary and benefits. The expendable income is determined in accordance with the UofG's policy, 'General Endowment Fund Management Policy' (see Appendix 1), as may be amended from time to time. If available, additional expendable income could be used as an expense allowance for research and appointment-related travel costs.

4. From time to time, Royal Canin will provide additional support to the Chair including research grant support (students and program funding). This research and student support will be considered as part of the overall package available to the appointee.

5. The UofG, OVC and Royal Canin will collaborate with each other for their mutual benefit and the benefit of the stakeholders. This will include, but not be limited to, discussion on the needs for nutrition education and research and ways to meet those needs.

6. An Advisory Committee will be created to support the Chair and to assure that the canine and feline clinical nutritional educational and research programs and activities align with the mission mandate of the UofG and Royal Canin. The members will be approved by both parties and will include two representatives from the UofG and two from Royal Canin. Terms of reference will be developed by this Committee for approval by the UofG and Royal Canin.

7. The appointees will be hired as regular full-time tenure-track faculty members by UofG and be subject to its policies and procedures. It is acknowledged that as a tenure-track faculty member, the appointee has the academic freedom to pursue interests in addition to the mission and mandate of the Chair. The Chair will not participate in any outside consultation or media activities that create a conflict of interest with the UofG or with Royal Canin.

8. Research carried out through the Chair will be consistent with Royal Canin's Research Policy (see Appendix B). If in future, a conflict arises between UofG's policies and procedures and Royal Canin's Research Policy, the conflict will be referred to the Advisory Committee. The

Advisory Committee will provide advice to UofG and to Royal Canin on possible resolution of the conflict.

9. The Chair will be expected to establish a successful teaching program in canine and feline clinical nutrition for veterinary students and graduate students. The Chair might also participate in undergraduate education as time permits. The Chair will maintain a superior program of research (as evidenced by publications and external grant support), and will play a leadership role in facilitating world-class research in feline and canine clinical research.

10. The home department for the Chair will be the Department of Clinical Studies. The Chair will have an appointment in the OVC Teaching Hospital (OVCTH) in canine and feline clinical nutrition. The Chair will provide learning opportunities for veterinary students, interns and graduate students in the OVCTH and will provide nutritional consultations for clinicians from other clinical services within the OVCTH (e.g. critical care, internal medicine, oncology).

11. The professorial rank of the appointee may be at the assistant, associate, or full professor level depending on the available funding from the Endowment for salary and benefits and the qualifications of prospective candidates. The first appointee, based on available funding, will be recruited as an assistant professor.

12. Faculty searches follow normal procedures for the UofG. Designates from Royal Canin will have an opportunity to meet with the candidates during their interviews and will be invited to the candidates' interview presentations.

13. In the event that the appointee leaves the UofG, UofG will fill the position as quickly as possible.

14. If the expendable income is insufficient to meet continuing appointment and expense costs, the Dean will consult with the Advisory Committee, the Provost, the OVC Director of Advancement and Royal Canin. A decision may be made to leave the position vacant intermittently, supplement the income from other sources, and secure additional investment or some combination of these measures.

15. During the period when the Chair is not permanently occupied such as when a candidate search is in progress, after consultation with the Department Chair, the Advisory Committee, and the Provost will use the Endowment's income to maintain the continuity of the research and teaching programs in canine and feline nutrition.

16. The capital gifts contributed to this Endowment shall be held in perpetuity.

17. This document may be amended by mutual consent in writing by UofG and Royal Canin.

Signed by the parties hereto this 22nd day of April, 2008.

Dr Alastair J.S. Summerlee
President and Vice-Chancellor
University of Guelph

Xavier Unkovic
Chief Executive Officer
Royal Canin Canada Company

UK codes of practice for the welfare of dogs and cats

The UK Government Department of Environment, Food and Rural Affairs (DEFRA) are in the process of drafting codes of practice for dog, cat and horse owners.

Apart from the muddled ideas, there's a general presupposition that dogs and cats should be fed junk food. Nowhere do the draft codes mention that dogs are modified wolves and that all carnivores need to consume raw meaty bones to ensure dental and general good health.

The UK government has been repeatedly informed about the biological imperatives and fundamental animal welfare implications arising from junk pet foods. But they refuse to learn; they refuse to change. How can the government enforce regulations against pet owners when the government itself is incapable of learning obvious oft-repeated truths?

Now's our chance to again repeat those truths. Let DEFRA know that the proposed codes are hopelessly misguided and rather than improve welfare, will reinforce the ongoing cruelty and suffering. Governmental support for the corrupt junk pet food/veterinary/fake animal welfare alliance should stop and stop pronto.

Please have a good look at what's proposed and then send your response before 31 December to:

Elaine Cannon, Area 8B, No. 9 Millbank, 17 Smith Square, London SW1P 3JR. Telephone: 020 7238 5332

Or email: animalwelfareconsultations@defra.gsi.gov.uk clearly stating the name of the consultation in the subject header, e.g. Code of practice—dogs.

Please send through any correspondence that might be useful or interesting for possible inclusion in future newsletters.

9

———

2009: A MOVEMENT UNDERMINED

Junk food makers, vets, and raw feeding factions (BARF, prey model etc.) undermine the RMB message, profiting from half-measures and confusion.

February 2009: Organised veterinary crime

Dear Reader,

Welcome to the first *RMB Newsletter* of 2009. How are you? In the midst of life's uncertainties, I trust that you are safe, well and making progress, however slow.

In the 8 December *Newsletter* we talked about the Animal Welfare Act draft Codes of Conduct for UK pet owners.

Thank you to the many readers who raised concerns with the UK Government Department of Environment, Food and Rural Affairs. You did a fine job and you've been noticed. More than that, the information is now permanently on the UK Government record. Will they take due account and act responsibly? Time will tell.

In the 8 November 'Partners in crime' edition of the *Newsletter* we looked at the Ontario Veterinary College (OVC) connivance with the Mars Corporation. (See p. 217.)

Thank you again to all those who wrote letters of complaint—whether to your local politicians or the Canadian politicians with responsibility for the OVC outrage.

In this newsletter we take another look at the Ontario Veterinary

College—one of the best veterinary schools money can buy. But first let's examine how Organised Veterinary Crime might be an apt descriptor of a global veterinary profession systematically abusing animals and exploiting pet owners.

Best wishes,
Tom Lonsdale

Organised veterinary crime

Frequently our (false) assumptions get in the way of clear understanding. And if we fail to understand our problems, then the chances of finding solutions are slim indeed.

Aren't vets supposed to care for and protect animals? Aren't they supposed to be a 'self-regulating profession' that identifies and resolves its own mistakes? Aren't vets supposed to be scientists who welcome inquiry and vigorous debate that tests established orthodoxy?

Aren't veterinary schools supposed to treat veterinary students fairly and to encourage the development of inquiring minds?

For too long I've fretted about a global veterinary profession that actively, knowingly spreads ill-health and suffering. A profession that connives with the mass poisoners (the junk pet food makers) to dumb down and exploit trusting pet owners under the full gaze of numerous government regulators whose role it is to protect the community from illicit, corrupt and fraudulent conduct.

Sadly, I believe it's time to stop pretending; stop hoping and face the reality that the veterinary profession (with notable exceptions) working on behalf of the junk pet food industry displays many of the features of an organised criminal network.

See what Wikipedia has to say about organised crime.[1]

> In order for a criminal organisation to prosper, some degree of support is required from the society in which it lives. Thus, it is often necessary to corrupt some of its respected members, most commonly achieved through bribery, blackmail,

and the establishment of symbiotic relationships with legitimate businesses. Judicial and police officers and legislators are especially targeted for control by organised crime via bribes.

Organised crime most typically flourishes when legitimate government and civil society is disorganised, weak, absent or untrusted. This may occur in a society facing periods of political, economic or social turmoil or transition, such as a change of government or a period of rapid economic development, particularly if the society lacks strong and established institutions and the rule of law. Under these circumstances, criminal organisations can operate with less fear of interference from law enforcement and may serve to provide their 'customers' with a semblance of order and predictability that would otherwise be unavailable.

For sure much organised crime is ruled by violent males in the mould of Al Capone, Tony Soprano and the Japanese Yakuza. A scary thought regarding organised vet crime—increasingly it's a female preserve operating in full public view.

Unfortunately, while legitimate government and civil society is disorganised, weak, absent or untrusted, and while fundamental truths about carnivore biology are obscured, organised vet crime will continue to flourish.

Take a look at how it's manifested at the Ontario Veterinary College.

Hill's contract with Ontario Veterinary College, University of Guelph, Canada

In the 'Partners in crime' edition we looked at the Mars Corporation $3 million commitment to the OVC. (See page 217.) Hill's, the junk pet food division of Colgate-Palmolive, have upped the anti.

My thanks to Carol Auld who conducted a Freedom of Information inquiry that revealed further OVC depravity:

University of Guelph (Ontario Veterinary College) and Hill's Pet Nutrition
Primary Healthcare Centre Proposal
Memorandum of understanding

1. Purpose

Hill's Pet Nutrition Inc. ('Hill's') and the University of Guelph (Ontario Veterinary College) ('OVC') propose a joint collaboration to educate and graduate the next generation of veterinary students who will be exceptionally skilled in delivering preventative healthcare to companion animals. This will be the model for companion animal primary healthcare and service delivery for the 21st century. OVC will build, staff and manage the operation of a state-of-the-art companion animal primary healthcare centre ('PHC') on the site of the University of Guelph campus and in accordance with the University of Guelph policies. The facility will be operational by 2009–2010 and is expected to be financially self-sustaining by 2013. Hill's will be the only nutritional company engaged with OVC in fulfilling the Purpose of the PHC for the terms of this Agreement.

2. Term

The term of this Agreement will be for a period of fifteen (15) years commencing on 1 January 2009. Hill's has the first right of renewal of this Agreement on terms as agreed to by the parties. If Hill's wishes to exercise its right of renewal, it shall notify OVC 12 months prior to the expiry of this Agreement.

3. Objectives

The key objectives of the PHC include to:
1. Create a talented and cohesive primary healthcare team that is energised, engaged, and open to shaping and delivering primary healthcare in veterinary medicine. This

team will include veterinary technicians, receptionists, clinicians, animal care attendants, students, and the director of the PHC.

2. Create new learning opportunities: from surgical and technical to business and communication skills for our student veterinarians and animal health technicians. Visiting veterinarians and staff will learn new methods for service delivery in primary healthcare.

3. Establish the critical role nutrition plays as part of general wellbeing of the pet as well as apply nutritional therapy as part of a multimodal protocol for sick pets.

4. Incorporate nutrition into all the programs and patient–client interactions within the PHC. For example, nutritional education will be included in the protocol for every client–patient visit and in the assessment and therapeutic plan for every patient.

5. Provide effective veterinarian-pet owner coaching and feedback, ensuring the veterinarian recognises his or her role in the healthcare team and delivering effective advice and education to the pet owner.

6. Develop veterinary leadership skills.

7. Establish the importance of the human–pet bond and its role in behavioural science and public health education.

4. Funding

i. Hill's will provide funding to aid in the development of PHC in the amount of $5 million dollars (Canadian) in cash. Hill's contribution will be paid in instalments of $500,000 over 10 years. These payments will be paid on 1 January each year, with the first payment scheduled for 1 January 2009.
[Details blacked out by Freedom of Information Officer here.]

Hill's financial commitment will be fulfilled no later than 1 January 2009.

ii. Hill's will provide $250,000 'in kind' funding. The 'in-kind' support will include curriculum resources contracted through Mark Morris Institute and support provided by Hill's local support staff (Director of Veterinary Affairs, Practice Development Veterinarian and Veterinary Account Manager, et al).

iii. The funding amount provided by Hill's will not be made public by the parties except as required by law.

5. Naming of the PHC

OVC has agreed to name the PHC 'the Hill's Pet Nutrition Primary Healthcare Centre at the Ontario Veterinary College'. This provision will survive expiry of this Agreement.

6. Supply of nutritional products

i. Hill's nutritional products will be the only such products displayed in the public area within the PHC for sale at retail prices set by the OVC. Other nutritional products which are supported by clinical trials and/or faculty approval may be used in the medical areas of the PHC. Such products, if prescribed by clinicians, may be sold to clients; however, these products will not be on display in the public areas.

ii. Hill's will also provide to PHC, the following as agreed to between the parties:

(a) use of Hill's client educational tools and literature;

(b) initial free food inventory and stocking of all wellness and therapeutic products; and

(c) food products at 70% of the wholesale price; funds generated from the retail sale of these products will support the PHC.

7. Joint Nutritional Curriculum Committee and curriculum resources

i. The parties will create a Joint Nutritional Curriculum Team including representatives from both Hill's and OVC. The team will be responsible for providing advice to OVC's Associate Dean (Academic Affairs) on the development of a nutritional curriculum which supports the Objectives of this Agreement.

ii. Hill's will provide resources through Mark Morris Institute for the development of a nutritional curriculum for training veterinary students in primary healthcare including the *Small Animal Clinical Nutrition* textbook. Free copies of the text and companion handbook and all current and future educational tools provided by Hill's will be distributed (atlas, clinical product guides, etc.) to all students in the PHC.

8. Partners in pet care

The parties agree to establish a 'Partners in pet care' team. The team will comprise representatives from Hill's, and the PHC healthcare team as deemed mutually appropriate. The team will work together to develop and implement global best practices in doctor–client education materials, merchandising systems and advice to the director of PHC on practice health strategies which include multimodal protocols incorporating wellness and therapeutic nutrition.

9. Access to Hill's facilities

Hill's will provide OVC's faculty and students access to the Hill's Pet Nutrition Centre in Topeka, KS, USA. Contingent on available funding, this access may include:

i. Orientation about Hill's Topeka research and education programs to OVC primary care faculty/staff current and new, on an ongoing basis;

ii. Opportunities for continuing education for undergraduate and graduate student; and

iii. Supplement education for new and emerging sciences such as nutrigenomics and clinical studies.

10. PHC Advisory Board

The PHC will have an advisory board wherein Hill's will have a permanent advisory representative. This group will meet at least three times per year to measure and evaluate the progress and effectiveness of further directives mutually agreed to by the Dean of the OVC and the General Manager of Hill's Pet Nutrition Canada. An annual report will be prepared and circulated to all interested parties. Determination of scope and terms of reference for the advisory board will be created by 31 December 2008.

11. Continuing education and outreach program

One of the goals of the PHC will be to promote opportunities to showcase best practice in teaching of clinical nutrition and take steps to attract fellow academics, practising veterinarians and government officials, to visit the Centre. This goal will be achieved through continuing education programs and outreach programs including the following:

- An annual Nutrition Symposium to be hosted at the University of Guelph. Hill's will provide the necessary annual financial sponsorship for the Nutritional Symposium. It is intended that the Symposium will provide an opportunity where scientists and academics including those from other pet nutrition companies from around the world will be invited to participate and present their research.
- A certificate program in clinical nutrition which will be a combination of distance education modules and time working in the PHC
- Certificates in continuing education for each of practic-

ing veterinarians, student veterinarians and veterinary technicians

- Development of a research program in service delivery with external funding. It is anticipated the research would include the development of a student survey to explore issues of confidence and perceived competence in clinical nutrition, overall healthcare and communication skills. The research program would also include how primary healthcare should be defined and delivered in veterinary medicine and education.
- Engagement of faculty members from other veterinary colleges to spend sabbatic leave or professional development time at the PHC
- Establishment of workshops, which may be with AAVMC, AVMA COE or other organisations to showcase the novel approach to primary healthcare and integrated primary healthcare and effective communication teaching
- Development of an elective training program for at least two clerkships for student veterinarians from other veterinary colleges to obtain training in primary healthcare and clinical nutrition at PHC. Funding to support travel and accommodation for the two clerkships would be awarded on a competitive basis from Hill's
- Development of a visiting educational training program for international veterinarians or student veterinarians that would showcase the novel approach to pedagogy including the importance of clinical nutrition.

12. Communication strategy

The parties will develop and implement a communication strategy to announce the Hill's–OVC collaboration outlined in this Agreement, highlighting the design of the facility, the pedagogical approach being used and the impacts and outcomes of the research into effective service delivery in a primary healthcare facility.

Public communication issued by the PHC will acknowledge, where appropriate, contributions of both Hill's and OVC and will include both Hill's and OVC logos in accordance with University policies.

Notices

All notices hereunder shall be delivered or sent by mail or fax at the following addresses:

If to University of Guelph at:
Dean's Office, OVC
University of Guelph, Guelph, Ontario, N1G 2W1
Fax (519) 837 3230

If to Hill's at:
General Manager
Hill's Pet Nutrition Canada, Inc.
6521 Mississauga Rd.
Mississauga, Ontario, L5N 1A6
Fax (905) 819 4984

Severability

If any provision of this Agreement shall, to any extent, be invalid or unenforceable, the remainder of this Agreement shall not be affected.

Governing law

This Agreement shall be governed by the laws of the Province of Ontario and the federal laws of Canada applicable therein. The parties hereto agree that the Courts of Ontario shall have the nonexclusive jurisdiction to entertain any action or other legal proceedings based on any provisions of this Agreement.

Entire agreement
With respect to the subject matter of this Agreement, this Agreement: (a) sets forth the entire agreement between the parties, (b) supersedes all prior communications between the parties, and (c) constitutes the entire agreement between the parties hereto. Any amendment to this Agreement must be made in writing and executed by both parties.

In witness whereof both parties have hereunto executed this Agreement,
University of Guelph 23 May 2008
Per: Alastair Summerless, President, University of Guelph
Per: Maureen Mancuso, Provost and Vice President, Academic

Hill's Pet Nutrition Inc. 23 May 2008
Per: Neil Thompson, President, Hill's Pet Nutrition Inc. Americas
Per: Gordon Dumesich, General Manager, Hill's Pet Nutrition Canada, Inc.

Can you believe it? Are you appalled? Do you want to do something to stop it—whether locally or on a global scale?

If the OVC were to experience community pressure leading to the abandonment of their contract of pet death and moral decay it might send a signal to organised vet criminals everywhere. Politicians are ultimately responsible for what happens at the OVC.

Ontario provincial members of parliament can be contacted at https://www.ola.org/en[2]

Members of the Canadian National Parliament can be contacted at http://www.parl.gc.ca/[3]

Besides complaining to politicians, it's a good idea to let the media know about the wholesale corruption pervading the vet profession. Google can provide contact details of newspapers, radio and TV.

If you know any vet students, please pass on the newsletter. One day students may rise up against the junk pet food vet school conspirators and seek compensation for the damage done.[4]

For the sake of animals and a better world I wish you good luck and much success. Please send progress reports.

Best wishes,
Tom

March 2009: RCVS Q&A

Dear Reader,

Regular *RMB Newsletter* readers know that the veterinary profession—self-appointed guardian of the public interest—has been hijacked by the junk pet food industry. Back in 1991 members of the RMB Lobby blew the whistle on the pet food/veterinary/fake animal welfare alliance. Rather than act responsibly, the veterinary establishment maintains denial, defends the indefensible and tries to suppress discussion.

One way to keep the matter on the agenda is to contest veterinary elections. In the UK, the Royal College of Veterinary Surgeons (RCVS) is a stuffy, archaic body responsible for the education and regulation of about 21,000 vets. The RCVS imposes a strict 500-word limit on election statements. This year there's been a quantum leap in the scope for discussions.

www.vetsurgeon.org is hosting a RCVS discussion forum for vets, vet students and allied professionals. On the same website there's a Raw Diet forum where Roger Meacock does sterling work explaining the health benefits of a more natural diet.

As one of nine candidates for six vacancies on the RCVS Council, I attempt to engage the other candidates about the junk pet food issue.

A vet asked me to explain:

After failing 12 times, what keeps you going? Why do you really want to become RCVS president? Is it just to promote RMB or do you have any other interests in the veterinary profession?

My answer appears below (as well as at www.vetsurgeon.org). I hope you'll get a moment to click through the links that set out what I believe to be important—and by implication what needs to be done.

Thanks and best wishes,
Tom

Cybernetics, U-turns and resolution of the junk pet food scandal

Hi F... and all,

Thanks for the questions.

Please think of the 12 previous attempts as 'rehearsals'. They've brought us to the point where you and I can discuss the issues.

What keeps any of us going? Why do we get out of bed each morning? What motivates a whistleblower turned campaigner? At one level: genes interacting with environment—I simply can do no other.

There's an expanded answer, from a whistleblower perspective, posted in the files accompanying my profile.

In the early days there was no single 'light bulb' moment, more a series of such moments akin to stadium floodlights gaining intensity. That was back in the late 1980s and early 90s.

We lived in a different environment before widespread use of the internet. Information was relayed in books and by word of mouth. So the 'wow' factor was huge when we stumbled on the explanation for why pets suffer a litany of easily preventable chronic and acute diseases.

As suburban veterinary practitioners, we had immense motivation to bound out of bed each morning. Every day provided new research, treatment and prevention opportunities. But one day stands in my memory. It was Christmas Day 1992, and I woke with the fully formed outline for the cybernetic hypothesis. I tiptoed out of bed at 4.30 in the morning, made for the study and wrote down the first draft.[5]

If, as I believe, cybernetics reinterprets existing information to form the basis of a new paradigm of health and disease leading to a renaissance in medical and veterinary thought, that will be special. If it helps us to better understand the homeostasis of our planet as it was in prehistoric times—regulated as it was by mammalian carnivores—then I believe we'll be onto something big.

I admit that it's been a slow burn—not least because any and all aspects of this story have been starved of oxygen. Although you can see an early attempt at getting the story aired in the Australian Veterinary Association 1994 election statement.[6]

There have, however, been some wonderfully uplifting events.

By chance, I heard Professor Lynn Margulis speak on the radio.[7]

Inspired by her enthusiasm and concepts about our co-evolved world I sent her a draft of the cybernetics paper and the lecture monograph: 'Petfoods' insidious consequences: a modern veterinary snafu'.[8]

When her handwritten reply arrived, it was one of my proudest moments:

> Your work is wonderful ... If you write this up as a book proposal, send it to our agent.

Fate smiled in other ways. I met with Professor Colin Harvey, at that time one of only two veterinary periodontists on the planet, who gave me advice on how to strengthen the paper 'Periodontal disease and leucopenia'[9]

He never said and I never asked, but I reckon Professor Harvey had a hand in ensuring that the cybernetics paper obtained pride of place in the *Journal of Veterinary Dentistry*.

When James Lovelock FRS endorsed the paper, I was confident this was no flash in the pan.[10]

Eventually in 2001, with the aid of two editors and a team of lawyers, *Raw Meaty Bones: Promote Health* was published.[11] The book has several themes and culminates in

Chapter 14 on cybernetics. Effectively, the other 13 chapters are there in a supporting role. (See suggested reading list.[12])

That the book received glowing endorsements from highly esteemed colleagues fills me with pride.[13] I'm motivated and grateful for the support from younger vets such as Roger Meacock (doing sterling educational work on the Raw Diet forum), family, friends and acquaintances.

You are right that I want to promote RMB the concept, and the book of the same name is currently available in the files. However, I hope you appreciate that's only an educational tool to help us deal with the crisis the profession now faces.

In 2006 I visited the UK and made a presentation at Parliament House as part of the U-turn Tour.[14] As agreeable as that tour was, please be assured, I do not relish the struggles to get the diet and health matter on the agenda. What I hope to see is action. I hope to see the veterinary profession making a U-turn and fixing the biggest problem of the age.

I hope to continue to play a useful role. Initially I seek a mandate from the electorate that will take me onto the RCVS Council to provide one clear voice amongst forty at the Council table. Thereafter, if enough Councillors agree on our collective obligations and opportunities, and if they decide to elect me as president, I shall be honoured to serve.

Of course it's a long-term project. For the benefit of pets, people and the planet let's get started.

Thank you.

———

Questions needing answers

So far the eight other candidates, five of whom include the current president and members of the RCVS Council, have not seen fit to answer the questions I raised in the RCVS Forum[15]

Your comments please

Dear Colleague,

Your comments on the raw diet question would be appreciated.

Judging by the 112 messages (and counting) on the Raw Diet forum, veterinarians are taking an interest in the subject.

Whereas the majority of auto mechanics are conversant with how to fuel the family car, many veterinarians appear unsure about the food (fuel) requirements of the family dog.

The British Veterinary Association policy and a rebuttal may be assessed here.[16]

Does the confusion about feeding pets concern you?

Do you believe that a committee of inquiry might help the profession to better understand and resolve the issues?

If elected, what might be your contribution?

Thank you for your consideration.

If they can't or won't answer basic questions, can they be trusted? Are they fit to run a so-called self-regulating profession?

May 2009: BARFer Billinghurst

Hello,

Welcome to this edition of the *RMB Newsletter*.

Back in the early 1990s the Raw Meaty Bones concept broke through the muddle and mystification of carnivore diets, and thus provided a firm three-cornered base for the RMB Campaign. In revulsion at the mass poisoning of the world's pet carnivores by the junk pet food/veterinary/fake animal welfare alliance, the RMB Campaign was born.

Cornerstone one
Carnivores need the chemical ingredients (nutrients) in broadly the same quantity, quality and frequency as is found in the prey of free-living carnivores. (For instance the progenitors of dogs—wolves, cats—wildcats, ferrets—polecats.)

Cornerstone two
Carnivores need the physical texture of their food to closely match that of their free-living carnivore progenitors, the simple reason being that it's the physical form of the food that governs the quantity, quality and frequency of teeth cleaning and the correct regulation of passage of foodstuffs down the intestinal tract.

Cornerstone three
Carnivores, be they domestic or captive wild carnivores, need to be freed from the corrupt and disgraceful yoke of the junk pet food/veterinary/fake animal welfare alliance.

At last, a coherent scientific theory, set in its social and economic context, offered an illuminated path to a better future. The original RMB Lobby of Dr Breck Muir, Dr Alan Bennet and me campaigned vigorously. And in the early days we met with some success.

Unfortunately, things started to go bad when Dr Ian Billinghurst joined the group. If you are an old Raw Meaty Bones hand you are likely aware of BARFer Billinghurst's exploits and the effective sabotage of the Raw Meaty Bones Campaign through the establishment of BARFmania.[17]

This newsletter adds another chapter to the BARF/vomit/spew saga and a couple of snippets on the venality and myopia of so-called veterinary researchers.

Unless we know and understand our problems, how can we hope to resolve them?

Until next time, keep on keeping on.

Best wishes,
Tom

BARFer Billinghurst

As a follower of Juliette de Bairacli Levy and Richard Pitcairn, Ian Billinghurst acknowledged the usefulness of raw meat and bones in a dog's diet. But otherwise followed his mentors up the garden path—literally and figuratively. Dr Billinghurst recommended that fruit and vegetables should comprise 30% to 60% of a dog's diet.

His diet sheet recommended:

Midday: carbohydrate meal
Rolled oats soaked in hot water until like porridge. Alternatively, Weet-Bix or muesli or vegetables. Add to this such things as dates, sultanas, prunes, raisins, grated apple or carrot. Add honey.

After reading Raw Meaty Bones information, Billinghurst saw the elegant simplicity of nature's teachings and applied to join the RMB Lobby. We freely supplied him with our research findings, and he availed himself of those findings—so much so that he used RMB information as foundation for his first book.[18]

Nowadays, Billinghurst has three books in print and each contains false and misleading information and each contradicts the other. Central in the enterprise is the misleading notion that dogs are omnivores. And where once he found it useful to extol the benefits of raw meaty bones, he now tells pet owners that his 'multi-mix patties contain all the ingredients in a finely ground and thoroughly mixed state. They are the only items fed.'

Dutch pet owners, believing that BARFer Billinghurst might have some useful information to impart, invited him to a discussion on their Natural Diet Forum.

The Forum members were less than impressed by the BARFer's commercially inspired madness. Here's a couple of their questions (which the BARFer refused to answer):

Raw meaty bones versus minced commercial raw food
When you launched your first book *Give Your Dog a Bone* you declared in a letter, advocating your book: 'the diets in this book all revolve around a central theme of raw meaty bones'.

Chapter 7 of the same book you wrote: 'the central message is that if a dog is to become and remain healthy, its diet must be based on raw meaty bones.'

So, for everyone, at that time, it was very clear that the key factor for a healthy carnivorous food was: raw meaty bones.

What was making you change your idea about this very important part and made you conclude that minced commercial prepared raw food was as good as the raw meaty bones?

Did you do research in one way or another about this matter?

Do you know about the study of a few Dutch veterinarian researchers at the Leiden (the Netherlands) University, study which is published in the US National Library of Medicine (NCBI PubMed) that food particles smaller than 3 centimetres probably are trigger factors for bloat or GDV [gastric dilatation and volvulus]?

More than 50 years ago, the kibble factories came out with one big lie, namely that wolves eat the stomach contents of their prey, to justify that they could mix leftovers from the grain mill factories and the leftovers from the canned vegetables industries into dog food.

Nowadays we know, from respectable wolf-researchers like Dave Mech, his books and his lecturing, that wolves don't eat stomach contents of their prey at all.

Did you do research or what was the reason for your conclusion by saying that vegetables are not an optional but an essential part of a dog's diet?

Is the BARF diet a compromise?
I have noticed on all the 'BARF' product websites that raw meaty bones are mentioned and encouraged. However, the emphasis is placed on the marketing of meat/veggie and fruit pulp.

As a veterinarian, isn't it best to set an example by promoting a diet which is wholly appropriate for our carnivorous pets? I understand that the vast majority of veterinarians have been hoodwinked by the likes of Hill's and Mars, but I cannot see how meeting them somewhere in the middle, effectively compromising, is the best thing for pets in general.

I understand also, the theory of providing a ready to feed, mince product in order to possibly entice more owners to feed 'raw'; essentially using the product as a stepping stone. However, I would venture to speculate that perhaps these same owners who are willing to feed uncooked meats to their animals, may also be willing to feed a proper, whole foods diet if provided with sufficient information about raw meaty bones and whole prey. Why not give them the benefit of the doubt? Why not arm them instead with information and resources which will enable them to feed their carnivores as nature has truly intended?

As a respected veterinary professional, you have the platform already established in order to persuade pet owners to follow your advice. If anything, promoting a mince product sets 'us' back, and further instils the belief into the public that they lack the ability to properly feed their own animals. It also gives further credence to processed pet food products in general, IMO.

With all that we know to be true about the natural feeding of carnivores such as dogs, cats and ferrets, why is ground up meat, veggies and fruits being marketed as a proper, *natural* diet?

I further wonder what it is that makes BARF mince products any different than the multitude of other pulverised meat and veggie pet foods?

Speaking of veggies, this also brings me to another question. I understand that you have been quoted as saying that veggies and fruits are a necessary part of the canine diet. Without seeing this paper, I cannot say if this was taken out of context, but is this really your view on the canine dietary requirements?

'Fruit and vegetables are an essential part of a dog's diet. An essential part, not an optional part. Meat is optional, fruit and vegetables are not.' ('Canine nutrition—a point of view', 1988)[17]

I truly hope that I have not offended you with this inquiry. I would hope to come to a better understanding of how you have arrived at your feeding philosophy which you currently promote. I think that we all share similar concerns about the health and welfare of pet carnivores. At the least, I would certainly love to foster that belief and give it justification.

With his past words and actions under scrutiny what did the BARFer do? He fled. Yes, that's right. Instead of attempting to justify the validity of his professional utterances and commercial output he disappeared back to the BARFer lair.

In his absence the Forum owners posted a rebuttal of the BARFer omnivore nonsense.

Nowadays BARFmania spews across the planet. Two essential cornerstones of the Raw Meaty Bones campaign, appropriate nutrients and appropriate texture, are obscured by BARF vegetable concoctions and sloppy textures. Regarding the vital third cornerstone, the need to combat the junk pet food/vet/fake animal welfare alliance, BARF manufacturers and retailers say and do nothing. They are a major part of the problem; they are dollar-hungry junk food merchants too.

BARFer Billinghurst's legacy will likely take a long time to remedy.

UC Davis vet school baloney

Michelle Rossi, long-time raw meaty bones feeder and campaigner, attempted to engage Jennifer A. Larsen, DVM, PhD, Dipl. ACVN, assistant professor in clinical nutrition at UC Davis in a discussion about natural diets for companion carnivores. Have a look at the nonsensical reply from Dr Larsen. See how instead of talking about natural diets, Dr Larsen switches discussion to 'home-cooked diets'.

Friday, 20 March 2009

Dear Michelle,

Thank you for sharing your concerns. Actually, we don't vilify home-cooked diets; in fact, our service may very well formulate more home-cooked diets that any other service in the world. We have a lot of experience with doing so, and are very comfortable with this way of feeding under controlled circumstances. I encourage you to visit our website to learn more about our activities.

Our approach is a bit less simplistic than you describe. We prefer to approach our cases more holistically; that is, we consider all aspects of an animal's underlying disease processes (including concurrent issues and specific clinical signs), owner preferences and concerns, and the home lifestyle of the client and the patient in order to develop a comprehensive nutritional management plan. Sometimes the plan will involve strategies that can be satisfied using commercially available diets; other cases require or prefer home-cooked diets. There is not a single best way to feed all animals.

However, it is critically important to properly formulate and prepare home-cooked diets to ensure their safety and nutritional adequacy. We frequently manage cases that have problems as the result of improper and inappropriate home-cooked diets. The pain and suffering of these animals is tragic, especially since it is completely preventable. It would be irresponsible to widely endorse home-cooked diets as a feeding option without providing prudent cautions with regard to potential adverse outcomes.

I can assure you that our approaches are based, as much as is possible, on evidence-based medicine, as well as our clinical experience and that of our colleagues at other institutions. Although we maintain mutually beneficial professional relationships with our colleagues employed by companies (which ultimately benefits our patients), our philosophies are not dictated or influenced by the marketing and preferences of pet food manufacturers.

Again, thank you for sharing your perspectives.

Sincerely,
Jennifer Larsen

———

Smokescreens and lies

News to hand indicates that vets with ties to the Hill's pet food monster have received a grant to report on (distorted) aspects of raw diets. See their research proposal. See how it's designed to mislead and deceive.

Nutritional adequacy and performance of raw food diets in kittens

Beth Hamper, DVM; Claudia Kirk, DVM, PhD, DACVN, DACVIM; Joseph Bartges, DVM, PhD, DACVN, DACVIM; University of Tennessee; $14,878

There are many benefits claimed for feeding raw food diets to cats, including improved immune function. Although 4% of US cat owners feed raw diets as all or part of their cat's diet, there are no published studies examining whether these diets are complete and balanced for feeding cats or whether immune function is improved in cats on a raw food diet. The goal of this study is to determine whether a commercially produced raw food diet and a homemade raw diet are nutritionally adequate for feeding kittens and whether these diets enhance immune function and improve digestibility. The outcomes to be measured include growth rate, feed efficiency, digestibility, and various blood and immune status parameters. The long-term goal is to evaluate ways of improving feline immune function through diet.

———

Our primary target must always be the cooked junk pet food/vet/ fake animal welfare alliance that does the greatest harm to the greatest number. Unfortunately, with BARF opportunists and other charlatans constantly on the make, we need to be vigilant and active on several fronts.

Wishing you fortitude and much success in your efforts.

Best wishes,
Tom

August 2009: UK veterinary scene

Dear Reader,

A majority of vets, when speaking about pet carnivore diets, say industrial food from the factory is *good*: nature's version, based on raw meaty bones, is *bad*.

Any sane person knows that's upside-down, back-to-front nonsense, made the more so since it's the collective view of so-called trained healthcare professionals. Why do the world's vets promote the bad and resist the good?

Could it be that vets and their institutions are tied up with the junk pet food factory owners, indeed the whole junk pet food industry? Does the first rule of medicine 'first do no harm' count for anything in the modern veterinary 'profession'? No, not much, judging by the performance of the UK veterinary profession.

In this newsletter we take a look at a few elements of the UK veterinary scene. I've included names and contact details in case you wish to address any concerns directly to the people involved.

Long term, I suggest we need to be more militant in our dealings with the aberrant vet profession. This year in the Royal College of Veterinary Surgeons Council Elections, I stood on a platform encouraging legal action against prominent vets and their junk pet food backers. 389 vets voted in favour.

Do your best, truth must finally out.

Cheers,
Tom

Pet Food Manufacturers Association dirty work

Do you know any unscrupulous, ignorant or desperate vets willing to do the dirty work? There's a job on offer (see ad below) at the UK Pet Food Manufacturers Association, the trade association for the junk pet food industry. They currently represent 56 companies including the vet John Burns and BARF suppliers Anglia Meat Products.[19]

Actually, it might be good fun if a few thousand pet owners, genuinely knowledgeable about pet feeding, applied for the job.

Please let us know if you get a response, interview appointment or are shortlisted. Good luck.

Nutrition and Information Executive—permanent London
Posted Wednesday, 15 July 2009
Pet Food Manufacturers Association

An exciting opportunity has come up to use your nutritional expertise working for the Pet Food Manufacturers Association, joining our young, energetic team based in central London.

One of your main responsibilities will be running our Veterinary and Nutrition Committee. You will also be responsible for taking forward the PFMA pet obesity campaign, which was successfully launched this year. Other responsibilities include our IT strategy, publications, as well as co-ordinating the running of the PFMA offices.

We are looking for someone with:
- excellent knowledge of pet nutrition
- experience dealing with pet obesity, possibly through running an obesity clinic
- well-developed writing skills
- good communicator and team player
- excellent administrative and organisational skills
- experience of Word, PowerPoint and Excel

Salary around £26,000 plus generous pension and health benefits.

How to apply
Please forward your application with CV and current remuneration to Michael Bellingham at michael@pfma.org.uk by Friday 7 August.

British Small Animal Veterinary Association (BSAVA) dog food study

As the name suggests, the British Small Animal Veterinary Association is the small animal division of the British Veterinary Association. They have a long history of conspiring with the junk pet food industry. Under the banner of Petsavers http://www.petsavers.org.uk/ the BSAVA produces publications and fronts 'research'. See what they say about feeding your kitten:

> Growing kittens have specific nutritional requirements, and the simplest way to fulfil them is to buy a good quality complete diet from a reputable manufacturer. For the first few days after your kitten comes home, continue to feed the food she's used to, to help prevent tummy upsets. Then you can gradually introduce a new food. Moist or dry? It's up to you. However, dried foods are more convenient to feed and help to keep your cat's teeth free from a build-up of tartar which can quickly lead to dental decay.

Of course, anyone with a modicum of knowledge knows that dental tartar is associated with rotten gums, not dental decay. But then the BSAVA have not been too concerned about either accuracy or empathy for their victims.

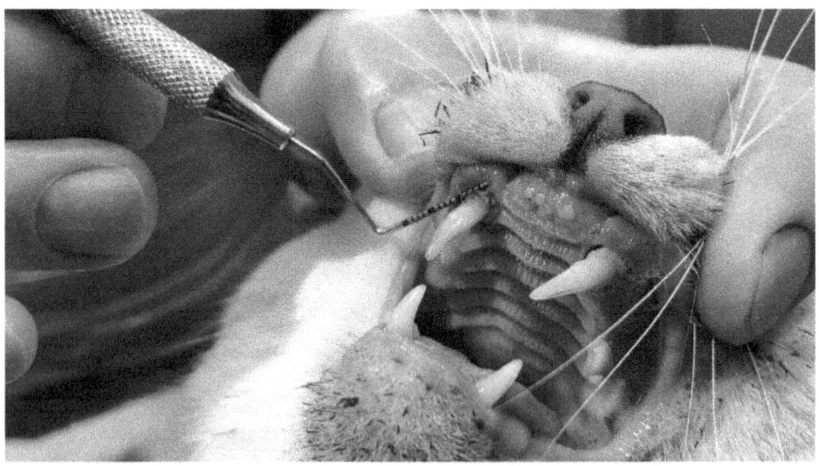

Kitty, six-year-old cat suffering the ravages of an artificial diet.[20]

See their 'pull'em out and chuck'em away' indifference to cats' teeth when they say in their junk pet food promotional booklet *Scamps Diary*:

> Don't worry if your vet says one or more of your cat's teeth need to be removed. Cats' gums are hard and tough, and even a toothless cat can eat crunchy dry food.

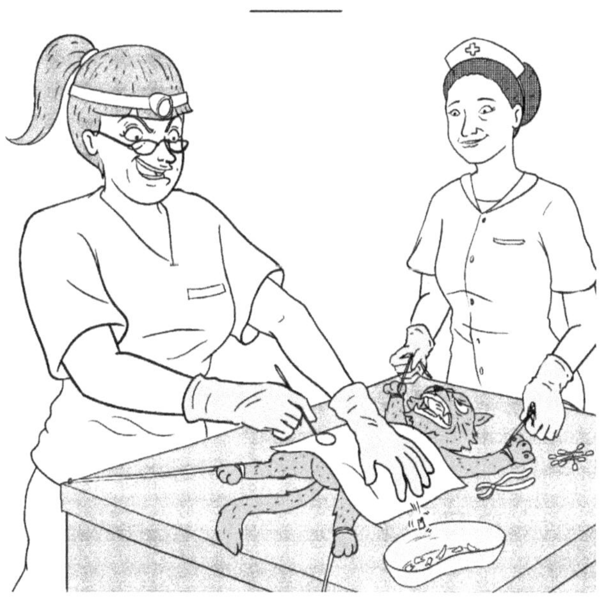

Lest there be any doubt, similar misleading and false information is promulgated by these BSAVA 'experts' for puppies too:

> Dog foods are broadly divided into two kinds, dry and moist. Provided that you get the correct food for his age, the choice of the food for your puppy is down to you and your pet.

BVA, BSAVA, PFMA—it's as if they are interlocked and interchangeable. Have a look at their policy brief condemning raw meaty bones.[16]

Seeing their open hostility to raw meaty bones, it should come as no surprise that the BSAVA Petsavers are funding a researcher at Glasgow Veterinary School, Emily Courcier MRCVS, Resident in Small Animal Evidence Based Medicine, to investigate the bacteria found in excrement from dogs fed a raw meaty bones diet.

If you've got a spare moment you might like to ask Ms Courcier what she knows about 'evidence-based medicine' and why this interest in the excrement of raw meaty bones fed dogs. Do they wish to raise a stink about bacteria in dog poo in an attempt to distract from the disgusting stench of veterinary corruption?

Royal College of Veterinary Surgeons elections 2009

In the March 2009 *RMB Newsletter* we talked about the discussion forums for vets, vet students and vet suppliers.[15]

During the several weeks of the campaign I posed six questions for the candidates to answer. Perfunctory answers were provided by three candidates to two of the questions. None of the sitting members of the RCVS Council replied to any question—however, they can never claim they did not know!

You can find the six questions together with the manifesto calling for legal action against the junk pet food collaborators in the endnote.[21]

RCVS election feedback

The RCVS asked for feedback on the discussions held on the www.vetsurgeon.org forum.[15] I replied as per the letter following. If you would like to add your voice then please contact the RCVS at registrar@rcvs.org.uk or profcon@rcvs.org.uk.

> Hi Lizzie,
>
> Thanks for the opportunity to comment.
>
> In my view, the RCVS Council forum was most definitely an improvement on previous years. Hustings ought to be a fundamental part of any democratic election process—free from interference by the establishment and the moderators.
>
> Whether a 'democratic process' is the best way to provide regulators for the profession is a question upon which I've written previously.

As can be seen from the debate or absence of debate on vetsurgeon.org and the *RMB Newsletter* that the profession at large and the candidates are woefully ignorant of the issues. (Some are arguably incompetent and corrupt.)

As part of my 18 years-long brief, I attempted to place information on the record—that being the least I could do in a hostile, uncomprehending environment.

As you know I stood on a platform recommending legal action against veterinary and pet food authorities. I believe that taking elements of my manifesto together with the discussions on vetsurgeon.org we can safely assume that the veterinary authorities have been put on notice. It may take time before these issues are finally actioned through the courts; however, it will not be possible to deny the historical record.[21]

Whether the courts use this information to arrive at their verdicts and whether this information assists the courts in arriving at penalties remains to be seen.

For my part, although the election forum was time consuming and taxing, I am grateful for the opportunity to serve the profession and the wider community.

Next year, I hope that you will continue this forum. Improvements could be made whereby all 40 existing councillors as well as the candidates could be encouraged to attend.

In the meantime, I trust that the RCVS Council will take note that 389 veterinary surgeons effectively lodged a complaint about massive corruption within our profession, that the RCVS is itself heavily implicated and that the RCVS should take urgent steps to resolve the issues.

Best wishes,
Tom

Translations

Have you noticed the array of brightly coloured flags at the bottom of the Raw Meaty Bones home page?[22]

Behind the flags is a story of countless hours of hard work by selfless volunteers who have translated *Work Wonders* and other documents. It goes without saying that the translators are busy people, but they still found time for this project and I am most grateful.

Thousands of pet owners now can access RMB information. Besides, if you want to learn another language, then here's an opportunity to read the English in tandem with German, French, Chinese etc.

There's scope for more translations. Japanese is missing, as is Italian. If you can translate into either of those languages or any other language and wish to give it a try, please let me know.

Perhaps the main two translations needed are the secret languages of 'Vetspeak' and 'Bureaucratese'. Try as we might, vets and bureaucrats fail to understand plain English—or for that matter any other language spoken by ordinary people. Any help, any suggestions, gratefully received.

By the way, exceptional vets Dr André Wassen translated the French, Dr Hanni Wienkoop translated the Finnish and vet student Sylvia Angélico translated the Portuguese.

Stop press: tidal wave of vomit

There's a tidal wave of vomit/puke/BARF coming your way according to a new report on the spread of junk raw pet food throughout North America.

They say:

Consumer demand for fresh pet food is on the rise, helped along by innovative new products based on technological advances and convenience features, frequent overlap into the high-growth natural/organic segment, heightened food safety concerns stemming from the sweeping pet food recalls of spring 2007, and the mobilisation of the raw/frozen pet food market via the formation of two industry groups: the North American Raw Petfood Association and the Canadian Association of Raw Pet Food Manufacturers.

Ominously they describe: 'competitive trends and forecasted market entry of mainstream major pet food players'.

OK, so it may be a good thing that cooked junk food is facing a challenge. Although it's basically an opportunity for Mars, Nestlé, Colgate and Procter & Gamble to enter the puke production business at a time of their choosing. And you can bet the lapdog vet schools and vets will do as they're told and promote their handlers' 'new best ever puke diet'.

But to me, it's all a travesty that need not be. In the early 1990s the Raw Meaty Bones campaign set the standard, promoting the essential three components of a coherent strategy for health. (See Three-part test, p. 150.)

BARFer Billinghurst, as long-time readers know, misappropriated key elements of the RMB strategy to launch his Altered Reality Fantasy Diet (BARF).[17]

After some years, some BARFers seeing the absurdity of their position plagiarised even more Raw Meaty Bones information and set themselves up as self-proclaimed experts. They renamed themselves prey modellers, and whilst they do espouse much Raw Meaty Bones theory, they retain their BARFer obsession with ingredients—the prey model cult being especially keen on some mad formula of 80% meat, 10% offal and 10% bone in the dog's bowl.[22]

What have the world's pets done to deserve this combined assault by cooked junk food makers, BARFers and prey modellers? Is there any high ground that pets and concerned owners can occupy until the tidal wave recedes?

Possibly there is, and I suggest a good start would be to seek sanctuary at the Raw Meaty Bones website.[23]

Until next time, try to stay afloat and keep cheerful.

Tom

November 2009: Introducing Professor Scarr

G'day Reader,

Forty-one degrees Celsius here today (105.8 degrees Fahrenheit) and hotting up for Christmas. How are you? How are your pets? Are you looking forward to the festive season and then soon 2010?

Will the pace of life slow down a bit next year? I hope so and I'm planning to ask Santa.

Do you contemplate what's needed to stop the junk pet food inspired madness; how to make vets accountable for the mass poisoning of their patients and the cynical exploitation of their clients; how to help pet owners see through the hollow vet profession?

For sure there can be many answers. Two things seem to me to be essential to the long-term success of our campaign.

First, we need a critical mass of pet owners who understand the fundamentals of the three-part test. (See p. 150.)

Second, we need champions who go out and about in the community and in the professions spreading the word. Since the junk pet food industry and the corrupted thinking arising contaminates many otherwise learned professions, then we need champions in those professions. We need medical researchers, dentists, biologists, ecologists, lawyers, social scientists, politicians and regulators who clearly see the damage done by the junk pet food cult and see in turn the benefits to be had when we turn through 180 degrees and start rebuilding nutrition, science, medicine and the pet feeding economy based on sound RMB principles.

Social scientist Professor Sandra Scarr was Commonwealth Professor of Psychology at the University of Virginia and an award-winning researcher in behavioural genetics and developmental psychology. See her Wikipedia entry.[24]

Nowadays Professor Scarr breeds Labradors on her coffee farm in Hawaii. She's also taken up the pen in support of the RMB cause. I've borrowed her blog entry 'How to feed a puppy to healthy adulthood' article for this newsletter. It's an excellent, practical reminder of how easy feeding raw meaty bones can be.

Wishing you a relaxing and healthful Christmas,
Tom

How to feed a puppy to healthy adulthood

As a breeder, I offer the following advice to puppy buyers, in the hope they will continue to feed my beautiful puppies a raw-meaty-bones diet that will nourish them to heathy adulthood.

History: I began breeding Labs eight years ago. At first I fed the dogs commercial kibble that I was told was 'premium quality', guaranteed to be '100% compete and balanced'. Several dogs had itchy skin, ear irritations/infections, and poor coats. One had sore joints. Veterinarians prescribed antihistamines, steroids and antibiotics. The poor dogs were constantly receiving some kind of medication to alleviate their 'allergy' and joint problems.

Fortunately, against vet advice, I also fed the dogs some raw meats and raw meaty bones three or four times a week to keep their teeth clean and gums healthy.

After seven months of feeding commercial pet foods, and observing 'allergy' problems, ear infections, itchiness and other irritations, I consulted an alternative vet, who told me she will not even treat dogs that are fed commercial pet foods, because those foods cause so many health problems.

Thus began my voyage toward raw feeding. The alternative vet recommended a BARF (Bones and Raw Food) diet, which I prepared at home. Almost immediately, the dogs' 'allergies', ear infections, and itchiness disappeared, and they became notably healthier and happier.

The 'super-premium', '100% complete and balanced' kibble

that other vets recommend and sell was causing my Labs' health problems (and even worse health problems for tens of millions of other pets).

Today I feed my 14 dogs (and cat) raw meaty bones (RMB). Remember, you are feeding a friendly wolf, whose normal diet consists of whole prey—raw meat, organs and meaty bones. Dogs are actually a subspecies of grey wolf. Dogs did not evolve to eat or digest grains and cooked foods. Commercial pet foods are not digested well and come out as huge, smelly poops. RMB-fed dogs have a third as much poop, and it doesn't smell! The health benefits of feeding a species-appropriate diet are enormous.

How to feed raw meaty bones

In Hawaii, we may not find the variety of meats that are available on the mainland or in Australia, especially various kinds of game, but we can feed a healthy variety of meaty bones and organ meats.

You don't have to cook anything. You just shop for meats and meaty bones, and hand your dog large hunks of meat and meaty bones, preferably outside where he'll make less of a mess.

Because I have so many mouths to feed, I buy beef soup bones (very meaty), whole beef hearts, whole beef livers, and green tripe from a local wholesaler. I buy cases of whole chickens from Costco. Also at Costco, I buy whole beef rounds, beef and pork ribs, and pork loins. At Thanksgiving, I stock my freezer with turkeys on sale.

Depending on how many pets and how much freezer space you have, you may want to order wholesale or purchase what you need at your local grocery store. Local grocery stores and meat shops can supply local meats that are not treated with hormones and antibiotics, and local fish, inexpensive beef hearts, meaty bones, fish trimmings, and scraps.

Puppies under a year should be fed approximately 2% to 3% of their adult weight (70 lb for a Lab) every day, which is 1.4 to 2.1 lb of food per day. They are growing very fast and need a lot of animal proteins and fats.

- From 2 to 4 months, puppies should be fed three times a day, so you can divide 1.4 to 2 lb of food into three servings. If he does not eat it all in 10 to 15 minutes, put away the remainder for another meal. Adjust how much you feed to his appetite. Young puppies do not usually overeat.
- Older puppies, 4 to 12 months, can be fed twice a day. Again, divide 1.4 to 2 lb of food into two servings. At this age, he will probably eat it all and act like he needs more. If he seems slim, increase his food allowance. If he is chubby, don't give into his 'I'm starving' tactics. Most well-exercised puppies don't get fat on a RMB diet, because they are growing fast and need all the protein and fat calories to grow.

Adult dogs, over 12 months, should be fed 1% to 2% of their adult weight once a day. **Watch your dog's waistline. Do not overfeed.** Adjust feeding to your dog's activity level and metabolism. You should be able to feel his ribs as you pass your hand lightly along his side. If you have to press hard to feel ribs, he's overweight. Reduce his portions. You should not be able to see his ribs, however. If he is too thin, increase the amount you feed. My dogs do not get fat on adult portions of raw meaty bones, but your dog is an individual with his own individual metabolism. Just keep an eye on his waistline.

Here are suggestions for a varied diet for a Labrador retriever in puppyhood and adulthood. Vary his food from day to day and week to week, just as you vary your family's food. You can mix and match within the daily ration. You don't have to 'balance' every meal—just try to get some poultry with bones, red meats and meaty bones, and organ meats into his weekly diet. Raw eggs three or four times a week are great in the diet.

- A quarter to a half a chicken. Raw chicken is a great basic food for your puppy, because he can chew up and digest the meat and bones.
- Whole chicken frames (carcasses after most meat is removed, have lots of edible bone)
- Meaty beef bones (lots of meat to chew off ribs or round bones with marrow). Do not feed hard beef leg or knuckle bones with little or no meat on them, because dogs can break their teeth trying to chew them.
- Beef hunks large enough that dogs have to tear them and chew, not swallow them whole.
- Beef or pork liver, kidney and green tripe hunks that require chewing. Organ meats should be 10% to 20% of the dog's diet. More may give him loose stools.
- Beef heart chunks, great for chewing.
- Whole small fish and big hunks of larger fish. Trimmings and guts from large fish are fine.
- Two to four raw eggs with crushed shells (good vitamin and calcium source).
- Pork and beef ribs—meaty slabs of 3 or 4 ribs. He won't eat all the rib bones, but he'll enjoy chewing on them. Throw away leftover bones.
- Lamb or mutton hunks and meaty bones (expensive here).
- Pork loin hunks, pork shoulder, if not too fatty.
- Whole rabbits, quail, venison parts, and other game you can find.

You can add or substitute turkey parts, chicken gizzards, chicken livers, goat, venison and any large meaty parts. Think whole prey and how to simulate that in your dog's RMB diet.

Some poultry and beef parts are too small to be safe. Puppies will be tempted to swallow them whole and may choke. Do not feed him chicken necks, chicken wings, or any small bones he can swallow.

Never feed cooked bones—they splinter and can damage your dog's throat or intestines.

Other foods

My dogs love avocados, which are a good source of vegetable fats and vitamins. Some also like bananas, apples, papayas and various cooked vegetables. These can be used as treats or occasional supplements to meaty meals. I also add 2 or 3 fish oil capsules once a day for more omega 3 and 6 fatty acids (probably not necessary but an old habit).

Do feed kitchen and table scraps occasionally. My dogs love meat trimmings and leftovers, cooked vegetables, pasta, cheeses of all kinds, yogurt and so forth. Table scraps should be a minor part of the diet, a little variety to round out his nutrition. Dogs do not need sweets, especially chocolate, which is poisonous to dogs.

Feeding large hunks of meat and meaty bones cleans his teeth, gets his digestive juices working, and provides all the vitamins and minerals he needs.

Remember you are feeding a carnivore, who will live a long, healthy life with a diet that is high in animal proteins and fats and low in carbohydrates. Even the most 'super-premium' kibbles and canned foods are largely cooked carbohydrates, an inappropriate diet for carnivores, a diet that causes periodontal disease, that stresses their immune systems, and makes them susceptible to major chronic disorders, such as diabetes, cancers, heart, liver and kidney diseases.

You will save a lot of money on vet bills throughout his

life. His teeth and gums will stay healthy and will not need expensive veterinary cleanings under anesthesia. He is not likely to develop chronic debilitative diseases that cost a fortune to treat and cause unnecessary suffering for the poor animal.

For more detailed guidance on why and how to feed Raw Meaty Bones, look at www.rawmeatybones.com[23] or read Tom Lonsdale's books, *Work Wonders*, and *Raw Meaty Bones*.

Your puppy will thank you for his raw meaty bones with great health and happiness.

Reproduced with kind permission of Professor Sandra Scarr.

Widespread hypocrisy and public lynching

Under the heading 'London vet struck off for dishonesty and misleading clients'[25] the Royal College of Veterinary Surgeons reported:

> On 19 May 2009, the Disciplinary Committee (DC) directed that Kfir Segev, of the Medivet practice in Stanmore, London, should be removed from the Register, having found him guilty of serious professional misconduct for deliberately concealing from his clients that their dog was terminally ill, whilst at the same time recommending that she undergo expensive and unnecessary procedures.

I don't presume to know the detail of the case nor the appropriate sentence for Mr Segev. Being struck off the register is potentially a life sentence that deprives a person of status and opportunity to earn a living. But I do know that the veterinary profession is a bastion of evil hypocrisy where the everyday activity of many vets involves concealment of known facts concerning the life-threatening consequences of the diets they recommend and sell. Capitalising on the progressive ill health of the unfortunate animals and their trusting owners, a majority of vets set about offering expensive and unnecessary procedures.

Does the public lynching of Mr Segev in some way exculpate the veterinary authorities? Just the opposite, is my view. I would like to see the veterinary authorities prosecuted to the full extent of the law. They are doubly accountable by virtue of their specialist knowledge and position of trust.

2009 Ferret Symposium, Sydney, Australia

Once again the organisers, Shirley Hewett, Shona Whaite and Saskia Hornig, did a terrific job and arguably it was an even more successful event than in 2008. Sydney tops Melbourne yet again!

International guests arrived from the US. Zooarchaeologist Bob Church gave a preliminary report on his wide-ranging survey of ferret diets and health in relation to lifestyle and environment. Suffice to say, the ferrets living and eating as did their wild polecat ancestors were much the healthiest.

Shona and Saskia spoke about their mouse breeding projects. In the space of a year they've researched, developed and are running highly efficient breeding programs providing excellent nutrition for hungry ferrets.

Dr Lyn Mathison and Dr David Neck showed X-ray images of multiple bone fractures in young ferrets fed calcium deficient diets. Precise dietary details were unknown. However, it was suggested that the young ferrets had been fed chunks of raw meat with occasional chicken wings (bones too big for tiny mouths and thus not eaten) and in another instance the young ferrets were fed predominantly day-old chicks.

Some years ago it was fairly common for butchers' puppies and kittens, fed exclusively raw meat, to suffer folding fractures. Instead of counselling the butchers to feed their carnivore pets on whole carcasses or a diet based on raw meaty bones, the vets intimidated the butchers into feeding junk food.

Dr Mathison and Dr Neck did not recommend junk food as the

solution. They cautioned the audience that when feeding a natural diet it's important to get it right. I was especially gratified that Dr Neck referred the audience to *Work Wonders* for the basic dietary recommendations: ideally feed whole carcasses of suitable size or in the absence of whole carcasses feed a diet based on raw meaty bones.

Raw Meaty Bones: U-turn Seminar (with Chinese translation)

On Sunday 11 October I had the special pleasure of speaking with the veterinary students at South China Agricultural University. Haven Qi, pioneer raw meaty bones feeder, did a terrific job arranging the event. Dr Yizhou Chen was our gracious host who introduced the event and then took us for a delightful lunch washed down with cool beer. The room was packed with students for what we believe to be the first RMB seminar in China. Here's looking forward to many more such events.

Thanks to all.

Subtle errors can be catastrophic

In 1983 Korean Air Lines Flight 007 was shot down over the Soviet Union with loss of all 269 passengers and crew. Due to navigational error the plane had strayed into Russian airspace.[26]

In a recent *Animal Lab News* article Barbara Mickelson PhD talked about minor dietary changes in rodent diets having the potential for significant impacts on the experimental results.

But dogs, cats and ferrets, whether or not in research cages, mostly consume diets varying enormously from the natural standard. What about the confounded experimental results being churned out by scientists who feed junk food to their experimental dogs, cats and ferrets?

Maybe the consequences are not as immediately shocking as 269 people being shot out of the sky, but erroneous research evidence can have adverse consequences for millions.

10

———

2010: TWO DECADES ON: PROGRESS AND ROADBLOCKS

After two decades of RMB campaigning, obstacles become ever more onerous. The RCVS remains a bastion of corruption. Sydney University's obduracy reaches new lows. BARFers are on the march and pet food corruption gains easy access to China.

March 2010: Plagiarism and sabotage

Hello,

Welcome to *RMB Newsletter 10:1*. Yes, this is the tenth year of publication and it's twenty years since the Raw Meaty Bones campaign got underway.

How were your last ten years? Can you remember events from twenty years ago? I hope you have lots of pleasant memories and are off to a good start for 2010 and the remainder of the decade.

Standing at this point on the journey, looking back over twenty years, I've got mixed feelings. In the early 1990s we had clarity and conviction. A small group of Australian vets had effectively cracked the carnivore code. Although a tiny realisation—and obvious enough if you think about it—carnivores need their food and medicine to be *raw*, *meaty* and contain *bones*.

I use 'carnivore code' to suggest a wonderful series of pathways regulating the internal environment of the carnivore which simultaneously brings about regulation of the carnivore's external environment.

Texture provided the key to the code. Elephants eat trees but fare badly on a diet of sawdust. Rabbits eat herbage. Their constantly growing teeth need the abrasion of tough bark, roots and dry vegetation to keep their teeth in good order. Carnivores, take lions for example, make a point of hunting large dangerous prey and thus obtain the nutrients and texture of food and medicine necessary for survival.

Although confronted by a hostile junk pet food, veterinary and fake animal welfare alliance, in the early days the Raw Meaty Bones Lobby made good progress. We were able to establish guidelines requiring that carnivorous pets (dogs, cats and ferrets) should be fed a Raw Meaty Bones diet—whole raw carcasses where possible and failing that a diet of predominantly raw meaty bones. The institutions, industries and professions that profited from and perpetuated the mass poisoning of pets were to be exposed and pressured to change.

But here's the conundrum: if the RMB Campaign is so important, why, after twenty years, isn't it more successful? Why isn't a Raw Meaty Bones diet every pet owner's first choice?[1]

How do the junk pet food collaborators get away with the mass poisoning of pets with hardly a murmur of protest anywhere?

An easy answer might be that the junk pet food collaborators are cashed-up and as strong as ever. Whilst this is undoubtedly true, I believe that the main reasons for poor progress, the muddle and confusion is directly attributable to the BARFers, prey modellers and holistics. Their pursuit of power, profit and prestige has seen essential RMB principles variously plagiarised, sabotaged and suppressed.

Let's take a look at the origins and activities of the prey model cult.

Best wishes,
Tom

Prey model cult

Have you heard of the so-called prey model diet—that obsession with dietary ingredients and percentages of ingredients that at one level imitates the Raw Meaty Bones diet, but then distorts and distracts from key principles? Imitation, they say, is the greatest compliment. Perhaps —but plagiarism and sabotage don't rate highly in anyone's estimation.

Some people use the term RMB diet and prey model diet interchangeably. By blurring the edges, those who plagiarise the RMB information gain some illicit credibility—they use stolen goods as if they were the rightful owners. However, the majority of people calling themselves prey modellers should not be blamed. They don't know the history and are prevented from knowing the detail. They are victims of the prey model leadership's ambitions.

Sordid history

Back in the early 1990s, BARFer Billinghurst misappropriated RMB principles in his bid to elevate his puke/vomit/BARF diet. Nominally and for a time he was a member of the RMB Lobby. However, at the height of the battle with the junk pet food/vet alliance, Billinghurst made a battlefield defection to the other side. At a crucial juncture, the defection served to sabotage the RMB Campaign and establish the BARFer as a junk food producer.[2]

Initially Dr Billinghurst, aided by Jane Anderson (formerly Johnson) gathered quite a following of people who called themselves Born Again Raw Feeders (BARFers). Proliferation of Anderson's BARF-ring of websites and discussion groups ensured that a naive and impressionable populace were duped into feeding their carnivores an omnivorous diet.

Things changed when in 2001 the BARFers read *Raw Meaty Bones: Promote Health*.

They were taken aback to discover that they had been hoodwinked and in the process hoodwinked a vast number of pet owners.

However, the BARF leadership had tasted power and prestige and experienced the ease with which it's possible to dupe a poorly informed and exploited community. Civil war broke out. Dr Billinghurst was ostracised from key BARF groups which then began, surreptitiously, to change their stance. Next Jane Anderson misappropriated the name 'RMB Lobby' and registered a Yahoo group under that name—effectively destroying key elements of the RMB Campaign.

Anderson and her associates then set about reinventing themselves as 'Prey Modellers'. Effectively this constituted a brazen misappropriation and relabelling of Raw Meaty Bones info. (Like a stolen car receiving a paint job.) Essential elements of the Raw Meaty Bones Three-Part Test were either trivialised or trashed. (See p. 150.) Instead Prey Model self-styled experts told pet owners they needed to feed a bizarre formula of 80% meat, 10% bone and 10% offal.

At that time, 2004–2005, there was some contact between the Raw Meaty Bones and Prey Model camps. In an attempt to get clear concise and practical information on the record, I published *Work Wonders*—against the wishes of the Prey Modellers. Yes, they told me not to publish the book.

Still taking an optimistic line, I tried logic and reason. But to no avail. Indeed, honest discussion is specifically banned. I was kicked off the Rawvet and all other Prey Model discussion lists for daring to challenge the authority of the Prey Model priesthood.[3]

So what's to be done? With the junk pet food/vet/fake welfare alliance in the ascendant, and the plagiarists and niche marketers peddling their influence—and simultaneously sabotaging sound RMB sense—we need a plan. We need to get the issues onto the table where the evidence can be seen and debated. Perhaps this newsletter will help get things underway.

Raw Meaty Bones medicine

We know that Nature knows best and that Hippocrates, more than 2,000 years ago, taught that food is the best medicine. Pet owners are beginning to rediscover the ancient wisdom and my mailbox often contains messages from delighted pet owners.

Tracey Slingerland, a client whose memory goes back to the beginning of the Raw Meaty Bones campaign, wrote:

> We have recently had to give dietary advice to family members who were given a bum steer by their vet. They have a beagle with severe skin itching and infection. They were told

to use 100s of dollars' worth of shampoos, scrubs and bedding sanitiser, to go along with the very expensive 'special' dog food they sell at the surgery. They did all that was recommended for more than a month to make absolutely no change other than to make her smell pretty, and to waste *a lot* of their time. After talking with them one weekend, we suggested a raw meaty bones diet, gave them your book to read, and told them of our 20 years of success on your recommendations. You will never guess ... well maybe you can. That's right ... the beagle was put on a strict raw meaty bone diet of lamb flaps, chicken carcasses and roo tails, and surprise surprise, after just 10 days she stopped her incessant itching, the bleeding stopped, the sores started clearing up and she no longer is a neurotic mental mess.

Christina wrote:

I was reluctant to feed RMBs to my dogs after being brought up to believe they cause damage. I am now a RMB convert and my dogs couldn't be better or happier. The skin conditions have gone, as have the anal gland problems and cleaning up poo up is almost a pleasure! It is great to see them happily gnawing at them and I wonder why I ever had doubts when it is all so natural. I have passed your book around and promoted the change to all doggy folk I meet, I am a trainee groomer so meet a lot of them! A lot of people tell me 'I thought it was dodgy to give dogs bones', so there is a lot of re-educating required, but they are all amazed by my enthusiasm and the huge changes my dogs have experienced, some even ask me how to make the change.

To my mind these are valuable firsthand experiences that need to be shared.

Do you have a similar experience to recount? Did your dog/cat/

ferret come alive after a change of diet—when all the modern treatments failed?

Some breeders report that puppies and kittens are born healthier and stronger; that births are easier and caesareans fewer when the mothers are fed a RMB diet. Often owners report improved skin health, recovery from liver disease and kidney ailments. Others tell me of the marked improvement in behaviour: how difficult, nervous and untrainable dogs become content on a raw meaty bones diet.

If you have documented cases of improvements or cure and instances where vet bills plummeted after switching to a raw meaty bones diet, please drop me a line. In particular, I would be pleased to hear about owners' experiences treating diabetes and exocrine pancreatic insufficiency (EPI).

Thanks in advance,
Tom

David Taylor MP

It's with sadness that I report the untimely passing of David Taylor MP. Many parliamentary colleagues and constituents offered up eulogies to the wonderful man of courage, integrity and kindness.

Paul Flynn MP's account of the funeral reflects the extent of our loss.[4]

You can find David Taylor's first ever statement in support of Raw Meaty Bones in the British parliament in the early day motions.[5]

See how Mr Taylor so skilfully leads pompous vets to skewer themselves on their own barbed rhetoric. (See p. 208.)

David Taylor's legacy lives and will thrive as we build on his work.

March 2010: Rotten callous venal sham

Dear Reader,

Welcome to this second *RMB Newsletter* for 2010. And a special welcome to all new subscribers.

Please take a moment to review previous editions of the *Newsletter* and thereby get a feel for the struggles against the junk pet food/vet/fake animal welfare alliance.

The practical aspects of feeding carnivores are the easy bit to understand and implement. Get the nutrients and texture right and you'll have the best food and medicine sorted out in one easy action. Don't let anyone complicate the issue with fanciful obsessions about the pet's bowl, ingredients and ratios. For easy, efficient, economical advice go to the pet owners section of the Raw Meaty Bones website.[1]

Now back to the hard part.

In this upside-down, back-to-front world those responsible for healing the sick and comforting the afflicted are in fact largely responsible for the mass poisoning of pets. Worldwide the veterinary profession perpetrates a rotten callous venal sham.

The trouble starts with governments who, when faced with the complexities of modern veterinary science, delegate authority to vets for all aspects of the health and disease of animals. After all, governments reason, if it takes four or five years at university to learn the intricacies then society must defer to the trained experts.

But straight away we can see the fallacy. By granting the vets absolute power in respect to the health and welfare of animals, governments set the the scene for absolute corruption. 'Power tends to corrupt, and absolute power corrupts absolutely.'

Let's take another look at the Royal College of Veterinary Surgeons, 18 years after they were first informed of the mass poisoning of pets and the mass deception of pet owners.

Best wishes,
Tom

Rotten Callous Venal Sham (RCVS)

Chances are that if you keep a pet you've been on the receiving end of the rotten, callous, venal sham that passes for veterinary care. Instead of the vet recommending a healthful, life-saving natural diet, you will likely have been cornered and coerced into a guilt trip. You will have been browbeaten and nigh-on ordered to feed your pet the packaged junk on the vet's shelves.

Professor Sandra Scarr comments: 'Some vets are quite crazed ... so blinded by pet food dogma, they can't practise medicine responsibly.' Others tell of ranting, apoplectic vets screaming about imagined bacterial diseases and blocked intestines. They speak about the same vets milking them of thousands of dollars pursuing worthless tests, prescribing dangerous medicines and still no solution for their pet's chronic ailments. But fortuitously, by searching the internet, the pet owners tell how they discovered the benefits of a raw meaty bones diet and the dog, otherwise condemned to a slow death, turns a corner and becomes like a puppy again.

Unfortunately, the junk food problem runs as part of the narrative at all levels of the vet profession in all countries of the world. Although it's true that some veterinary regulatory bodies and some veterinary associations have not yet been confronted over their disgraceful activities. (Hint to those in America, start badgering the state veterinary boards now.) Whilst ignorance is no defence, they can purport to be unaware of the depravity of their crimes.

In the UK, the Royal College of Veterinary Surgeons, governing body of the vet profession overseeing some 21,000 registered vets, cannot plead ignorance. Since 1992 they've received numerous documents[6] and several copies of *Raw Meaty Bones: Promote Health*. Every year since 1997 I've contested the RCVS council elections.[7]

In the early days my esteemed college lecturers, the late Oliver Graham-Jones FRCVS (longtime RCVS councillor) and Arthur Hayward MRCVS, provided nominations and testimonials. More recently Bill Miller, Roger Meacock and Alan Bennet have lent their support.

Each year about 10% of voters support the campaign. That's around 350 vets who, by voting for RMB, register a complaint of massive malfeasance against the veterinary authorities—nigh on a complaint that the RCVS actively or passively condones the mass poisoning of pets, dupes pet owners and veterinary students throughout the UK.

Here's the 500-word RCVS election statement for this year:

Biography

I graduated from the RVC (University of London) in 1972. Some fifteen years later I gained first inkling that most of my carnivore patients were suffering diet-induced diseases. Careful investigation revealed that the veterinary profession, colluding with pet food makers and so-called animal welfare groups, had falsified the records regarding preventable diseases and premature death affecting millions of pets. (Harold Shipman,[8] a notorious medical practitioner and mass murderer, hid in plain sight behind falsified records too!)

Despite establishment disbelief and denial, there is a scientifically sound solution understood by thousands of conscientious pet owners: raw meaty bones promote health. In 1991, part blowing the whistle and part sharing a simple concept with profound health benefits, I published 'Oral disease in cats and dogs'.[9]

In 1992 I delivered the 'Pandemic of periodontal disease' lecture, chaired by Richard Le Couteur (now professor at UC Davis) and attended by six academic vets including Professor David Church and Dr Jill Maddison (now of RVC). Dr Richard Malik attended and has since made significant contributions.[10] Otherwise, the information was treated with contempt by an arrogant assembly.

If the vet establishment refused to act, then I would. Since 1992 I have worked to solve the gravest issue facing pet health and the veterinary profession in the 21st century.

Manifesto

From the outset a corrupt veterinary establishment fought back. I was subjected to several bogus disciplinary actions and threatened with jail. To avoid harassment and find time to write, I sold the practice in 1997 and in 2001 published *Raw Meaty Bones: Promote Health*.

During the election period the book can be downloaded for free at www.vetsurgeon.org. Please read the book and consider the range of options available for reforming our sick profession.

Clearly our veterinary 'educational' institutions, political structures and representatives have not helped; in fact they've done untold harm. We need a wide-ranging inquiry leading to the creation of a new Veterinary Surgeons Act. The prostitution of our profession must stop, and a scientific renaissance could follow. For wider commentary see *RMB Newsletter* archives.[11]

Institutions and individuals should be held accountable. Veterinary students deserve a better deal. We can launch lawsuits against veterinary schools that perpetuate false and misleading information in support of their junk pet food sponsors.[12]

Junk pet food companies have infiltrated the highest levels of our profession. A chief scientist for Mars and a sales manager for Hill's are past presidents of the RCVS! Another past president is in receipt of junk pet food largesse and a councillor coordinates the 'Pet Smile' scam. Twelve councillors represent the vet schools—all in receipt of junk pet food hush money.

On a community level we can hold client information evenings and generally encourage discussion and understanding. Roger Meacock and I are available to address student groups, university faculties and professional meetings.

> In our daily work we can practise what we preach: to ensure the welfare of the animals committed to our care.
>
> Please use your vote strategically. Vote only for those who can be relied on to deal with the gravest issue facing our profession in the 21st century. Thank you.

Given the magnitude of the issues, you might expect that other candidates might campaign for reform of the Rotten Callous Venal Sham. Alas, we are dealing with a veterinary profession corrupt to the core; rather than hide in the shadows; pimps and pet food tarts solicit for votes.

Invoking the ghost of Harold Shipman

We expect doctors to be conscientious and kind to their patients—not to knowingly, systematically kill them. So imagine the trauma in the UK when it was discovered that medical doctor Harold Shipman had murdered 250 and possibly more of his elderly patients. See Wikipedia.[9]

Shipman's killing spree led to the establishment of a major inquiry costing the UK government £21 million and resulting in a major shake-up in the medical profession.[13] Shipman hanged himself in Wakefield prison in 2004. Nowadays his ghost surely hovers over the UK medical profession as it seeks to guard against future such atrocities.

I mentioned Shipman in the RCVS election manifesto (above) for one very important reason. Shipman killed 250 of his patients. For vets, the mass killing of their patients, numbering in the thousands, is a regular part of the job. And I'm not talking about the euthanasia of pets or the humane destruction of farm animals. No, I'm referring to the disease and death most vets mete out to their small animal patients as a matter of course.

By steadfastly insisting that pets be fed junk food, vets either know or should know that they are killing their patients. They bluff, they bluster and seek to deny the obvious. But it's increasingly clear to anyone with an ounce of common sense that a majority of vets are hiding behind transparent lies.

So let's invoke the ghost of Harold Shipman, let's lobby political leaders the world over to set up commissions of inquiry into the corrupt, death delivering vet profession. Please send this newsletter and any supporting information to your political representatives, to your local newspapers, radio and television and demand that the widespread maiming and killing of pets by vets be stopped.

Google and other search engines can provide all the contact details you need.

Please let us have feedback and good luck. Our pets and the wider community need us to succeed.

July 2010: Conniving veterinary establishment

Dear Reader,

How are things in your neck of the woods? I trust you and your carnivore companions are well and enjoying life.

How time flies! Back in April my wife, stepdaughter and I were treated to fine hospitality during a two-week lecture tour of Auckland, Christchurch and Tauranga, New Zealand.

Dr Lyn Thomson, family, staff and friends worked wonders to make the event a success. Lyn runs Raw Essentials, a diet consultancy and RMB supply service in Auckland. As the leading pioneer turning feral pests (rabbits, hares and possums) into food for urban carnivores, Lyn sets the standard.

A big thank you to Lyn, Richard, Libby, Olly, Kathy, Hailey, Conny and all.

———

As a reader of this newsletter, you know that we seek to combat the multifaceted pet food fraud. You know that:

1. Junk food (BARF pap included) neither cleans teeth nor massages the gums. Foul-smelling septic mouths then poison the rest of the body.
2. Junk food 'nutrients' flood through a pet's system via the capillaries and lymph vessels of the small intestine. Internal organs and the immune system are under constant siege.
3. Junk food residues sitting in the large bowel feed trillions of harmful bacteria. Toxic waste products in contact with the bowel wall create local damage before passing into the blood stream to adversely affect the rest of the body.
4. Arising from the above three assaults on their health, the majority of pets become prematurely aged with stinking breath, vile skin, dysfunctional immune systems, and diseased kidneys, hearts, livers and joints, all of which lead to a miserable life and an untimely death. But before death brings a merciful relief, the helpless, voiceless

pets are poked full of toxic pharmaceuticals, costing owners billions of dollars.

When you contemplate the suffering of millions of junk pet food affected pets, who do you blame? Do you blame the dogs, cats and ferrets for eating the stuff? What about the owners? Do you think they should be pilloried for their inattention to the basic needs of carnivores? Do you blame the RSPCA, People for the Ethical Treatment of Animals (PETA) and other fake animal welfare societies? Many folks put the responsibility squarely at the feet of the massive multinational poisoners: Mars, Nestlé, Colgate-Palmolive and Procter & Gamble.

As a vet who's seen the reality up close, I'm disappointed that pets become addicted to the junk food and that their owners are caught in a trap feeding their pets' addiction. Unfortunately, they are easy prey for the cashed-up and unscrupulous. And as much as I despise the multinational corporations, I do understand that they are simply working the capitalist system within, for the most part, participatory democracies. So who do I hold chiefly responsible for the cruelty, ill health, economic and environmental disaster flowing from the junk pet food industry? The conniving veterinary establishment, that's who I blame.

Worldwide, vets are presented with the evidence in their surgeries every hour of every working day. Sadly, though, the vet practitioners have mostly been dumbed down and rendered insensible to what appears before them. They enter the vet schools as impressionable young people and sit with open mouths as they are spoonfed junk pet food inspired nonsense by their university teachers. Let's be clear: the folks who run the system and place their imprimatur on the mass poisoning of pets are the universities, the veterinary associations and the veterinary regulatory authorities.

In Sydney, a key pillar of the conniving veterinary establishment is Sydney University.

Let's take a look.

Best wishes,
Tom

Sydney University conniving veterinary establishment

Undergraduate students receive a thorough brainwashing in the veterinary faculty of the University of Sydney. Visitors to the veterinary outpatient clinic might suspect that it's a showroom for Hill's junk pet foods. Flashy posters and racks of Hill's Science Diet proclaim the allegiance of the university to their benefactors Hill's, a division of Colgate-Palmolive.

In 2009 I lodged a freedom of information inquiry in an attempt to learn more about the University's Faustian pact with junk pet food makers. The university disclosed that it had a memorandum of understanding with Hill's Pet Nutrition, but refused to reveal the contents.

Besides brainwashing undergraduate vets, Sydney University also runs a Centre for Veterinary Education (CVE) specialising in the postgraduate education (more brainwashing) of vets in the community. In a previous incarnation the CVE was known as the Post Graduate Foundation in Veterinary Science. And for some years the directors actually lent support to the Raw Meaty Bones Lobby. You can see comments made by Dr Tom Hungerford OBE and Dr Douglas Bryden AM.[14] Dr Michele Cotton, associate director, wrote a review of *Raw Meaty Bones: Promote Health*.[15]

These days the CVE hosts a procession of pet food stooges who lecture at seminars and write in the CVE newsletter. Imagine the surprise, in June 2007 when two pet owners were permitted to comment about their dismal experiences at the hands of the veterinary profession in the newsletter of the Post Graduate Foundation (soon to be renamed the Centre for Veterinary Education).[16] Their cat Sefi was subjected to hundreds (perhaps thousands) of dollars of tests and investigations, all of which were shown to be worthless when a junk food diet was identified as the culprit. Familiar story, you say?

Two months later I submitted a follow-up article asking the Sydney University Centre for Veterinary Education to conduct a thorough review as a means to stopping the abuse of pets by vets. In other words, for the CVE to stop their connivance with the junk food makers and their front people and instead of being part of the problem become part of the solution.

Article submitted August 2007, finally rejected November 2008

Sefi's ear discharge

Than and Nichola Wright, owners of Sefi, the six-year-old cat, have done us a great service. They are to be congratulated on their stoicism and forbearance in the face of counterfeit science and techno veterinary medicine.

In the June 2007 Post Graduate Foundation (PGF) *Control & Therapy*, they recount the sorry tale of how a discharge from Sefi's ear led them through an obstacle course of first opinions, expert opinions, bacteriological tests, radiographic tests, test therapies and radical surgery.[17]
After spending several months, and doubtless hundreds of dollars, the Wrights say:

> We were highly concerned and frustrated at the lack of progress we had made and the costs outlaid which had provided no answers as to why she had the condition or what was causing it. As a last resort, our vet told us about Dr Richard Malik at the PGF.

Dr Malik recommended that the owners discontinue feeding the prescription dry cat 'food' and provide a more natural diet which straightaway had the desired effect: 'After changing her diet, it didn't take long for us to see a rapid improvement in the condition of her ear and the happiness of our cat.'

In conclusion the Wrights state:

> We have learnt that while our vet went through appropriate routine testing to find the cause of Sefi's ear problems, there isn't always an obvious diagnosis and factors such as diet and environment should be investigated in the first instance.

Let's face it, we all make mistakes from which we can hope to learn. The discharge from Sefi's ear contains lessons old and new.

At the 1993 Australian Veterinary Association (AVA) annual general meeting the members approved a motion brought by the then PGF director, Dr Douglas Bryden:

> That in keeping with the AVA policy of providing forums for the membership, the AVA establish an independent committee to prepare a report on the interaction between diet and disease in companion animals.

In the event the AVA executive restricted the terms of reference to an investigation of existing literature on the diet and periodontal disease nexus. The committee was 'assisted' by a pet food company employee. Notwithstanding, in February 1994 *AVA News* carried the front-page article:

Diet and disease link—final report

In summary the committee found that, 'there is sufficient evidence to incriminate an association between diets of predominantly soft consistency and periodontal disease' and that veterinarians 'need to be concerned about the relationship between diet and health'.

The reasons for restricting the terms of reference as compared to the very broad specification in the motion were as follows:

- The committee believed the concerns raised required urgent attention and comment. It was considered that within the time frame set by the AVA it was not possible to explore every aspect of dietary interaction with disease.
- Information which could be gathered on the broader issues would be unlikely to add more than is already well known.

- Concentration should be placed on periodontal disease and diet because this was the principal area of current concern to the Australian veterinary profession.
- It was felt that if periodontal disease could be prevented then any secondary complications from this problem would be reduced.

There is *prima facie* evidence to justify concern by veterinarians. Pet owners should consider the need to provide some 'chewy' material as well as the basic nutrient intake of their dog or cat. Periodontal disease may be associated with the occurrence of other diseases but the available evidence is inconclusive. Periodontal disease is arguably the most common disease condition seen in small animal practice and its effects on the gums and teeth can significantly affect the health and well-being of affected animals. This is sufficient in itself to give reason for concern. Proof of additional systemic effects is not necessary to justify further action.

Further research is required to better define the relationship between particular diet types and oral health in dogs and cats. Those investigating small animal health problems should also take diet and diet consistency into account when researching systemic diseases—possible confounding effects of diet and poor oral health must be considered in such studies.

Clearly the AVA Diet and Disease Committee, in 1994, established an ethical and professional benchmark applicable to Australian clinicians, researchers and educators. Previously in the June 1993 Post Graduate Committee Veterinary Dentistry Proceedings 212, a NSW lawyer's opinion was published indicating that processed pet food related matters may become issues of relevance in the future:

1. Potential claims by pet owners under various pieces of consumer legislation throughout the states and territories of Australia.
2. In the federal sphere potential Trade Practices Act claims for false or misleading claims may be made either in relation to advertising or promotional material or labels.
3. The new truth in labelling activities instituted by the Federal Government.
4. Potential problems or claims under the recently introduced Product Liability provisions in Part V of the Trade Practices Act.
5. The, as yet, unknown effect of class actions which have been lawful in Australia since 5 March 1992, which may tend to overcome the existing drawbacks to actions brought by individual pet owners, namely the high cost of litigation and claims which may amount to only several hundreds of dollars in relation to an individual pet.

The foregoing relates to potential claims against manufacturers, distributors and possibly even retailers of processed pet food. Query what may be the legal problems of veterinarians who fail to consider the issues in this paper or fail to address those issues in advising pet owners who make known to the veterinarian that they rely wholly and solely on processed pet food to supply their pets' diet. Is it too much to suggest that, as pet owners—in common with everyone else in the community—become more litigious, veterinarians may some day share top billing on a writ?

It seems to me that we know, or at least should know, the biological, ethical and legal imperatives regarding the veterinary treatment of carnivores in our care. Sadly though, in respect to Sefi the cat and thousands like her, these things are more honoured in the breach than the observance. What's to be done and by whom? May I suggest that perhaps the Board of the Post Graduate Foundation* may have a role to play?

As a way forward, and in the first instance, I suggest that the Board could review:

a. The content of PGF courses and publications, as they relate to both wild and domestic carnivores, in light of biological imperatives.

b. The objectivity, affiliations and possible conflict of interest of PGF course teachers.

c. The diverse legal implications of the pet diet and disease issue as may apply to veterinary clinicians, researchers and educators.

Publication of the review findings would honour the good work started by Than and Nichola Wright and would help the veterinary profession to learn from history, keep faith with Sefi the cat and better secure our future.

Notes
1. T. Wright and N. Wright, 'Waxy ear canal in a cat', *Control & Therapy*, no. 4803, 2007, Post Graduate Foundation in Veterinary Science, University of Sydney.[17]
2. 'Pet food produces lively AGM', *Australian Veterinary Association News*, June, 1993, pp. 1 and 9.
3. 'Diet and disease link—final report', *Australian Veterinary Association News*, February, pp. 1 and 6.
4. T. Lonsdale, 'Preventative dentistry', *Veterinary Dentistry*, Proceedings of the Post Graduate Committee in Veterinary Science, University of Sydney, 1993, p. 212.[17]

*In August 2007, at the time of submission of this article for publication, the Post Graduate Foundation in Veterinary Science of the University of Sydney was overseen by a board of directors. The name changed in August 2008 to Centre for Veterinary Education (CVE), overseen by an advisory council.

At first the CVE agreed to publish the article. However, the new Director, Dr Hugh White, was reluctant and consulted one of his predecessors, Dr Doug Bryden AM. Dr Bryden suggested that the CVE should 'bite the bullet' and publish the article. This, he said, would serve to 'put the CVE on the map'. (Yes, honesty and integrity would stand out like a beacon in the corrupt veterinary environment.)

But 15 months later and after several changes of mind, the CVE finally refused because they said: 'The role of CVE is to provide continuing education, not act as the conscience of the veterinary profession.'

So there you have it. Those controlling the Sydney University conniving veterinary establishment will not be swayed. And whilst their disgraceful ongoing actions speak much louder than words, we who are concerned about the mounting fraud are not allowed even a few words of protest.

For details of the CVE discussions revealed by a Freedom of Information inquiry go to the Raw Meaty Bones website.[18]

'Free advertising for your business with Pet Oral Health Month'

Mars Petcare Australia in league with the Australian Veterinary Association are about to work their annual pet dental scam. August is the month when Mars will run radio ads encouraging pet owners to visit their vet for a 'free' dental check.

In the lead-up to this disgraceful event Mars are funding lectures for vets and vet students at Sydney and Melbourne universities. In the lecture blurb Mars say:

We all know that four out of five dogs over the age of three have periodontal disease [PD], so why not get involved in Pet Oral Health Month this August?

Help us to lower the incidence of PD for our favourite little friends by inviting your clients in for a 'free oral health check'.

Mars don't say that:

- Food, junk food made by Mars and other manufacturers, is the reason four out of five dogs (and cats and ferrets) suffer this easily preventable disease.
- By meeting the periodontal disease problem head-on, Mars create the impression that they are the experts in control, earnestly working to find a solution, and thus deflect attention from their poisonous junk.
- By creating the impression that they, Mars, are the vets' benefactors, they draw unsuspecting vets into a web of lies and deceit.
- Once the vets, the Australian Veterinary Association and the universities are partners in the scam, it becomes easier to substantiate the use of extruded rice sticks 'To keep your dog's teeth and gums healthy and strong, use great tasting Pedigree® Daily Dentastix™ everyday'.

Sucked into the Mars orbit, vets become the front-line sales force. 'Health' and 'welfare' may get a mention—as camouflage for the elaborate con trick. But no, it's dollars, billions of dollars that drive the entire disgusting, avaricious fraud. Suggesting that the health checks are 'free' is another cruel twist when in fact it's pet owners and their long-suffering pets that pay and pay for the excesses of the junk pet food companies and their vet stooges.

On Friday 9 July my wife and I attended the falsely named 'Improving periodontal health' lectures at the CVE building at Sydney University. As expected, Mars DENTAstix girls made us welcome and a tasty buffet dinner was on offer. Propaganda packs complete with DENTAstix samples were waiting on every chair. A film cameraman moved amongst the young vets recording the event for use in forthcoming marketing scams.

We knew to expect a stream of factoids and disinformation. However, we were not prepared for the poor calibre of the speakers, paucity of ideas or the often illegible PowerPoint presentations. Dr Rod Salter was introduced as an old hand who had been part of the Australian Veterinary Dental Association since its inception in 1990. As a vet dentist he was a participant in the Australian veterinary civil war that raged in the early 1990s and led to the Diet and Disease study commissioned by the Australian Veterinary Association. Even though 'assisted' by Mars Corporation flunkeys, the study raised concerns about junk food and made favourable mention of raw meaty bones. You can find the draft version on the Raw Meaty Bones website[19] and the published version at the UK Raw Meaty Bones site.[20]

Dr Salter, however, treated the AVA official review with passing contempt. His last PowerPoint slide carried a large DENTAstix logo with the words:

> Wayne [Fitzgerald] and I would [like] to thank
> Pedigree for the opportunity to
> present this lecture and spread the 'gospel'

They know no shame. We must take action. Let vet schools know that you know they are engaged in a monstrous fraud. Let university vice-chancellors know that their veterinary faculties are bringing the universities into disrepute. Tell politicians and the media. Eventually we can expect a breakthrough. It's just a question of when.

Best wishes, Tom

December 2010: Pet food curtain

Dear Reader,

Another year flashes by and in a few days it will be Christmas. I hope this finds you well and looking forward to the festivities.

This year, as usual, many people have written to tell how their pets glow with health when fed a raw meaty bones diet. Many tell how their vets remark on the health of the animals. But as soon as the healthful RMB diet is mentioned, the hapless owner is treated to a sermon on the alleged evils of natural food. It's a bizarre world when the positive evidence before one's eyes is condemned by so-called health professionals and the fabricated data generated by faceless corrupt pet food companies and veterinary schools is hailed as gospel truth.

Pet owners caught in the one-on-one confrontations with their vets flinch and seek evasive action. Recently I spent three months in discussion with predominantly American vets on an internet site. If you are a registered vet you can pay $720 per year to access http://www.vin.com. VIN stands for Veterinary Information Network (although Mis-Information Network more accurately describes their club). It's said that there are 40,000 VINers and 242 so-called expert consultants who minister to the educational and professional needs of the subscribers. Paul Pion the cofounder says he was offered over $40 million for the business.

Of course, just like the wider vet profession, VIN teachings are founded on fallacy; the VIN cult is living a lie. Although it's almost 20 years since the whistle was blown on the corrupt petfood/veterinary alliance[10] it seems VIN vets are not yet ready to hear the message.

Besides being rabid in defence of junk food—they maintained a barrage of personal abuse against me the messenger—VINers are also cowards. Repeatedly I asked them to set out their opinions and that I would happily publish those for all to see at the raw meaty bones website. Despite their aggressive tone and unshakable certainties expressed in the privacy of the VIN website, not one of the critics would permit their comments to be published in an open forum. And then, completely without warning, Paul Pion expelled me from the list.

Back in the days of the Cold War an Iron Curtain divided the Soviet bloc from the West. For the majority trapped behind the Curtain, life was a drudge. For the power elites, life was full of benefits. They found ways to amass power, prestige and profit under cover of the oppression and propaganda governing the masses.

The Iron Curtain partitioned Europe; the Pet Food Curtain envelopes the entire globe. These days, by controlling the flow of information, the junk pet food/veterinary conspiracy maintains a global population in thrall to the contents of the pet food can and bag. Veterinary associations, vet schools, Paul Pion and thousands of vets get their power, prestige and profit. Others cash in by creating and occupying an alternative niche. In this newsletter we take a peek at how some 'alternative' authors and cults promote their interests—and distract from the main task of tearing down the Pet Food Curtain.

Perhaps by shedding a bit of light and truth we can improve the lot of pet owners and their pets in time for Christmas.

Wishing you compliments of the season and a wonderful New Year, Tom

BARFers and associated cults behind the pet food curtain

After years of muddled ideas about the ideal carnivore diet, 'raw meaty bones' represented a major breakthrough. Raw meaty bones provide the key to the carnivore code. Raw meaty bones are the super food, the wonder drug for carnivores.

Instead of going round and round in interminable circles arguing about recipes, raw meaty bones info proclaimed the need for ingredients to be (a) in their natural chemical state, and importantly (b) in their tough chewy physical state. Once armed with this key to the carnivore code, it was easy to see that stopping the diet problems at source offered the best way to assist the world's pets. Accordingly, this led to (c), the third component of the RMB approach, requiring that every effort be made to overturn the cruelty and corruption associated with the junk pet food/veterinary conspiracy.

See one pet food maker enlist vets to kill dogs and cats and you are rightly appalled. See hundreds of pet food makers enlisting thousands of vets to kill millions of pets and it's time for action. Unfortunately, things took a turn for the worse when Dr Ian Billinghurst joined the Raw Meaty Bones Lobby of concerned veterinarians based in Sydney, Australia. We shared our RMB information, which resulted in Billinghurst misappropriating, bastardising and ultimately sabotaging the RMB concepts and campaign.

Dr Billinghurst initially joined us in our war on the global pet food/vet system. But spontaneously and without warning he resigned from the RMB Lobby. That would have been OK had he stuck to telling people about the simplicity and benefits of the RMB diet. Unfortunately, Billinghurst's agenda included encouraging pet owners to feed grains, dairy products, leafy vegetables, lashings of fruit and bottled supplements all ground to a pulp. Billinghurst's recipes caught the attention of Jane Anderson and her acolytes, who helped Billinghurst promote his Born Again Raw Feeder (BARF) madness. In a just and equitable world, with the veterinary profession doing its job as source of sound dietary and health information, Billinghurst's BARF would have been exposed long ago.

Alas, according to an article in the December 2010 edition of the *Whole Dog Journal* (*WDJ*), misinformation and confusion is not only alive and well, it's heavily promoted. What have dogs and their owners done to deserve such ill-treatment? Let's take a look at some verbatim extracts from the *WDJ* article: 'How-to books for feeding raw diets: a review of books on feeding your dog a raw meaty bone diet'. My comments are marked 'TL'.

WDJ: [Mary Straus the author writes] I'll start this month by looking at books that focus on diets based on raw meaty bones (RMBs). Next month, I'll review some excellent new books that offer guidelines for diets where RMBs are optional. Last, I'll discuss books that have only boneless recipes, either raw or cooked.

TL: At first Mary Straus appears to identify the importance of RMBs. But any credibility gained is instantly lost when she suggests that there could be 'excellent new books' where RMBs are 'optional'! We accept that the Earth is round and spend no time looking in books proclaiming that the Earth is flat/oval/cuboidal or any other whimsy. Now that we know, or should know, the significance of RMBs in the carnivore diet, why do authors and journals devote any time to consideration of weird, wild and whimsical notions?

WDJ: Australian veterinarian Ian Billinghurst wrote the first popular book on diets that include RMBs, which he called BARF diets, for 'bones and raw food' or 'biologically appropriate raw food'.

TL: Yes, Billinghurst misappropriated RMB information and mixed it with misinformation gleaned from Juliette de Bairacli Levy and Richard Pitcairn. His followers coined the term Born Again Raw Feeders —contracted to BARF, the slang word for vomit—as self-deprecating humour. Despite the puke/vomit/spew connotations Billinghurst saw the opportunity to register the trademark 'BARF' and thereby take ownership of the name.

WDJ: He [Billinghurst] later wrote two more books, *Grow Your Pup with Bones*, on feeding puppies and dogs used for breeding, and *The BARF Diet*, an updated and condensed version of his first book.

TL: BARFer Billinghurst's 2001 *The BARF Diet* does indeed condense and compound the errors in his 1993 book. Nowadays, Billinghurst has three misleading and mutually contradictory books on the market at the same time. With an increasing following of Born Again Raw Feeders, Billinghurst saw his chance to market BARF/vomit/spew pap. Timed to coincide with the 2001 launch of his commercial junk food, *The BARF Diet* is little more than a promotional pamphlet. Imagine my surprise when the BARFer sent me a signed copy. Did he think his BARF pamphlet trumped the 389 pages of facts and analysis in *Raw Meaty Bones: Promote Health*?

WDJ: Billinghurst's books can be frustrating, though. The information is disorganised. None of the books contains an index. If you want recipes or simple, clear instructions, you will not like Billinghurst's books.

TL: Very true. Why no indexes? Why no references? Where did Billinghurst get his information? With no coherent theory, the books are a blight on the landscape. They have set back the interests of pets, pet owners and the wider society by decades.

WDJ: Even those who appreciate the details on the nutritional benefits of each type of food may find it difficult to extract the specific elements needed to formulate a diet and determine how much to feed.

TL: Very true. Pet owners, with no specialist knowledge, are treated to a confusing mix of misleading and wrong information.

WDJ: Billinghurst recommends feeding a diet that is approximately 60 per cent RMBs.

TL: It's the misappropriated RMB information that provides Billinghurst's narrative with traces of credibility. However, he soon loses the plot as per the following passage from the *WDJ*.

WDJ: [Billinghurst recommends] 15 to 20 per cent vegetables and fruits, 10 to 15 per cent organs, and the rest a variety of 'additives', including eggs, fish, muscle meat, oils, table scraps, grains, legumes, yogurt and raw milk. Billinghurst also adds whole food supplements: cod liver oil, apple cider vinegar, brewer's yeast, honey, kelp, alfalfa and garlic. He suggests supplementing with vitamins A, B complex, C, D, and E, and offering the dog larger (recreational) bones.

TL: But as previously remarked, and despite his convoluted recommendations, Billinghurst provides no sources or scientific justifications for his recipes. And so-called 'recreational bones' are dangerous.

WDJ: Billinghurst stresses the need for variety in all three books, but he's not consistent. ... Feeding methodology varies between the three books.

TL: Seeing as how the *WDJ* is alert to Billinghurst's inconsistent ramblings, the big question is: Why do they recommend the books at all? Indeed, why does anyone recommend the BARFer books?

WDJ: In the first [book], Billinghurst suggests feeding different foods at different meals. Over three weeks, you would feed 10 meals of RMBs, four vegetable, one starch, one grain/legume, one meat, two milk, and one or two organ meat meals.

TL: Yes, it was the BARFer's first book of recipes that snared thousands of Born Again Raw Feeders. Little did they realise that the primary health benefits they saw in their animals did not stem from adopting the BARFer recipes, it stemmed from *stopping feeding commercial junk*. The secondary benefit arose from feeding raw meaty bones.

WDJ: The second book introduces the 'patty', a mix of all foods except RMBs (though those can be included in small amounts).

TL: Here the BARFer shows his true colours. Having enticed a band of followers by virtue of his inclusion of raw meaty bones information, the BARFer now discounts and discards the importance of raw meaty bones. Instead, he grinds carnivore food to a processed pap. Ripping, tearing and chewing, teeth cleaning and polishing are no longer significant factors in the BARFer's scheme of things.

WDJ: The third book offers two feeding choices: alternating RMB meals with a combination of other foods, such as meat (some including bone), organs, vegetables, fruit, and additives; or feeding 'multi-mix patties', consisting of all foods, including RMBs, ground together. The latter ties in with the introduction of 'Dr. Billinghurst's Meat and Bone Minces' from a company, BARF World, that he helped found.

TL: Exactly. Having thoroughly confused his readers, Billinghurst encourages consumers to buy his Meat and Bone Minces, conveniently supplied (at enormous prices) by his BARF World enterprise. The *WDJ*, instead of condemning the BARF hoax then go on to review and recommend another BARF book by Carina Beth MacDonald entitled *Raw Dog Food*.

WDJ: Carina Beth MacDonald uses a light-hearted approach to cover the basics of a RMB diet.

TL: Wrong. Carina MacDonald does not deal with a RMB diet, she promotes BARF/spew/puke dogma that she learnt from Billinghurst as illustrated by the following passage in the *WDJ*.

WDJ: [Carina Beth MacDonald's] recommended proportions are 50 per cent RMBs, 20 per cent boneless meat, 5 to 10 per cent organs, and 20 to 25 per cent veggies, eggs and fruit. ... Optional ingredients include dairy products, grains, apple cider vinegar, blackstrap molasses, garlic, ginger, nuts, legumes and leftovers.

TL: After endorsing the irrelevant and erroneous BARF books, the *WDJ* turns its attentions to *Work Wonders: Feed Your Dog Raw Meaty Bones*.

WDJ: Alternative paradigm: The 'whole prey' diet Tom Lonsdale, another Australian vet, advocates a raw diet based on whole prey.

TL: Quite right he does. It's called the Raw Meaty Bones diet because raw meaty bones are the essential element. They are the super-food and wonder drug for carnivores.

WDJ: I am not a fan of this style of feeding, as I feel it is impractical.

TL: Nonsense. It's the easiest, most economical most efficient way we have for feeding domestic carnivores as articulated in 1991.[10]

WDJ: This book [*Work Wonders: Feed Your Dog Raw Meaty Bones*] is the best guide available, however, for people who choose this feeding method.

TL: Thank you for the recommendation *WDJ*. Lots of people say the same thing.

WDJ: Lonsdale asserts that RMBs should come preferably from whole carcasses, such as: rats, mice and quail for small dogs; calf, goat, pig, kangaroo and lamb for larger dogs; and rabbit, fish and chicken for all dogs. Other recommended RMBs include chicken and turkey backs and frames (meat removed); poultry heads, feet, necks and wings (small dogs only); sheep, deer, pig and fish heads; lamb and pork necks; ox and kangaroo tails; sides of lamb; slabs of beef; and ox brisket. Table scraps and fruit are also allowed. Large meals of liver are fed once every two weeks. Other offal deemed suitable by Lonsdale include lung, trachea, heart, omasum (part of the stomach of ruminants), tripe, tongue, pancreas and spleen.

TL: The *WDJ* provide a fair precis of the Raw Meaty Bones Diet and for which I'm grateful.

WDJ: Lonsdale and his followers are adamant that there is only one right way to feed dogs; no deviation is permitted.

TL: That's not true. Raw Meaty Bones followers know that there is one best way: feed whole carcasses of other animals. There's a second-best way: feed a diet based on raw meaty bones with considerable variation available.

Perhaps the *WDJ* don't know their RMB history and are thinking about those folks who were once BARFer Billinghurst's main supporters but now call themselves Prey Modellers.[2]

The Prey Modellers misappropriated RMB information, distorted it and changed the name from Raw Meaty Bones Diet to Prey Model Diet. They are adamant that dogs should be fed a formula of 80% meat, 10% bone and 10% offal, no deviation permitted. I tried reasoning with the Prey Modellers but to no avail and for my troubles was banned from all their Yahoo chat lists.[3]

WDJ: Lonsdale has another book, *Raw Meaty Bones: Promote Health* (Rivetco Pty Ltd, 2001), which is not a how-to book; it's mostly a history of Lonsdale's war with the pet food industry.

TL: *Raw Meaty Bones: Promote Health* represents several books in one.

Diet 'how-to' advice is but one of several threads contained within the 389 pages. Pet diet and disease information is presented in a historical context, helping the reader understand how new information struggles into existence.

Ultimately the book is about a new theory of health and disease as set out in Chapter 14 with the other 13 chapters in a supporting role. Alison Tyler recommends that by reading the book five times you gain the full benefit.[21]

Developments behind the pet food curtain in China

This past week my wife and I have been attending the first South China Small Animal Veterinary Conference in Guangzhou, China.

At the entrance to the conference centre we were greeted by the Mars Corporation's Royal Canin Veterinary Diet logo, which was blazoned throughout on hoardings, posters and stationery. Inside the trade hall the Royal Canin stand dominated the refreshment area—on the TV screen a video pushing the Royal Canin dachshund diet!

Moving on we noticed the Hill's logos framing the podium in conference room A. Royal Canin logos dominated rooms B and C.

A veterinary student from the local university handed out promotional material for the Pet Food Institute (PFI). Their logo proclaims 'PFI promotes products of the USA'. In fluorescent colours with cartoon animals gathered around bowls of junk food, the PFI tells how the whole shebang is endorsed by Association of American Feed Control Officials (AAFCO) and the US Food and Drug Administration.

Yes, this is a detailed, planned invasion by American companies in concert with the American government into the minds and pockets of unsuspecting Chinese vets and their clients. The mass poisoning of Chinese pets gets underway.

In the interests of research, we decided to look in on two lecture sessions. Previously I'd encountered Kurt Verkest as an especially arrogant combatant on the Veterinary (Mis-)Information Network (http://www.vin.com). And back in 2004 he attacked Raw Meaty Bones concepts in an ill-conceived article published in Australia. As it turned out he'd been in receipt of research funds from Nestlé Purina and worked with the notorious Linda Fleeman in a junk-food-funded department at the University of Queensland researching insulin requirements in obese dogs.

These days Verkest resides in Hong Kong and 'specialises' in cancer treatment. He told his audience 'lymphoma is one of the most common serious malignancies that we see in dogs'. Diagnosis and treatment were Verkest's focus. Treatment, of course, involves toxic chemotherapy that costs a fortune. No mention that in all probability the rise in malignant cancer is connected to junk food diets. No mention that in a developing country vets need to keep things simple and get the basics right. Their focus needs to be prevention, prevention, prevention—left, right and centre.

Next, we endured a nauseating session listening to Hong Kong vet Dr Carla Chow recite junk pet food/veterinary propaganda about obese cats. Carla Chow has a vet degree from Edinburgh in Scotland and further qualifications gained in Australia. Impressionable Chinese vets could be expected to soak up her recommendations. Feline obesity, she said, is very common in domestic felines. There's an increased risk of diabetes mellitus, glucose intolerance, skin problems, joint disease, hepatic lipidosis, exercise/heat intolerance and feline lower urinary tract disease. High-calorie palatable *ad libitum* diets lead to overeating, remarked Dr Chow.

So far so good, you say. But when Carla Chow showed a slide of the Nestlé Purina Body Condition System for assessing obesity you knew that she was on the wrong track. Instead of advising Chinese vets to chuck out the junk food (and be sure to pay attention to any dental disease) and get the animals back on a natural diet, Chow's recommendations were to:

- reduce dry food, increase canned food ration
- or try high-protein, low-carbohydrate diets, e.g. Hill's.

Similarly, when Dr Chow spoke about the problems associated with urine and faeces elimination, she simply didn't get that the cats' body systems are severely stressed when forced to eat junk food. Faecal volumes increase threefold, are often liquid and give off an appalling stink. No wonder bloated cats experience problems with their urine and faeces. The one obvious, essential piece of advice—feed a natural diet—was withheld from her audience.

I grieve for the cats of Hong Kong and southern China confined to apartment blocks, their bowels straining under the impact of fermenting grain, bladders inflamed and the best solution on offer is a visit to Carla Chow.

Next year the Second South China Small Animal Veterinary Conference is to be held in Shenzhen. Will the organisers take urgent action to reverse the damage done by Dr Verkest, Dr Chow and their ilk? Or will they continue to compound the errors—help Royal Canin, Hill's and Nestlé Purina to tighten their grip on the Chinese veterinary mind?

Watch this space.

11

———

2011: FINAL WORDS: THE FIGHTCONTINUES

The final edition of the RMB Newsletter looks back over the Campaign, records the egregious failings of the veterinary profession and slams the fad raw diet opportunists. The edition closes with expressions of hope for a better future informed by integrity and common sense.

December 2011: 20th anniversary

Dear Reader,

Twenty years ago this month Dr Breck Muir and I blew the whistle on the junk pet food/veterinary alliance.

Breck's letter appeared in the *Australian Veterinary Association News* and my piece was published in the Sydney University Post Graduate Committee in Veterinary Science newsletter. At the time we were optimistic that our appeal to the better nature and professional integrity of vets would strike a chord. Now, twenty years on, I believe we've seen some of the worst professional blindness, cruelty, incompetence and corruption that is possible to contemplate.

Instead of investigating and addressing the massive junk pet food fraud and the highest veterinary involvement in the scam, the global veterinary profession has aligned itself ever more closely with the mass pet poisoners.

Of course, there are exceptions—vets who put their heads above the parapet in support of a natural diet. They deserve recognition.

However, I won't name names. In vet circles it's seen as something of a crime or at least a mark of insanity if a vet advocates a natural diet according to Nature's teachings. In this junk pet food dominated world, vets are expected to be tame lap dogs who regurgitate junk pet food inspired dogma.

Had the vet profession shown some leadership then I believe it could have achieved massive benefits for pets, pet owners, the wider community and the planet itself. The medical profession speaks out against junk food. Increasingly doctors investigate the mechanisms whereby junk food and periodontal disease give rise to morbidity and mortality of their patients. Vets by contrast peddle ever more expensive brand-name products—as their patients get sicker and sicker.

Twenty years of failed veterinary leadership created a vacuum filled by opportunists, quacks and hucksters. Some vets manufacture junk cooked and raw food and bogus supplements. Profit is their goal. And the internet is alive with self-styled experts who seek power and prestige through promoting their confected concepts.

Perhaps this is a low point. Let's hope so. In an effort to keep the original ideals alive I've reproduced both of the opening statements below. Let's hope that integrity and common sense come back into fashion over the next twenty years.

With only days until Christmas, I'd like to end on a happier note. We all enjoy the gift of life on a wondrous planet. This year I turned 62 years of age and I look back with gratitude for the life lived. What does the future hold? Who knows? But I'm eager to find out. I hope that you've got lots of wonderful memories and lots of extraordinary experiences to come.

Wishing you and your pets a merry Christmas and a happy, healthful New Year,

Tom

Canned pet food not the healthiest
Dr Breck Muir, *Australian Veterinary Association News*, December 1991

The pet food situation has concerned me for some years, my feelings brought to this by the current competitive marketing of various dental workstations for veterinary use.

The scene as I see it goes like this: 'Here is the best food ever made for your dog, Mrs Jones', handing her a can of commercial dog food or dry food, 'but he may develop problems with his teeth, so here is a special toothbrush and paste for you to use to clean his teeth regularly, and then if that doesn't keep the periodontal disease at bay then we have the very latest in dental equipment just like our own dentist has, and we can give Fido that perfectly enamelled ivory grin'— that he would have had had you not fed him the commercial food in the first place.

Here we have the perfectly engineered commercial circle—a problem doesn't exist, so we create one, and then come up with all the remedial treatments.

Infiltration

The infiltration of the commercial pet foods into our lives is one of the great success stories of the business world. Gross sales figures for a single product type are probably only bettered by petroleum products worldwide.

We as a profession have been led by the nose by vested interests in to a current situation where most younger vets actually recommend commercial pet foods as the best available way of feeding domestic pets—because they have never known of any other way. Before they had their first pet they were bombarded with constant mass media advertising instilling into them that the various commercial foods were the only way to go, and when they graduated and went to postgraduate nutrition courses, again they had this idea reinforced by visiting lecturers who actually mentioned brand names in their notes.

My experience with commercial canned and dry pet foods is that they:

- are a prime cause of periodontal disease in all breeds of dogs and cats are associated with an increased incidence of gastric dilation and/or torsion.
- are a cause of diarrhoea in a substantial number of dogs
- cause intestinal 'allergies' with associated dermal pruritus and behavioural changes in a significant number of cases
- are a prime cause of flatulence and offensive odour in dogs—some brands more than others.

We are objectively educated, of above average intelligence, trained to observe and reason as undergraduates. We should develop the ability to assess products for what they are in spite of extremely effective advertising claiming otherwise. This is a mammoth and ongoing task for all of us and certainly not just with pet foods.

In this case we should be giving clients advice to correct their pets' diet towards more natural one and not justify the financial outlay on the latest dental equipment available by advocating the wholesale feeding of commercial pet foods.

Oral disease in cats and dogs
Dr Tom Lonsdale, December 1991, Control and Therapy Series No. 3128; Mailing No. 163, Post Graduate Committee in Veterinary Science

The stench of stale blood, dung and pus emanating from the mouths of so many of my patients has finally provoked this eruption of dissent.

The sheer numbers passing through the practice, when extrapolated to the world situation, tells me that oral disease is the source of the greatest intractable pain and discomfort experienced by our companion animals.

This is a great and mindless cruelty we visit upon our animals from the whelping box to the grave. Just imagine having a mouth ulcer or toothache for a lifetime.

The internal factors are these:
Puppies and kittens cut their deciduous teeth between two and six weeks of age. An inevitable consequence of this is gingivitis. A diet of processed food ensures lack of gum massage and the gingivitis persists. The growing animal develops grooming behaviour and adds hair and faecal materials to the accumulated food scraps clogging the interdental spaces.

Between four and six months of age the permanent teeth erupt into a soup of blood, pus and saliva. The gingivitis is now well established and not infrequently one finds a young kitten or puppy with a complete set of deciduous teeth hanging from inflamed gingival shreds.

Even on a diet of processed food the deciduous teeth must eventually fall out. The permanent teeth come to occupy a diseased mouth and by this time the animal has learned not to chew on anything because of the pain involved.

The exquisite mechanism of teeth and gums, designed by nature to be cleaned, massage and stressed daily, is left to rot. Compare mining machinery properly maintained which can excavate a mountain but by disuse can be rendered useless.

A lifetime of inescapable pain is bad enough. The sequelae of endocarditis, iliac thrombosis, nephritis and all those other entities attributable to a permanent septic focus finally condemn this situation as being intolerable.

The external factors are these:
Foremost are the pet foods which are promoted as 'complete diets, only water needed'. Along with petroleum and coffee, pet food is one of the biggest industries worldwide.

Reacting to the now universal dental needs of our animals the dental instrument, the dental machine and even the imitation bone industries have flourished.

I believe many veterinary practitioners have reacted passively, perhaps providing some dental care as an afterthought and virtually no advice. Since cats and dogs don't complain, owners don't realise and don't seek advice. Many vets just don't seem to be proactive in this vital area. As vets we need to provide more than palliative care. Brushing teeth and regular prophys (dental cleaning under general anaesthetic) are not enough when advice on diet and food to massage the gums is so vitally important.

What's to be done?
(a) The internal system
Help puppies and kittens to control their two bouts of physiological gingivitis before it becomes pathological. Older larger dogs need raw bones and cats need raw meat on the bone.

(b) The external system
The external commerce-driven system did not exist before the fifties and now it seems such an inescapable part of life. It may take a while to alter course.

The profession can do much to re-educate itself and in turn the public. A few practice surveys and university-based research projects would set the tone.

The pet food manufacturers will need advice on the problems caused by processed food. One pet food company gives biannual 'prophys' to its research animals (personal communication).

However, they may be persuaded to voluntarily print cautionary advice on their packaging.

What benefits can we expect?

Innumerable. Pets will be fed on cheap unprocessed by-products some of the time. The environment will benefit, clients will be an average $1,000 per animal/per lifetime better off. Certainly, the pets can be expected to live longer as they enjoy their lives seeking to 'steal bones out of the freezer'.

As vets we will be happy to see more pain-free, healthier pets and grateful owners.

POSTSCRIPT

As the first decades of the 21st century recede in the rear-view mir-ror, we should ask what, if any, progress has been made. And what we need to do next.

Sad to say, the faceless pet food giant has ever more willing partners in crime. Vets live in his pockets, sell themselves cheaply and climb the ladder of success to whisper in his ear.

Mainstream print, radio and television media provide active propaganda channels for the pet food scam. That's to say they broadcast a steady stream of sanitised, sugar-coated misinformation. And seldom if ever do they broadcast insights into the junk pet food cruelty and fraud. Pictures of 'happy' dogs and cats illustrate media articles, whether or not those articles relate to pet keeping—product placement worth thousands of dollars in product sales and vet services.

Digital media—Facebook, LinkedIn, Instagram, TikTok, X—carry endless streams of pet food spin and gloss. And it's here that the 'alternative' BARF, Prey Model and assorted holistics ply their trade too. Podcast influencers attract thousands of followers like moths to the flame.

What's next?

In the face of apparently overwhelming odds, there may be a glimmer of hope, there is some good news. And that mostly centres around concerned, motivated and well-informed citizens. When Rachel Carson published *Silent Spring* in 1962 there was little public knowledge of the chemical pollution of farmlands and waterways. In the 1980s the risks of climate change barely rated a mention. Nowadays everyone wants a better environment and most folks support action on climate change.

Edward Morrow commented: 'The obscure we see eventually. The completely obvious, it seems, takes longer.'

The animal cruelty and consumer fraud perpetrated by the vet-pet food industrial complex, once pointed out, is indeed obvious. And if cruelty and fraud are criminal offences, then the perpetrators should be prosecuted to the full extent of the law.

It's also clear, after decades spent pitting truth against lies, that truth alone will not prevail. It's a losing strategy. The truth has only one version, it cannot be bent and twisted and remain the truth. The rigid truth struggles to persuade. Lies, however, deceive with ease. Lies are flexible and able to contort to fit any circumstance. Of course we must be ever faithful to the truth; however, for the future we must look beyond the lies, and focus on the source of the lies. Let's give the spin doctors and partners in crime their day in court. Let them explain to judges the world over why they are indifferent to animal suffering, why they engage in a multibillion-dollar fraud.

Let's band together. Let's help the lawyers counter the spin and obtain justice for all. Onwards and upwards, we can make the world a better place.

APPENDIX A

Diet guide for domestic dogs and cats

Wolves, dingoes and feral cats keep themselves healthy by eating whole carcasses of prey animals. Ideally we should feed our pets in the same manner. Until a dependable source of whole carcasses becomes available, pet owners need a satisfactory alternative. The following recommendations, based on raw meaty bones, have been adopted by thousands of pet owners with excellent results.

The diet is easy to follow and cheap, and pets enjoy it.

- Fresh water constantly available.
- Raw meaty bones (or carcasses if available) should form the bulk of the diet.
- Table scraps both cooked and raw (grate or liquidise vegetables, discard cooked bones).

Puppies and kittens

From about three weeks of age puppies and kittens start to take an interest in what their mother is eating. By six weeks of age they can eat chicken carcasses, rabbits and fish.

During the brief interval between three and six weeks of age it is advisable to provide minced chicken, chicken carcasses or similar for young animals (as well as access to larger pieces that encourage ripping and tearing). This is akin to the part-digested food regurgitated by wild carnivore mothers. Large litters will need more supplementary feeding than small litters. (The meat and bone should be minced together. Meat off the bone can be fed, but only for a short time, until the young animals can eat meat and bone together—usually about six weeks of age.)

Between four and six months of age puppies and kittens cut their permanent teeth and grow rapidly. At this time they need a plentiful supply of carcasses or raw meaty bones of suitable size.

Puppies and kittens tend not to overeat natural food. Food can be continuously available.

Natural foods suitable for pet carnivores

Raw meaty bones

- Chicken and turkey carcasses, after the meat has been removed for human consumption, are suitable for dogs and cats.
- Poultry by-products include heads, feet, necks and wings.
- Whole fish and fish heads.
- Goat, sheep, calf, deer and kangaroo carcasses can be sawn into large pieces of meat and bone.
- Other by-products include: pigs' trotters, pigs' heads, sheep heads, brisket, tail bones, rib bones.

Whole carcasses

- Rats, mice, rabbits, fish, chickens, quail, hens.

Offal

- Liver, lungs, trachea, hearts, omasums (stomach of ruminants), tripe.

Quality—Quantity—Frequency

Healthy animals living and breeding in the wild depend on the correct quality of food in the right quantity at a correct frequency. They thereby gain an appropriate nutrient intake plus the correct amount of teeth cleaning—animals, unlike humans, 'brush' and 'floss' as they eat.

Quality

Low-fat game animals and fish and birds provide the best source of food for pet carnivores. If using meat from farm animals (cattle, sheep and pigs) avoid excessive fat, or bones that are too large to be eaten.

Dogs are more likely to break their teeth when eating large knuckle bones and bones sawn lengthwise than if eating meat and bone together.

Raw food for cats should always be fresh. Dogs can consume 'ripe' food and will sometimes bury bones for later consumption.

Quantity

Establishing the quantity to feed pets is more an art than a science. Parents, when feeding a human family, manage this task without the aid of food consumption charts. You can achieve the same good results for your pet by paying attention to activity levels, appetite and body condition.

High activity and big appetite indicate a need for increased food, and vice versa.

Body condition depends on a number of factors. The overall body shape—is it athletic or rotund—and the lustre of the hair coat provide clues. Use your fingertips to assess the elasticity of the skin. Does it have an elastic feel and move readily over the muscles? Do the muscles feel well toned? And how much coverage of the ribs do you detect? This is the best place to check whether your pet is too thin or too fat. By comparing your own rib cage with that of your pet you can obtain a good idea of body condition—both your own and that of your pet.

An approximate food consumption guide, based on raw meaty bones, for the average pet cat or dog is 15% to 20% of body weight in one week or 2% to 3% per day. On that basis a 25 kilo dog requires up to five kilos of carcasses or raw meaty bones weekly. Cats weighing five kilos require about one kilo of chicken necks, fish, rabbit or similar each week. Table scraps should be fed as an extra component of the diet. Please note that these figures are only a guide and relate to adult pets in a domestic environment.

Pregnant or lactating females and growing puppies and kittens may need much more food than adult animals of similar body weight.

Wherever possible, feed the meat and bone ration in one large piece requiring much ripping, tearing and gnawing. This makes for contented pets with clean teeth.

Frequency

Wild carnivores feed at irregular intervals. In a domestic setting regularity works best and accordingly I suggest that you feed adult dogs and cats once daily. If you live in a hot climate I recommend that you feed pets in the evening to avoid attracting flies.

I suggest that on one or two days each week your dog may be fasted—just like animals in the wild.

On occasions you may run out of natural food. Don't be tempted to buy artificial food, fast your dog and stock up with natural food the next day.

Puppies, cats, ferrets and sick or underweight dogs should not be fasted (unless on veterinary advice).

Table scraps

Wild carnivores eat small amounts of omnivore food, part-digested in liquid form, when they eat the intestines of their prey. Our table scraps, and some fruit and vegetable peelings, are omnivore food which has not been ingested. Providing scraps do not form too great a proportion of the diet, they appear to do no harm and may do some good. I advise an upper limit of one-third scraps for dogs and rather less for cats. Liquidising scraps, both cooked and raw, in the kitchen mixer may help to increase their digestibility.

Things to avoid

- Excessive meat off the bone—not balanced.
- Excessive vegetables—not balanced.
- Small pieces of bone—can be swallowed whole and get stuck.
- Cooked bones—get stuck.
- Mineral and vitamin additives—create imbalance.
- Processed food—leads to dental and other diseases.
- Excessive starchy food—associated with bloat.
- Onions, garlic and chocolate—toxic to pets.
- Grapes, raisins, sultanas, currants—toxic to pets.
- Fruit stones (pits) and corn cobs—get stuck.
- Milk—associated with diarrhoea. Animals drink it whether thirsty or not and consequently get fat. Milk sludge sticks to teeth and gums.

Take care

- Old dogs and cats addicted to a processed diet may experience initial difficulty when changed on to a natural diet.
- Pets with misshapen jaws and dental disease may experience difficulties with a natural diet.
- Create variety. Any nutrients fed to excess can be harmful.
- Liver is an excellent foodstuff but should not be fed more than once weekly.
- Other offal, e.g. ox stomachs, should not exceed 50% of the diet.
- Whole fish are an excellent source of food for carnivores, but avoid feeding one species of fish constantly. Some species, e.g. carp, contain an enzyme which destroys thiamine (vitamin B1).
- There are no prizes for the fattest dog on the block, nor for the fastest. Feed pets for a lifetime of health. Prevention is better than cure.

Miscellaneous tips

- Domestic dogs and cats are carnivores. Feeding them the appropriate carnivore diet represents the single most important contribution to their welfare.
- Establish early contact with a dependable supplier of foodstuffs for pet carnivores. Buy food in bulk in order to avoid shortages.
- Package the daily rations separately for ease of feeding.
- Refrigerated storage space, preferably a freezer, is essential.
- Raw meaty bones can be fed frozen just like ice cream. Some pets eat the frozen article; others wait for it to thaw.
- Small carcasses, for example rats, mice and small birds, can be fed frozen and complete with entrails. Larger carcasses should have the entrails removed before freezing.
- Take care that pets do not fight over their food.
- Protect children by ensuring that they do not disturb feeding pets.
- Feeding bowls are unnecessary—the food will be dragged across the floor—so feed pets outside by preference, or on an easily cleaned floor.
- Ferrets are small carnivores that can be fed in the same way as cats.

Important: Note that individual animals and circumstances may vary. You may need to discuss your pet's needs with your veterinarian.

For an expanded description of dietary requirements, including the potential hazards, please consult:

Raw Meaty Bones: Promote Health
Work Wonders: Feed Your Dog Raw Meaty Bones
Multi-Billion-Dollar Pet Food Fraud: Hiding in Plain Sight

APPENDIX B

Artificial intelligence or artificial nonsense?

A pet owner asked AI program ChatGPT a simple, uncomplicated question: 'What is the best food for dogs?'

The answer confirms worst fears. In March 2025, ChatGPT surveyed the internet electronic record. But instead of intelligent information the answer provides a summary of artificial pet food nonsense—nowadays made worse by fad raw (Righteous And Wrong) recipe books and con artists.

It's all a cruel hoax.

ChatGPT presents three harmful options and no good option. It preserves the illusion consumers have a 'choice' and are sufficiently informed to decide what's best. Unfortunately, the experts' (dogs') opinions are not part of the electronic record. They have neither choice nor voice about the options on offer.

ChatGPT answer

> The best food for dogs depends on their breed, age, size, activity level, and any health conditions. Here are some general recommendations:
>
> **1. High-quality commercial dog food**
> Look for dog food that meets **AAFCO (Association of American Feed Control Officials)** standards and contains:
> - Real meat as the first ingredient (chicken, beef, lamb, fish, etc.)
> - Healthy grains or grain-free (depending on your dogs needs)
> - Vegetables and fruits for vitamins and fibre
> - Omega-3 and omega-6 for skin and coat health

Avoid:

✗ Fillers like corn, soy, and wheat (low nutritional value)
✗ Artificial preservatives, colours, and flavours
✗ By-products of unknown origin

Some top brands include:

- **Premium:** Orijen, Acana, Blue Buffalo, Taste of the Wild
- **Budget-friendly:** Purina Pro Plan, Iams, Hill's Science Diet

2. Raw or fresh food diet

Some dog owners prefer a **raw diet (BARF—Biologically Appropriate Raw Food)** or **fresh-cooked meals**, which can include:

🍗 Raw or lightly cooked meats (chicken, beef, turkey, fish)
🥦 Vegetables (carrots, spinach, pumpkin)
🍳 Cooked eggs
🦴 Raw meaty bones (NEVER cooked bones—they splinter!
⚠️ **Be cautious:** Raw diets require careful balancing of nutrients, and some dogs may not tolerate them well. Consult a vet first.

3. Homemade dog food

If you prefer to cook for your dog, ensure the diet is **well-balanced**. A basic recipe might include:

🥩 Lean protein (chicken, beef, turkey, fish)
🥔 Carbohydrates (sweet potatoes, brown rice, quinoa)
🥬 Vegetables (spinach, carrots, peas)
🫒 Healthy fats (olive oil, fish oil)
🚫 **Avoid toxic foods for dogs:**
✗ Chocolate, grapes, raisins, onions, garlic, avocado, xylitol (found in sugar-free gum), macadamia nuts

Notice that the AI-generated list emphasises human culinary concepts focusing on *ingredients*. Raw meaty bones get a brief mention. Otherwise, the first imperative, the tough chewy *texture* of a carnivore diet receives no mention.

Dogs, if able to speak, would point out the obvious. They crave to spend hours ripping, tearing and gnawing on raw meaty bones—it's their birthright and how carnivores obtain essential ingredients. Cats know that their prolonged wait at the mousehole may be rewarded with a fur-wrapped 'toothbrush' and parcel of nutrients. Ripping and tearing at raw meaty bones provides medicinal benefits—mental stimulation leading to immune system stimulation, clean teeth, massaged gums and a gastrointestinal system primed to digest meat and bone.

How many years will it take before the electronic record is purged of artificial nonsense and replaced with intelligent information? How long before ChatGPT realises that the food for carnivores must provide essential raw nutrients coupled with medicinal benefits too?

2025 Royal College of Veterinary Surgeons Council Election

The veterinary communication channels are clogged with marketing spin falsely labelled as 'science'. True, relevant information is banned. The result is a cult-like profession peddling lies, never or almost never being exposed to truth.

Contesting Royal College of Veterinary Surgeons elections provides a small window of opportunity to publish relevant objective information. Unfortunately, though, that information is mostly not read or acted upon.

Heres the 2025 election manifesto with links to supporting information and previous election campaigns.

2025 Royal College of Veterinary Surgeons council election
Dr Tom Lonsdale BVetMed, MRCVS

Candidate biography

1972 Royal Veterinary College, London graduate. In the late 1980s, I realised I had harmed patients and defrauded clients by endorsing the feeding of industrial pet foods.

Conscience-stricken, I blew the whistle on the reprehensible cruelty and corruption.[1]

From 1991 to the present, I have researched and written about the pet food fraud[2] and its impact on animal health, human wellbeing, and stewardship of the planet.

In 1992, I formulated the 'Cybernetic hypothesis of periodontal disease in mammalian carnivores' (*Journal of Veterinary Dentistry*, vol. 11, issue 1, 1994),[3] a new hypothesis of health and disease applicable to animals and humans.

Raw Meaty Bones trilogy

- Raw Meaty Bones: Promote Health (2001)—Essential science and practical know-how for all pet professionals.[4]
- Work Wonders: Feed Your Dog Raw Meaty Bones (2005) —Practical, easy-to-read guide for pet carers.[5]
- Multi-Billion-Dollar Pet Food Fraud: Hiding in Plain Sight (2023)—Foundational science providing an indictment and prosecuting brief against the pet food/vet alliance.[6]

2023–2024 Petition to Parliament: 'Inquiry into the pet food industry and its relationship with the vet profession'.[7]

For 24 consecutive years from 1997 to 2020, I contested RCVS elections[8] on the single most important issue confronting our profession.[9]

This year marks my 26th appeal for your vote.

Candidate statement

Why do you want to stand to be a member of RCVS Council?

If possible, we should choose to make the world a better place.

I believe the RCVS is criminally negligent and in breach of its undertakings:

> To enhance society through improved animal health and welfare. We do this by setting, upholding and advancing the educational, ethical and clinical standards of veterinary surgeons and veterinary nurses.

In 1995, I believe Henry Carter acknowledged core failings[10] but denied RCVS regulatory accountability, writing to me:

> For 45 years, I have observed Pedigree Petfoods (and its predecessor, Chappie Ltd) seeking to influence veterinary students and practitioners.
>
> For over 25 years, I have observed Pedigree Petfoods and other pet food manufacturers exerting what some may consider to be undue influence on the BSAVA.
>
> As a past president of the RCVS, I believe that your complaints about the BSAVA and the BVA are of no concern to the Royal College.
>
> As a past chairman of the disciplinary committee, I do not believe that the activities of any of the individuals you have named could be considered to be unprofessional or calculated to bring the profession into disrepute.
>
> ...
>
> You may use these comments in any way you choose.

For the greater good, my choice—our choice—remains clear.

What do you think you can bring to RCVS Council?
With the Veterinary Surgeons Act up for review, I bring a unique and essential perspective gained from 55 years of experience.

As a London vet student, I first became concerned about the difficult choices confronting our profession. I noted that human medicine and dentistry have clear-eyed goals for the health of their patients. As vets, we suffer constant cognitive dissonance. We're mostly available to the highest bidder. Factory farms receive acceptance despite the widespread animal suffering. Pets in terminal decline receive lavish care whilst puppies and kittens are euthanised en masse.

I enrolled at the London School of Economics in search of answers. But it was only after establishing a group of vet clinics in Sydney, Australia, that I came to understand the economic foundations of the profession: the junk pet food industry's relentless promotion of dog ownership—modified wolves with hereditary defects—and relentless promotion of ultra-processed junk.

The veterinary bubble economy[11] depends on a population of diet-affected dogs and cats.[12] When bureaucrats take over regulatory control of the profession, the junk pet food industry's fraudulent bubble may receive scrutiny. I believe that my know-how and experience can help restore confidence, leading to a renaissance for the profession.

What relevant experience do you have?
At 75 years of age, I have extensive life experience. My relevant experience and leadership are second to none.

Vet testimonials and manifestos from 26 years of standing in RCVS elections are published on the RawMeatyBones website.[13] ThePetFoodCon website[14] carries new information.

Whilst researching junk pet food-induced disease, I saw the co-evolutionary role periodontal disease plays in carnivore biology, with consequent significance for human medicine, dentistry, and science more generally. In 1992, I proposed a new paradigm of health and disease—the 'Cybernetic hypothesis of periodontal disease in mammalian carnivores'.[3]

Nowadays human periodontists identify patterns of systemic disease[15] triggered by gum disease—although they fail to grasp the co-evolutionary significance.

I have gained inspiration from the struggles of Ignaz Semmelweis and Joseph Lister and the following books:[16]

> *The Sleepwalkers: Man's Changing View of the Universe*, Arthur Koestler
> *Gaia: A New Look at Life on Earth*, James Lovelock
> *Silent Spring*, Rachel Carson
> *Animal Farm*, George Orwell
> *The Age of Propaganda*, Pratkanis and Aronson
> *The Double Helix*, James Watson
> *The Structure of Scientific Revolutions*, Thomas Kuhn
> *Microcosmos: Four Billion Years of Microbial Evolution*, Lynn Margulis and Dorion Sagan
> *Effectiveness and Efficiency*, Archie Cochrane

Is there anything else you would like to add in support of your candidacy?

Since 1991, from the beginning of the Raw Meaty Bones (RMB) Campaign, the vet establishment has been in denial. Veterinary schools continue in partnership with pet food makers.

Multi-Billion-Dollar Pet Food Fraud was awarded Best of the Best Book Award 2023[17] by the Dog Writers Association of America. Pet owners give the book five stars.[18] But vet journals refuse to review the book.[19]

The RCVS administration refused to disseminate the book to councillors.[20] Which, for lay councillors, is especially disadvantageous.

I hereby request for copies of the RMB trilogy to be

shared with *all* councillors. Better still, I ask that *all members* on the RCVS mailing list be provided with clickable links to the three books.

I believe that the RCVS is obliged to facilitate full, fair and easy access to information—especially where that information disproves vet dogma and helps bring the profession into line with universally accepted medical and dental teaching.

If the RCVS administration fails in its function and declines to provide internet links for members, then I offer free pdf copies of the RMB trilogy to all veterinarians, their staff and clients. Please send an email request to receive pdf books by return. Audiobooks are also available.

Candidate answer to question from the profession
Question:
'Feeding vs nutrition: have we lost the plot in small animal dietetics?', *Australian Veterinary Practitioner*, 23(1), March 1993, makes clear:[21]

> Existing laws prohibit manufacturers and suppliers from recklessly or knowingly making false or misleading statements. Other clauses of the Trade Practices Act and Cruelty to Animals Act may also apply.

Please indicate, with reasons, if you are for or against invoking existing laws against pet food companies, veterinary schools and the RCVS.

Answer:
In my opinion, manufacturers of processed products, whether cooked or raw, veterinary schools and the RCVS should be held accountable for widespread animal cruelty and consumer fraud. Unless they change course, I believe that existing laws should be invoked and criminal and civil proceedings should commence.

For fuller presentation of the facts and my reasoning, please download free Raw Meaty Bones trilogy:

- Foundation facts and suppressed science: *Raw Meaty Bones: Promote Health.*[4]
- Baseline reference standard: *Work Wonders: Feed Your Dog Raw Meaty Bones.*[5]
- Indictments and prosecuting brief: *Multi-Billion-Dollar Pet Food Fraud: Hiding in Plain Sight.*[6]

I welcome questions and hope that the veterinary authorities will facilitate informed discussions. I propose to visit the UK during the months of June, July and August. Visits to other countries may be included.

Thank you for your consideration.

———

Media Release 5 June 2025[22]

Call to prosecute pet food companies, vet schools and RCVS

The Pet Food Con

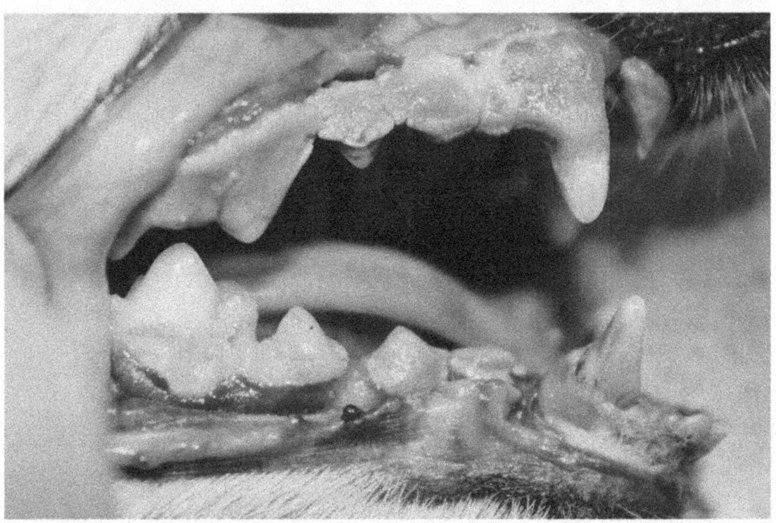

Is the UK government regulator of all things to do with vets, the Royal College of Veterinary Surgeons (RCVS)**, protecting and thus facilitating widespread animal cruelty and consumer fraud? At least 260 registered vets appear to agree with me that it is.

Please allow me to explain. As a basic tenet of civil society, we expect government regulatory authorities to take the initiative, identify major issues of concern, investigate those issues and provide recommendations and guidance to a dependent public. With these thoughts in mind, I sent details of my 1992 Australian Veterinary Association presentation and video recording of 'Pandemic of Periodontal Disease, A Malodorous Condition' to the President of the RCVS. (Periodontal disease, gum disease, is now accepted to be a major contributor to heart disease, stroke, diabetes, cancer and host of inflammatory diseases affecting humans and animals alike.)

The paper set out what the authorities should already have been seeking to remedy: Namely the serious health, cruelty and consumer fraud issues associated with a monotonous diet of ultra-processed 'food'.

In reply, the RCVS wrote: "The President thanks you for your letter of 26th August and the attached paper which we will draw to the attention of the members of the College."

Alas, since that first seemingly positive acknowledgement, things have not gone as hoped. Instead of gratitude for helping them do their job over the past 33 years, the RCVS has stonewalled. The veterinary journals refuse to air discussions. Vets and vet students are deliberately kept in the dark by the vet authorities—whilst simultaneously they are fed a constant diet of junk pet food propaganda.

In 1997, in an attempt to counter the relentless brainwashing, I commenced standing for election to the RCVS Council. Once per year for 26 elections vets, if they happen to look, get to see a 500-word manifesto statement alerting them to the pet food devastation.

In 2004, 2014 and 2016 I travelled to London for face-to-face meetings with three separate RCVS presidents to no avail. Briefly, in 2004, Members of Parliament took an interest with an Early Day Motion signed by 55 MPs.

PROCESSED PET FOODS AND VETS

EDM (Early Day Motion)335:

tabled on 07 December 2004

That this House deeply regrets the professional endorsement of processed food for domestic dogs, cats and ferrets by some members of the veterinary profession; is concerned at the level of incidence of malodorous gum disease and associated diseases of the kidneys, liver and other organs amongst the domestic pet population; recognises that their health and welfare is best served by foods, such as raw meaty bones, that reflect the full range of nutritional need; applauds and recommends the work of veterinary surgeon Tom Lonsdale and others in this field; recognises also that vets in the UK are trusted and independent advisers on the health of our pets; is therefore concerned by the nature of the relationship between some vets and producers of foods that cause illnesses in pets; and calls upon the Royal College of Veterinary Surgeons to make a definitive statement on the active endorsement and promotion of processed pet foods by vets.

The RCVS made no 'definitive statement' and continued to give succour to the mass poisoning of pets by the veterinary-pet food industrial complex.

Nothing, but nothing seems to shake their determination to resist examining and dealing with the junk pet food monster in the room.

Decades passed. The pet food industry, through advertising and vet school sponsorships, tightened its grip on the veterinary mind. Millions of pets have died of preventable diseases and pet owners have been fleeced of $millions.

In 2024 I sent a letter and copy of the award-winning book *Multi-Billion-Dollar Pet Food Fraud: Hiding in Plain Sight* for circulation to all 24 Members of the RCVS College Council. But the RCVS Executive, unlike their 1992 predecessors, refused to draw the evidence "to the attention of the members of the College".

Also in 2024 I tabled a petition for a full Parliamentary "Inquiry into the pet food industry and its relationship with the vet profession".

And in this 26th year of standing in RCVS elections I called on the membership to consider:

If possible, we should choose to make the world a better place.

I believe the RCVS is criminally negligent and in breach of its undertakings:

To enhance society through improved animal health and welfare. We do this by setting, upholding, and advancing the educational, ethical, and clinical standards of veterinary surgeons and veterinary nurses.

I asked voters to further consider:

In my opinion, manufacturers of processed products, whether cooked or raw, veterinary schools and the RCVS should be held accountable for widespread animal cruelty and consumer fraud. Unless they change course, I believe that existing laws should be invoked and criminal and civil proceedings should commence.

260 registered Members of the Royal College of Veterinary Surgeons voted in support.

However, legal action will be costly and time consuming. Meanwhile, pet owners must protect themselves from the failings of a corrupt system; inform themselves of the multi-billion-pound pet food fraud, collusion of government authorities and the cruel effects on pets, people and the planet.

** RCVS provides accreditation for Australian and USA veterinary degrees.

Key Facts:

The ravages of a junk pet food diet on the health of pets has been well known in the veterinary profession at least since

1991. Despite accumulating further evidence the veterinary schools continue to promote commercial propaganda with devastating effects on animal health, human economy and the natural environment.

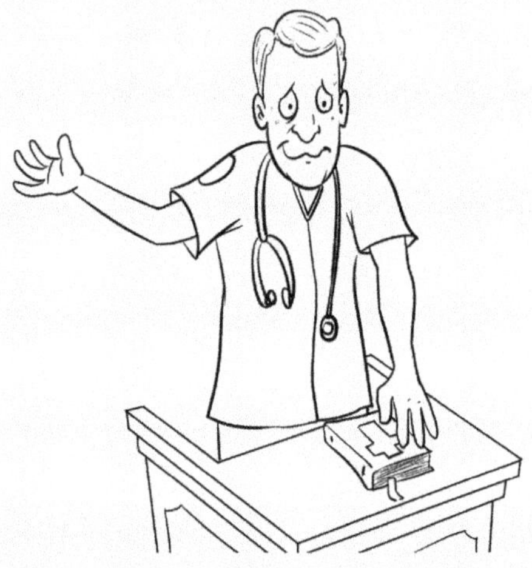

About us:

Dr Tom Lonsdale first blew the whistle on the veterinary-junk pet food industrial complex in 1991. Since when he's been campaigning for a global reckoning with potential for a renaissance in veterinary and medical science and improvement in animal health, human economy and natural environment. His 2025 Royal College of Veterinary Surgeons election manifesto provides much background information.

Contact details:

For all media enquiries, contact The Double Agents London: enquiries@capitallmedia.co.uk

For any non-media enquiries, please send email: team@ThePetFoodCon.com

ENDNOTES

Introduction

1. https://www.youtube.com/watch?v=4muH5_qWZ00

Chapter 1
2001: Laying the foundations

1. From the newsletter at http://www.crikey.com.au

Chapter 2
2002: Industry strikes back

1. *A Current Affair program, with a segment on the pet food industry.* https://www.youtube.com/watch?v=g4g8uyHzAGU&t=216s
2. Dr Michele Cotton, associate director of the Foundation, has reviewed the book *Raw Meaty Bones.* https://rawmeatybones.com/pgf/rmb_doc.htm
3. Full text at https://rawmeatybones.com/hungerford.php
4. *Sunday Times* article at https://rawmeatybones.com/sunday_times.html
5. Letter from Dr Douglas Bryden at https://rawmeatybones.com/bryden.php

Chapter 3
2003: Spreading the word, facing resistance

1. Full transcript at http://www.rawmeatybones.com/PFIC.html
2. 'Pushers of poison or dispensers of medicine—you choose.' http://www.rawmeatybones.com/RCVS/RCVS2003.html
3. Letter sent to the journal of the British Veterinary Association at http://www.rawmeatybones.com/RCVS/vet_record.pdf
4. Transplantation in cats at https://www.rcvs.org.uk/news-and-views/news/guidelines-approved-for-kidney-transplantation-in-cats/

Chapter 4
2004: The vet-industrial pet food complex tightens its grip

1. Reading for seminar students at https://rawmeatybones.com/suggestedreading.php
2. See the Royal College of Veterinary Surgeons at www.rcvs.org.uk
3. You can read Professor Greenhalgh's article at http://bmj.bmjjournals.com/cgi/content/full/327/7424/1175-a?etoc?eaf?eaf
4. T. Lonsdale, 'Cybernetic hypothesis of periodontal disease in mammalian carnivores', *Journal of Veterinary Dentistry*, vol. 11, issue 1, 1994, pp. 5–8. https://rawmeatybones.com/pdf/periodontal-cyber.pdf
5. 'Your pet's health: nature's way'. http://www.rawmeatybones.com/speaking.html

6. International Working Dog Breeding Association Conference. http://www.iwdba.org/

7. T. Lonsdale, *Raw Meaty Bones: Promote Health,* Rivetco, pp. 295–315. http://www.rawmeatybones.com/pdf/RMB-14-A%20cybernetic%20hypothesis.pdf

8. Widespread serious misconduct. http://www.rawmeatybones.com/nsw_parliament.html

9. *Time Magazine.* https://rawmeatybones.com/Images/20130731210441_00001.jpg

10. Channel 7 TV. https://www.youtube.com/watch?v=fFnsEOHS_Os

11. The manifesto. https://rawmeatybones.com/RCVS/RCVS2004.html

Chapter 5
2005: Hitting walls: legal and institutional barriers

1. Processed pet foods and vets. https://edm.parliament.uk/early-day-motion/26858

2. Early day motions. https://www.parliament.uk/globalassets/documents/commons-information-office/p03.pdf

3. Comments on *Raw Meaty Bones.* https://rawmeatybones.com/vetsay.php

4. T. Lonsdale, 'Putting feline lower urinary tract disease in context', *Journal of Small Animal Practice,* vol. 34, 1993, pp. 592–3. http://www.rawmeatybones.com/FLUTD.html

5. T. Lonsdale, 'Cybernetic hypothesis of periodontal disease in mammalian carnivores', *Journal of Veterinary Dentistry,* vol. 11, issue 1, 1994, pp. 5–8. http://www.rawmeatybones.com/Cybernetic.html

6. T. Lonsdale, 'Periodontal disease and leucopenia', *Journal of Small Animal Practice,* vol. 36, pp. 542–6. https://rawmeatybones.com/pdf/periodontal-leuco.pdf

7. Tony Buffington, on National Public Radio, 8 August 2002. https://thekojonnamdishow.org/audio/#/shows/2002-08-08/feeding-our-pets/78339/@00:00

8. 'Human and veterinary medicine'. http://bmj.bmjjournals.com/cgi/content/full/330/7496/858

9. *BMJ* rapid responses. https://www.bmj.com/content/330/7496/858/rapid-responses

10. Readers' comments on *Work Wonders.* https://www.amazon.com.au/Work-Wonders-Feed-Meaty-Bones/dp/0975717405 and https://rawmeatybones.com/book-ww.php

11. BVA policy brief. https://rawmeatybones.com/pol-brief.html

12. British Veterinary Association. http://www.bva.co.uk/

13. British Small Animal Veterinary Association. http://www.bsava.com/

14. Pet Food Manufacturers Association in the UK. https://www.ukpetfood.org/

15. What the MPs wrote in the early day motion. https://edm.parliament.uk/early-day-motion/29343

Chapter 6
2006: Confidence tricksters and censorship

1. Diet sheet. http://www.rawmeatybones.com/diet/exp-diet-guide.pdf

2. Translations of *Work Wonders* under the national flags. www.rawmeatybones.com

3. Contact Tom Lonsdale. tom@rawmeatybones.com

4. Ten years of election statements. https://rawmeatybones.com/elections.php

5. British Veterinary Association policy brief. http://www.rawmeatybones.com/pol-brief.html

6. Jackie Marriott's letter to the *BMJ.* https://www.bmj.com/content/330/7496/858/rapid-responses

7. Submission for the College Prize of the ACVS. https://rawmeatybones.com/vetsay.php

8. Mars Corporation website. http://www.mars.com/

9. Public interest with Kojo Nnamdi. https://thekojonnamdishow.org/audio/#/ shows/2002-08-08/feeding-our-pets/78339/@00:00

10. Transcript and slides. https://www.youtube.com/watch?v=MHLhdL-sCfk&t=9s

Chapter 7
2007: Feeding fads and false prophets

1. Veterinary reviews of *Raw Meaty Bones*. https://rawmeatybones.com/vetsay.php

2. Information for pet owners at www.rawmeatybones.com

3. Lifelong diet-induced ill health. https://rawmeatybones.com/newsletters/11-1%20 Dec%202011%20-%2020th%20Anniversary.pdf

4. Predator–prey population dynamics. http://www.stolaf.edu/people/mckelvey/envision. dir/lotka-volt.html

5. Raw Meaty Bones Diet. http://www.rawmeatybones.com/diet/exp-diet-guide.pdf

6. Discussion on RawVet List. http://www.rawmeatybones.com/pdf/RawVet%20Prey%20 Model%2006.pdf

7. *Nexus* article. http://www.rawmeatybones.com/presscoverings.php

8. Articles from outside sources. http://www.rawmeatybones.com/papers-others.php

9. Social benefits of owning pets. https://rawmeatybones.com/articles-others/ AustInstitute_Wellbeing_Feb2004.pdf

10. Overconsumption of pet food. https://australiainstitute.org.au/wp-content/ uploads/2020/12/WP60_8.pdf

11. Feeding cats for health. https://rawmeatybones.com/articles-others/Malik_feedingcats_ Aug2007.pdf

12. Rats reveal risks of junk food. https://rawmeatybones.com/articles-others/VetRecord_ rats_Aug2007.pdf

13. *Veterinary Record*. http://www.rawmeatybones.com/pol-brief.html

14. 'They eat what we are', *New York Times*. https://rawmeatybones.com/pdf/NYT2007.pdf

15. Brushing your cat's teeth. http://www.youtube.com/ playlist?list=PLgyMKAquGJOZHeMX7VmuAuCrujjBPPY1O

16. Raw feeding. http://en.wikipedia.org/wiki/Raw_feeding

17. Dog food salmonella outbreak. https://www.cidrap.umn.edu/foodborne-disease/more-salmonella-cases-linked-dry-pet food

18. Burns Pet Nutrition fined. https://dogforum.co.uk/threads/burns-pet foods-defra.16597/

19. *Nexus* article. https://rawmeatybones.com/articles/Nexus07_pub_articletext.pdf

20. Early day motion 335. https://edm.parliament.uk/early-day-motion/26858

Chapter 8
2008: Smokescreens and red herrings

1. *International Journal of Epidemiology*. http://ije.oxfordjournals.org/cgi/content/full/32/6/910?ijkey=43550467984937d6bfcf635ddb730a45f4715739&keytype2=tf_ipsecsha
2. *Medical Journal of Australia*. http://www.mja.com.au/public/issues/185_10_201106/martin_201106.html
3. World Small Animal Veterinary Association. http://www.wsava.org/
4. 'Continuing education'. http://www.vin.com/proceedings/Proceedings.plx?CID=WSAVA2007&O=Generic
5. Company 'consultant' Jill Madison. https://www.youtube.com/watch?v=f7XhE5hOBgI&t=228s
6. 'A malodorous condition'. https://rawmeatybones.com/lectures.php
7. Veterinary Dental Conference presentation. https://www.youtube.com/watch?v=5mkQNLdILgE&t=9s
8. Preventative dentistry. http://www.rawmeatybones.com/PrevDent.html
9. ACVSc Nomination Statements. www.rawmeatybones.com/vetsay.html
10. 'Periodontal disease and leucopenia'. http://www.rawmeatybones.com/pdf/periodontal-leuco.pdf
11. 'Cybernetic hypothesis of periodontal disease in mammalian carnivores'. http://www.rawmeatybones.com/pdf/periodontal-cyber.pdf
12. 'George Bernard Shaw, *The doctor's dilemma*', *International Journal of Epidemiology*, vol. 32, issue 6, December 2003, pp. 910–15. https://doi.org/10.1093/ije/dyg233 and http://ije.oxfordjournals.org/cgi/content/full/32/6/910
13. Royal College of Veterinary Surgeons (RCVS) Council. http://www.rawmeatybones.com/elections.php
14. Revitalising veterinary science. https://rawmeatybones.com/revitalise.php
15. Recommendations to the UK government. http://www.publications.parliament.uk/pa/cm200708/cmselect/cmenvfru/348/34802.htm
16. Tiptoeing around the issues. http://www.publications.parliament.uk/pa/cm200708/cmselect/cmenvfru/1011/101104.htm
17. 'Pandemic of periodontal disease: a malodorous condition'. https://rawmeatybones.com/pdf/popdamc.pdf
18. More monographs mailed out. https://rawmeatybones.com/lectures.php
19. Mexico's police forces. https://time.com/archive/6944961/in-mexicos-drug-war-bad-cops-are-a-mounting-problem/
20. Royal Canin Canada press release. http://www.uoguelph.ca/news/2008/04/royal_canin_can.html

Chapter 9
2009: A movement undermined

1. Organised crime. http://en.wikipedia.org/wiki/Criminal_organization
2. Ontario provincial members of parliament. https://www.ola.org/en
3. Members of the Canadian National Parliament. http://www.parl.gc.ca/

4. Actions against veterinary schools. http://www.rawmeatybones.com/campaign/legal-vet.php

5. First draft of the cybernetic hypothesis. http://www.rawmeatybones.com/pdf/periodontal-cyber.pdf

6. AVA 1994 election statement. http://www.rawmeatybones.com/pdf/AVA%2094.pdf

7. Professor Lynn Margulis on the radio. http://en.wikipedia.org/wiki/Lynn_Margulis

8. 'Petfoods' insidious consequences: a modern veterinary snafu'. http://www.rawmeatybones.com/PFIC.html

9. 'Periodontal disease and leucopenia', *Journal of Small Animal Practice*, vol. 36, 1995, pp. 542–6. http://www.rawmeatybones.com/pdf/periodontal-leuco.pdf

10. James Lovelock FRS endorsed the paper. http://en.wikipedia.org/wiki/James_Lovelock

11. *Raw Meaty Bones: Promote Health.* https://www.thepetfoodcon.com/raw-meaty-bones/

12. Suggested reading list. https://rawmeatybones.com/suggestedreading.php

13. Glowing endorsements. http://www.rawmeatybones.com/vetsay.php

14. The U-turn Tour and presentation at Parliament House. http://www.rawmeatybones.com/speaking_2006.php

15. RCVS Forum. www.vetsurgeon.org

16. BVA policy and rebuttal. http://www.rawmeatybones.com/pol-brief.html

17. BARFmania. http://www.rawmeatybones.com/petowners/whynotBARF.php

18. Foundation for Billinghurst's first book. http://www.rawmeatybones.com/pdf/93ab.pdf

19. UK Pet Food Manufacturers Association. http://www.pfma.org.uk/

20. Kitty, six-year-old cat suffering the ravages of an artificial diet. https://www.youtube.com/watch?v=deyz0-G-jyg

21. Six questions and manifesto. http://www.rawmeatybones.com/RCVS/RCVS2009.php

22. Prey model. http://www.rawmeatybones.com/pdf/RawVet%20Prey%20Model%2006.pdf

23. Raw Meaty Bones home page. www.rawmeatybones.com

24. Professor Sandra Scarr Wikipedia entry. http://en.wikipedia.org/wiki/Sandra_Scarr

25. London vet struck off. https://www.rcvs.org.uk/news-and-views/news/london-vet-struck-off-for-dishonesty-and-misleading-clients/

26. Korean Air Lines Flight 007. http://en.wikipedia.org/wiki/Korean_Air_Lines_Flight_007

Chapter 10
2010: Two decades on: progress and roadblocks

1. RMB Campaign and owners' choice. http://www.rawmeatybones.com/petowners.php

2. BARFer as junk food producer. http://www.rawmeatybones.com/petowners/whynotBARF.php

3. Prey Model discussion lists. http://www.rawmeatybones.com/pdf/RawVet%20Prey%20Model%2006.pdf

4. Death of David Taylor. http://paulflynnmp.typepad.com/my_weblog/2010/01/funeral-of-david-taylormp.html

5. David Taylor's statement. https://edm.parliament.uk/early-day-motion/26858

6. Numerous documents received by the Royal College of Veterinary Surgeons. http://www.rawmeatybones.com/lectures.php

7. RCVS council elections. http://www.rawmeatybones.com/elections.php

8. Harold Shipman, notorious mass murderer. https://en.wikipedia.org/wiki/Harold_Shipman

9. T. Lonsdale, 'Oral disease in cats and dogs', December 1991; Control and Therapy Series No. 3128; Mailing No. 163, Post Graduate Committee in Veterinary Science of the University of Sydney. http://www.rawmeatybones.com/No_3128.html

10. A significant contribution by R. Malik, 'Feeding cats for health and longevity—an idiosyncratic perspective', paper delivered at Australian College of Veterinary Scientists, Science Week 2007, Small Animal Medicine Chapter meeting. https://rawmeatybones.com/articles-others/Malik_feedingcats_Aug2007.pdf

11. *RMB Newsletter* archives. http://www.rawmeatybones.com/newsletters.php

12. Lawsuits against veterinary schools. http://www.rawmeatybones.com/campaign/legal-vet.php

13. Shipman Inquiry. http://en.wikipedia.org/wiki/The_Shipman_Inquiry

14. Dr Douglas Bryden and Dr Tom Hungerford. http://www.rawmeatybones.com/vetsay.php

15. Review of *Raw Meaty Bones: Promote Health*. http://www.rawmeatybones.com/pgf/rmb_doc.htm

16. The cat Sefi. http://www.rawmeatybones.com/pdf/Sefi.pdf

17. Lonsdale, 'Preventative dentistry'. www.rawmeatybones.com/PrevDent.html

18. Freedom of Information inquiry. www.rawmeatybones.com/pdf/C+T%20cat's%20ear%20IIaa.pdf

19. Draft version. http://www.rawmeatybones.com/articles-others/docArticle1.pdf

20. Published version. http://www.ukrmb.co.uk/images/WatsonReport.pdf

21. Alison Tyler's recommendation. http://www.rawmeatybones.com/alisontyler.php

Chapter 11
2011: Final words: the fight continues

Appendix C

1. I blew the whistle on the reprehensible cruelty and corruption. https://rawmeatybones.com/newsletters/11-1%20Dec%202011%20-%2020th%20Anniversary.pdf

2. I have researched and written about the pet food fraud. https://www.thepetfoodcon.com/

3. T. Lonsdale, 'Cybernetic hypothesis of periodontal disease in mammalian carnivores', *Journal of Veterinary Dentistry,* vol. 11, no. 1, 1994, pp. 5–8. https://www.thepetfoodcon.com/cybernetic-hypothesis-of-periodontal-disease-in-mammalian-carnivores/

4. *Raw Meaty Bones: Promote Health* (2001)—*Essential science and practical know-how for all pet professionals.* https://www.thepetfoodcon.com/

5. *Work Wonders: Feed Your Dog Raw Meaty Bones (2005)—Practical, easy-to-read guide for pet carers.* https://www.thepetfoodcon.com/work-wonders/

6. *Multi-Billion-Dollar Pet Food Fraud: Hiding in Plain Sight (2023)—Foundational science.* https://www.thepetfoodcon.com/multi-billion-dollar-pet-food-fraud/

7. 2023–2024 Petition to Parliament: 'Inquiry into the pet food industry and its relationship with the vet profession'. https://petition.parliament.uk/archived/petitions/651425

8. From 1997 to 2020, I contested RCVS elections. http://www.rawmeatybones.com/

elections.php

9. The single most important issue confronting our profession. https://www.youtube.com/watch?v=4muH5_qWZ00

10. Henry Carter's acknowledgement of core failings. https://rawmeatybones.com/pdf/Henry%20Carter%201995.pdf

11. The veterinary bubble economy. https://www.thepetfoodcon.com/vet-shortage-in-the-bubble-economy/

12. A population of diet-affected dogs and cats. https://www.thepetfoodcon.com/vet-shortage-in-the-bubble-economy-ii/

13. Testimonials and manifestos. https://rawmeatybones.com/elections.php

14. ThePetFoodCon website. https://www.thepetfoodcon.com/

15. Nowadays human periodontists identify patterns of systemic disease. https://onlinelibrary.wiley.com/toc/16000757/2024/96/1

16. Inspiring books. https://rawmeatybones.com/suggestedreading.php

17. Best of the Best Book Award 2023. https://dogwriters.org/tom-lonsdale-bvetmed-mrcvs-challenging-the-status-quo/

18. Pet owners give the book five stars. https://www.thepetfoodcon.com/reviews-for-tom-lonsdales-books/

19. Vet journals refuse to review the book. https://www.thepetfoodcon.com/centre-for-veterinary-education-refusal/

20. RCVS administration refused to disseminate book to councillors. https://www.thepetfoodcon.com/wp-content/uploads/2024/03/RCVS-Coms.pdf

21. T. Lonsdale, 'Feeding vs nutrition: have we lost the plot in small animal dietetics?', *Australian Veterinary Practice*, vol. 23, issue 1, 1993. https://rawmeatybones.com/pdf/avp.pdf

22. Media release, 5 June 2025: https://newshub.medianet.com.au/2025/06/call-to-prosecute-pet-food-companies-vet-schools-and-rcvs/104424/.

ACKNOWLEDGEMENTS

From the beginning of the Raw Meaty Bones Campaign in 1991 many people have helped me understand and communicate the 'good diet, good health' message. Chance remarks, random comments and examples from a wide circle of people have found their way into the inner recesses of my brain and helped me list the facts and opinions expressed in the Raw Meaty Bones trilogy and now in this compilation of *Raw Meaty Bones Newsletters*.

Dr Breck Muir, from our first meeting in 1982 until today, has been a source of knowledge, inspiration and support. Bill Bowes arrived with impeccable timing in 2000 to help me with the sprawling IT needs of research and publishing. He's the mentor, friend and IT guru who provides extraordinary 24-hour support without which there would be no campaign.

Many colleagues, clients and staff have supported the campaign. Dr Richard Malik is the sole veterinary academic who provides support. Roger Meacock is mentioned throughout the book and has been a source of inspiration and strength since our first meeting in 2002. Other names appear in the text, but there are many whose names are not included. I extend my thanks to all.

Sadly, there are mentors and colleagues who are no longer here. Despite the 'heretical' nature of the Raw Meaty Bones Campaign, notable veterinary academics and administrators provided support and credibility. My tutors at the Royal Veterinary College, Dr Arthur Hayward and Dr Oliver Graham-Jones, were solid in support, as were directors of the Centre for Veterinary Education at the University of Sydney, Dr Tom Hungerford OBE, Dr Douglas Bryden OAM and Dr Michele Cotton. Eminent psychology professor Dr Sandra Scarr wrote articles in support. Old friends Dr Jon Lumley and Dr Johan Joubert were enthusiasts for the cause. I acknowledge my debt and salute them all.

Many books, periodicals and films have provided important information. I acknowledge all sources referenced in the Endnotes section and the many more that came across my desk this past fifty years.

Dr Juliet Richters provided vital guidance, copyediting, proofreading and indexing of *Multi-Billion-Dollar Pet Food Fraud* and returns here in the same essential role. Saul Symonds arrived with perfect timing and contributed laser sharp recommendations and succinct chapter summaries. Simon Goodway provided inspiration and created the illustrations. My admiration and thanks go to Joy Lankshear of Lankshear Design for book design and typesetting. The London agents, Jon Kirk and Anthony Harvison of Palamedes and The Double Agents, have shown immense faith in the direction and purpose of the Raw Meaty Bones Campaign. I acknowledge my lasting debt to all.

Over the fifty-plus years of my veterinary career, many thousands of animals have taught me about stoicism and the silent endurance of suffering. I hope that this book provides some acknowledgement and provides the animals with a voice. Lastly, I acknowledge you, the reader, for your interest in our unfinished work. Thank you.

Also by Dr Tom Lonsdale

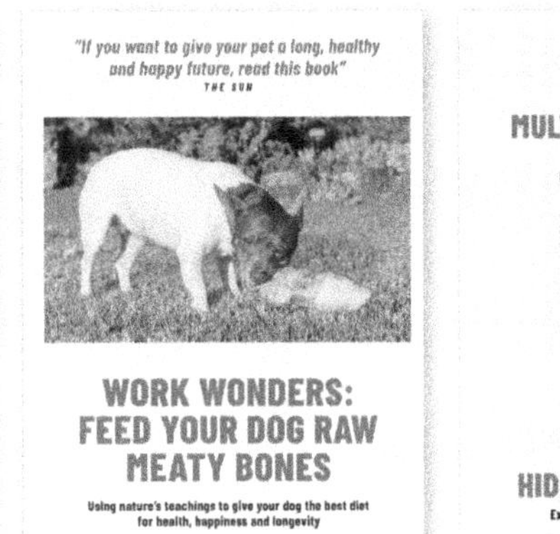

Raw Meaty Bones: Promote Health (2001) provides scientific foundations for a pet health revolution. Thirteen chapters anticipate and support Chapter 14, 'A cybernetic hypothesis of periodontal disease', a co-evolutionary hypothesis of relevance to veterinary and human medicine, dentistry and biological science more generally.

Work Wonders: Feed Your Dog Raw Meaty Bones (2005) provides the easy, practical information for feeding our dogs. It's also applicable to the feeding of cats and ferrets.

Multi-Billion-Dollar Pet Food Fraud: Hiding in Plain Sight (2023) provides a manifesto for change. It sets the scene for scientific, political and legal action leading to a potential renaissance in veterinary care and pet health.